LEWES

THROUGH TIME

Bob Cairns

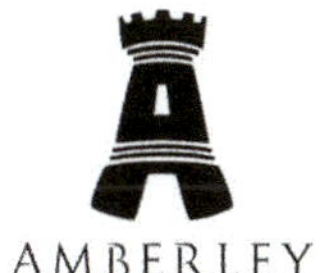

AMBERLEY

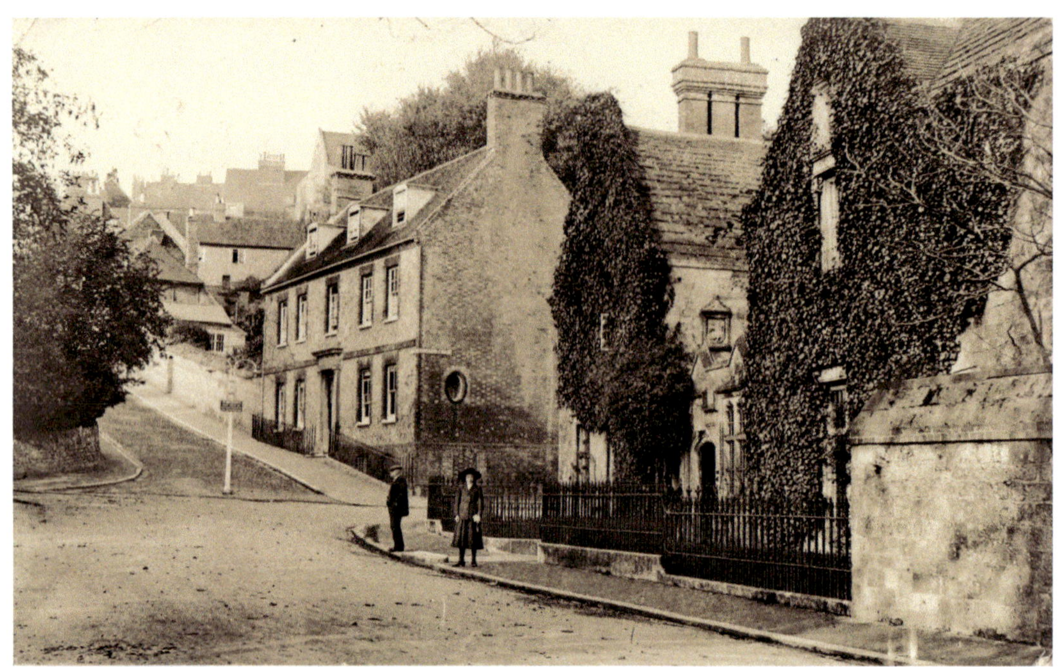

Southover Grange and Keere Street look rather grand and present an unchanged picture. Elsewhere the town has seen wholesale decimation in the name of progress.

First published 2012

Amberley Publishing
The Hill, Stroud, Gloucestershire, GL5 4EP
www.amberley-books.com

Copyright © Bob Cairns, 2012

The right of Bob Cairns to be identified as the
Author of this work has been asserted in accordance with
the Copyrights, Designs and Patents Act 1988.

ISBN 978 1 84868 807 0 (print)

British Library Cataloguing in Publication Data.
A catalogue record for this book is available from the
British Library.

Typesetting by Amberley Publishing.
Printed in Great Britain.

Introduction

Given the amount that has been written about Lewes over the centuries, there seems little new I can add.

Each author, however, brings a fresh perspective. I hope this modest book does so through my choice of Edwardian postcards and the accompanying photographs. It has not been possible to always replicate the postcards' views because of trees, traffic and new buildings, so I have been liberal with my interpretation. Also, it has been difficult in ninety-six pages to fully capture the character of *Lewes Through Time* and fully represent a 2,000-postcard collection. This is not a history book either – it's just my reflection of Lewes.

Lewes is like the proverbial curate's egg — good in parts. Much of its fine architecture and Saxon/Norman layout has survived but, conversely, a lot has gone, particularly in the name of two twentieth-century curses – slum clearance and the motor car. It could have been far worse, though, had not Lewes citizens and organisations, such as the Friends of Lewes, steadfastly opposed the more extreme plans for improvement and development.

Similarly, Lewes has been blessed with outstanding photographers. Between them they captured most aspects of Lewes' life and topography over the past 150 years. The quality of their work still cannot be beaten and we should be grateful for their legacy.

Pride of place goes to Edward Reeves & Son. Established in 1857, it is now run by Tom, the founder's great-grandson. Its extensive archive is a veritable treasure house and photographs from it have appeared in the majority of books published about the town. Surprisingly, the family did not jump on the postcard bandwagon, although they did publish cards. Tom thinks this was due to the demands on his grandfather's time for traditional portrait and commercial work.

The best-quality photographic postcards were produced by James Cheetham, about whom Kim Clark wrote in her book *Lost Lewes*. His distinctive style, with the description in white at the bottom of the card, features heavily in this book. He was an amateur photographer and worked variously at Lewes Prison and as a schoolmaster.

The most prolific was Bliss & Co. Alfred Marsh Bliss moved to Lewes in 1889 and opened a studio at 34 Lansdowne Place, over which premises he and his family lived. His tenure was short-lived and the business was run during the Edwardian period by James Worthington and then John Leedaford.

Finally, a number of non-attributed cards were clearly taken by Henry John Bartlett. They are distinctive for their rounded corners, sepia tone, neatly written descriptions and the excellence of the photographs.

The images of these and other Edwardian photographers present a better description of Lewes than most of us could ever do with words. My photographs are those of a very amateur photographer flattered by being able to use a complex digital camera. Even so, I have not been able to match the quality or depth of field of the old-timers' photographs.

Despite these limitations, I hope you will still enjoy my eclectic view of *Lewes Through Time*.

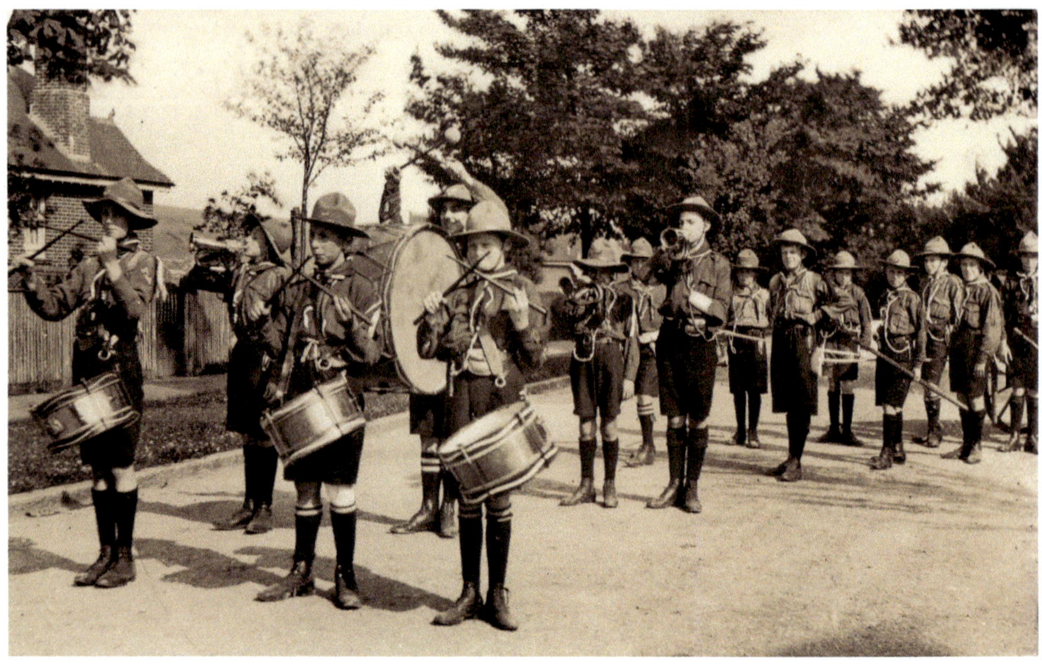

The bugler of the 1st Company of Lewes Boy Scouts' Band, whose leader was Mr Pym Browning, organist at St Michael's church, plays a fanfare to announce the start of this trip of *Lewes Through Time*.

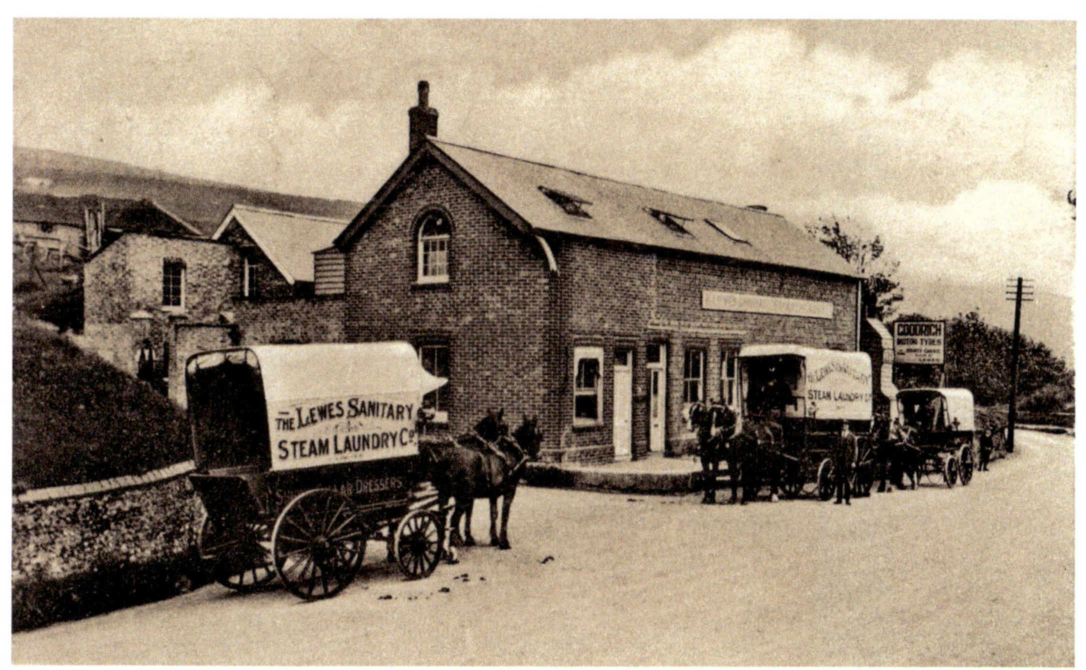

Lewes Sanitary Steam Laundry

The laundry burned down in March 1941. It occupied an extensive site at the top of Malling Hill and had a large workforce, many of whom lived in Malling Villas and Mill Road. There was no mains water and the business and employees relied on supply from a reservoir at the top of Mill Road. They went without on a Sunday as the supply was turned off. The drying grounds were on the green in front of the Villas, now lost under the north-side houses of Mill Road and Malling Down.

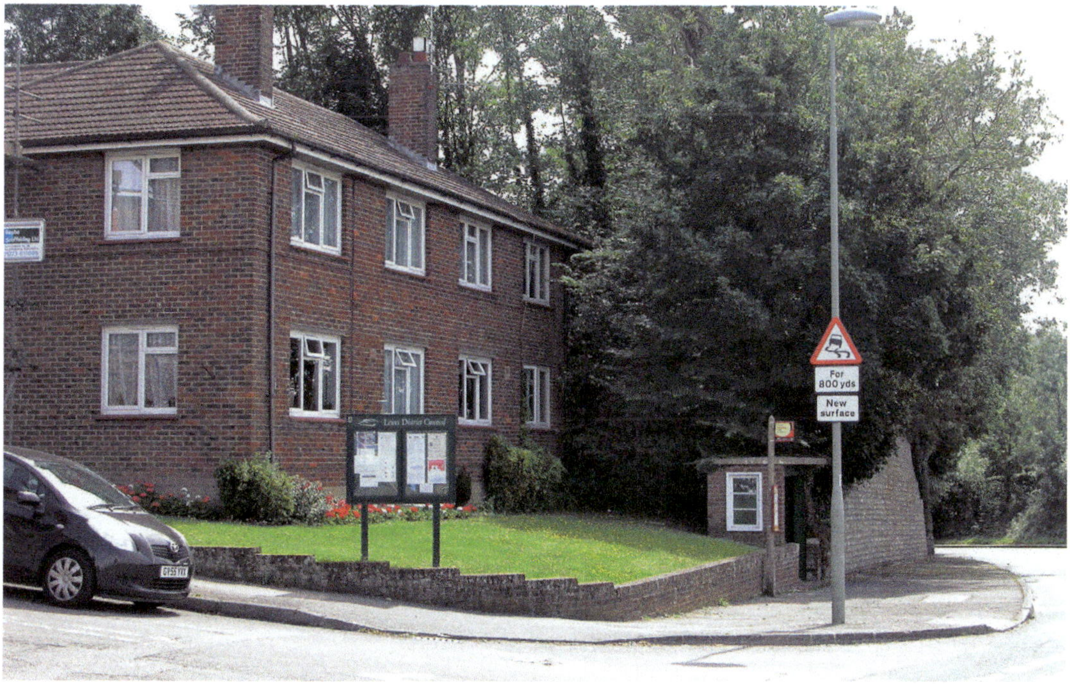

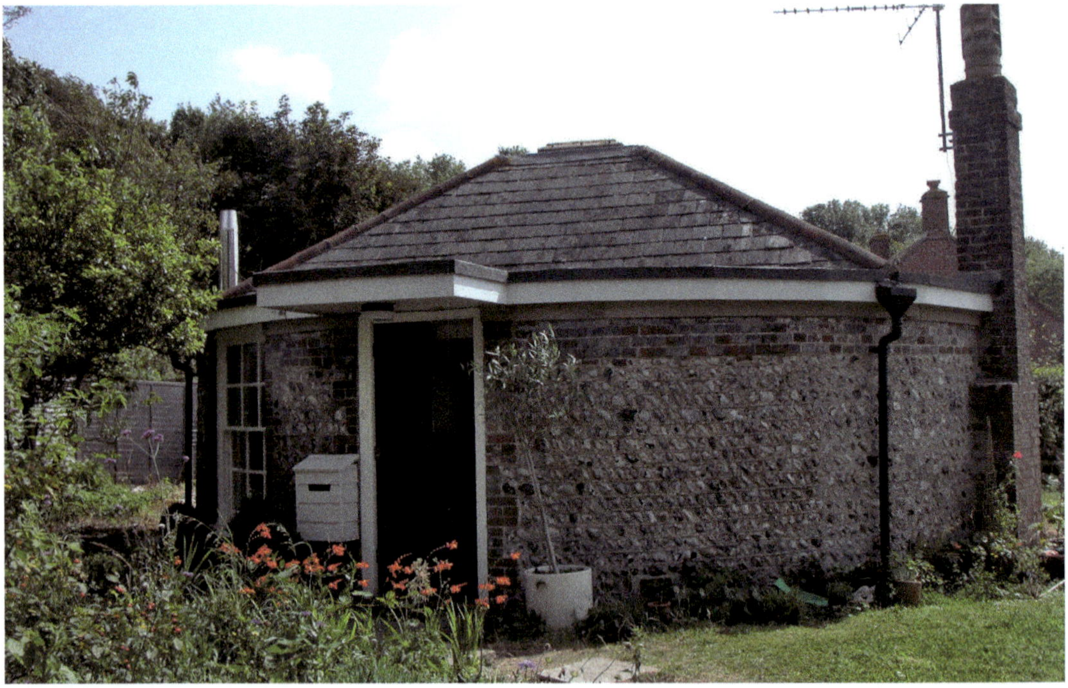

Malling Mill

This was one of a ring of windmills circling Lewes a century ago. When it burnt down on 8 September 1908 it was being used as a store by the Lewes Sanitary Steam Laundry. Without a plentiful water supply, it was destroyed totally although the nearby cottages and Mill House suffered no more than cracked windowpanes and scorched blinds. The base is now a delightful tucked-away cottage owned by Edward Underwood, Liza Jones and their lovely son Orson.

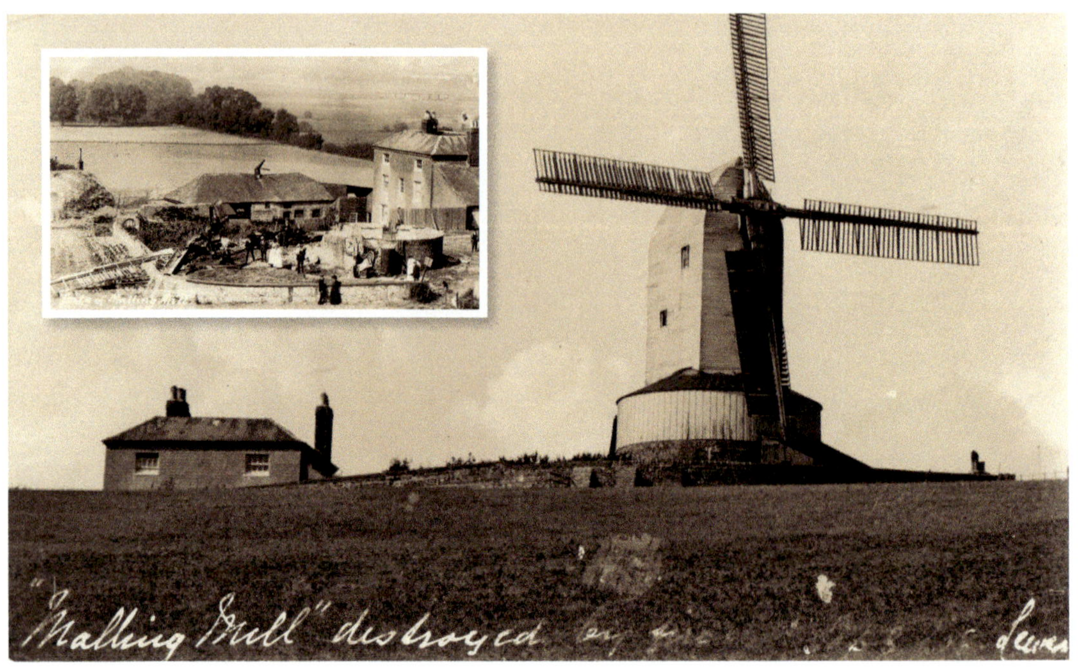

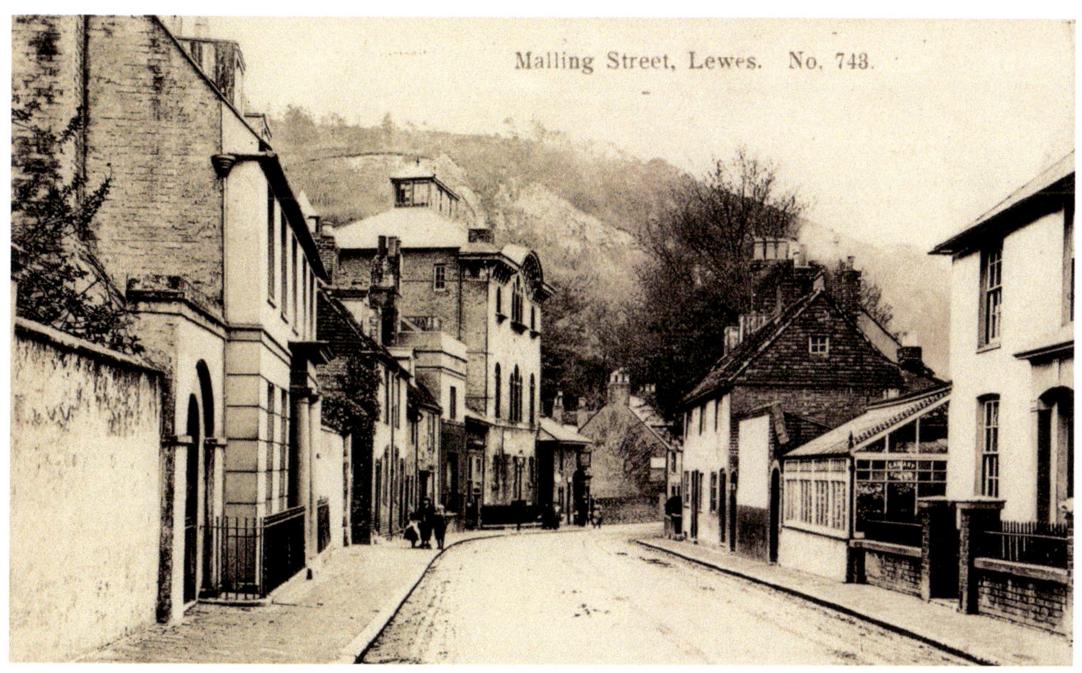

Elmsley's Brewery in Malling

Malling Street, formerly known as North Street, has probably changed more than any other in the town and owes its demise to the motor car. The Master's House, the Georgian house and the row of cottages on the left are the only survivors of road widening in the 1960s. Elmsley's Brewery is in the middle ground, with the Brewery Tap nearby at 135. It was formerly the Tanners Arms, there having been tan yards behind the cottages opposite. One of these, below the current road level and at right angles to it, survives.

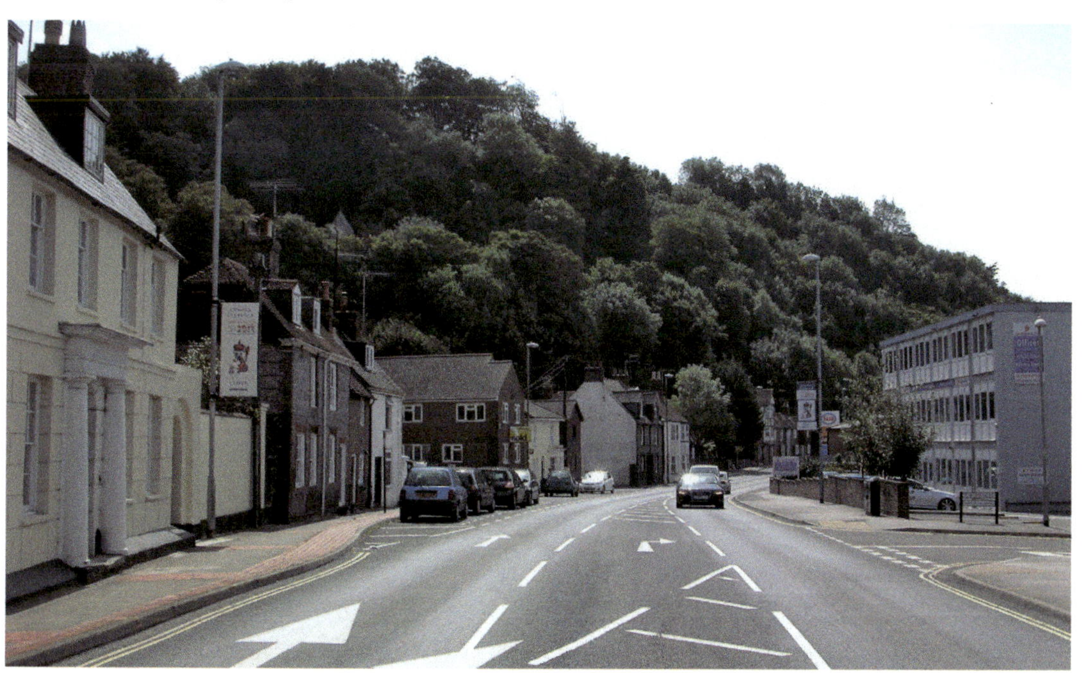

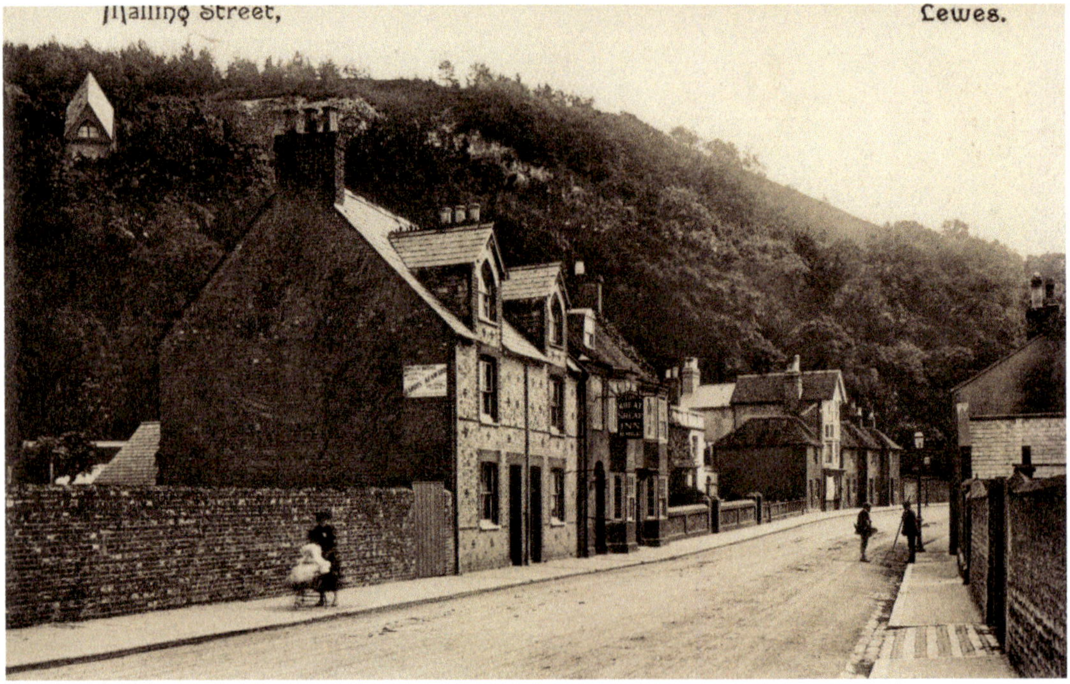

The Wheatsheaf in Malling

Beyond the brewery was The Wheatsheaf public house, which became The Cleopatra and then Cleo's nightclub in the 1970s. Next door, Coombe House still has charm despite its incongruous position facing the Esso garage that replaced the run of attractive cottages.

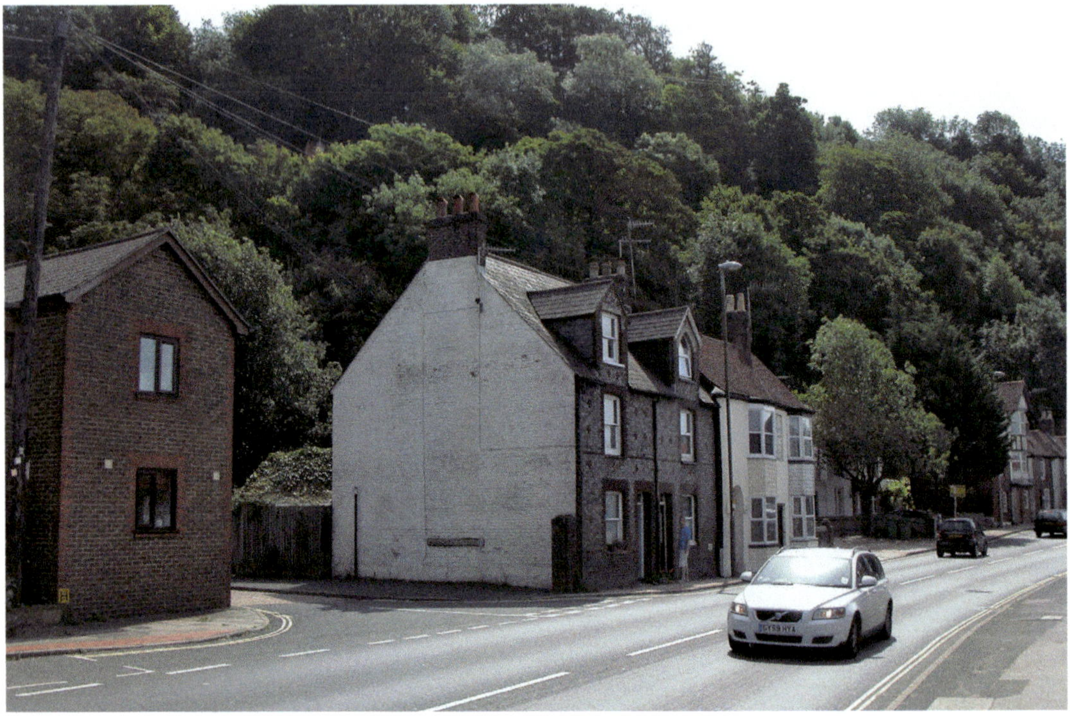

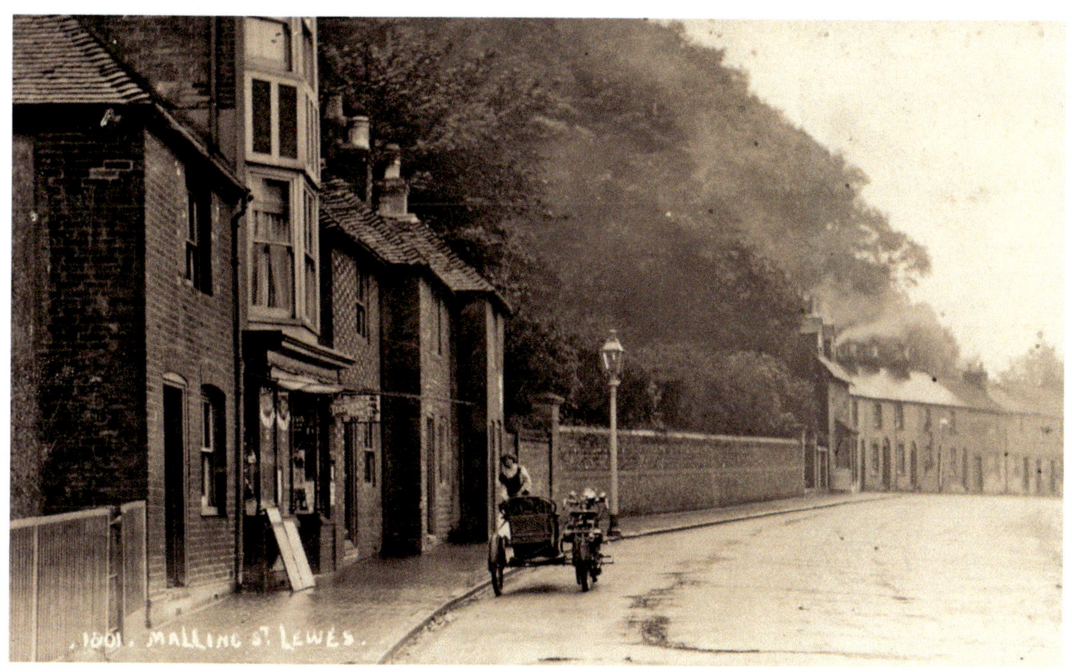

The Malling Sub-Post Office

Now appropriately called Penny Black Cottage, it was the three-storey building. It gained its third floor in about 1910. The wall that fronted the Cliffe Cemetery is now under the dual carriageway, as are all the cottages beyond. The remains from the Cliffe and All Saints Cemeteries were re-interred in the main Lewes Cemetery following an Act of Parliament.

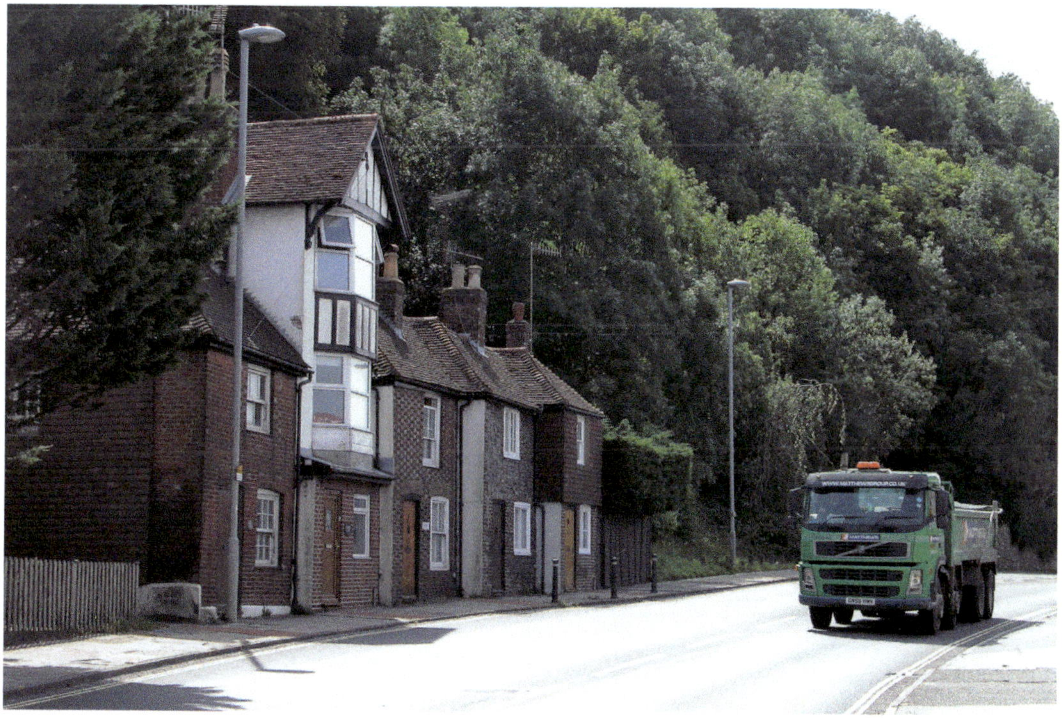

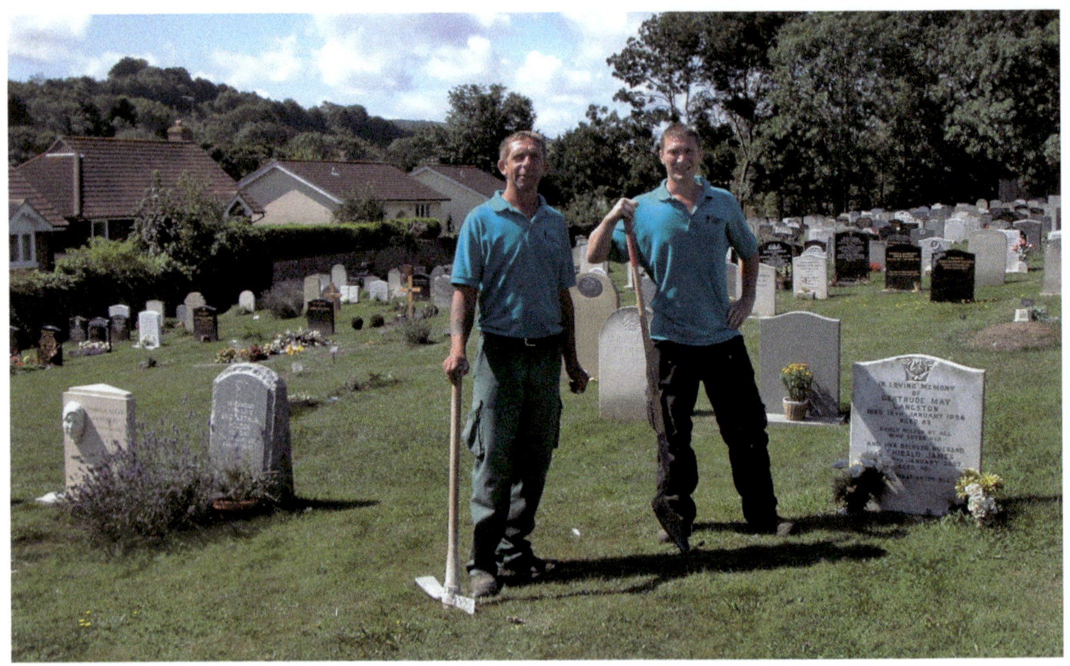

Mrs Steere, Gravedigger

Mrs Steere became the cemetery's gravedigger after the death of her husband, who had been sexton. The card carries an earlier photograph as she died in 1903. Apparently she was helped by a male lodger, but the postcard suggests that she also carried out her full duties when required. Ian Hutchinson, left, and George McMasters now look after the town's cemetery in Rotten Row. It is kept immaculately by them, but where will burials be held when it is full in a few years' time?

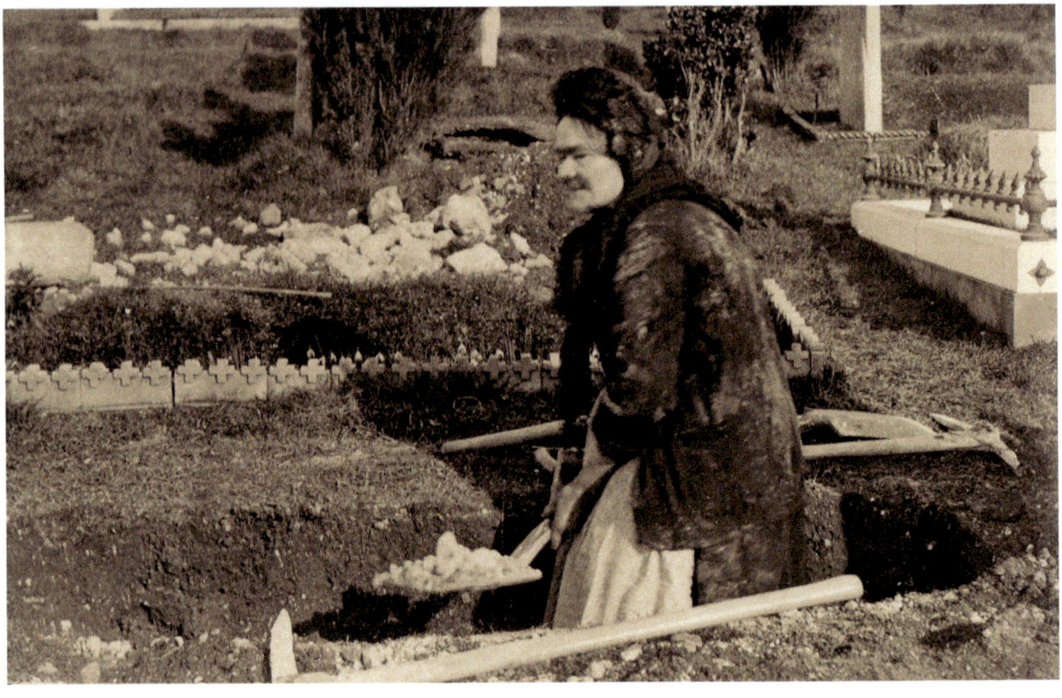

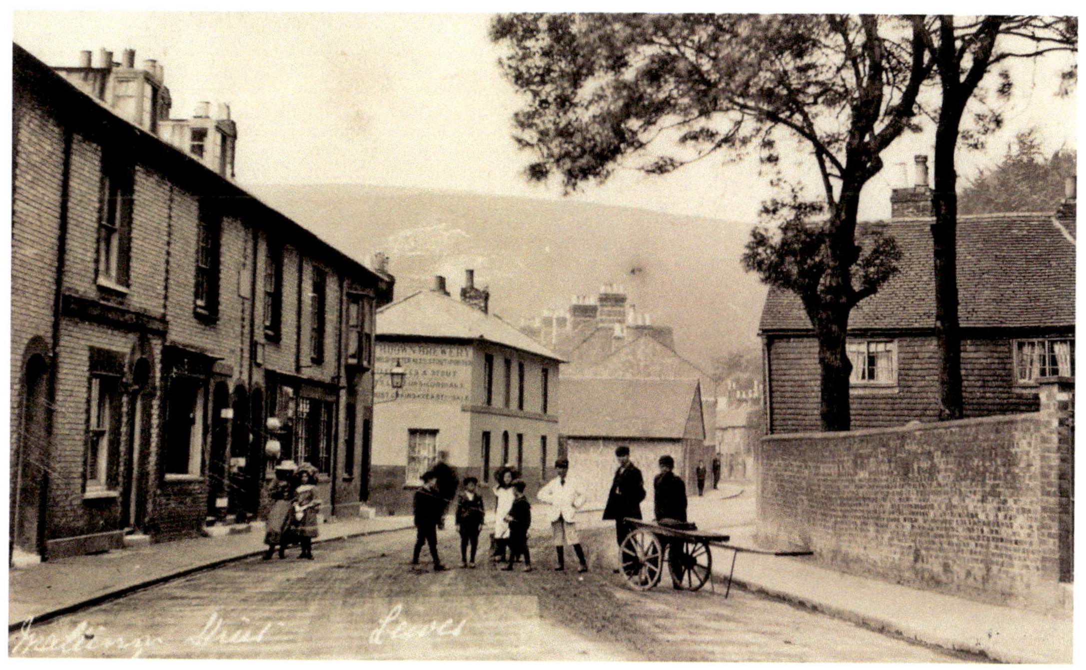

Lower Malling Street

Close to the Cuilfail roundabout the survival rate of cottages has been better, although the east side was cleared along with the previously mentioned cemetery. The advertising on the building refers to the Southdown Brewery, which was in Lewes from 1838 to 1920 and had its headquarters in Thomas Street, which cuts down on the left. The fine premises are still there but at the time of writing are up for sale and need urgent TLC.

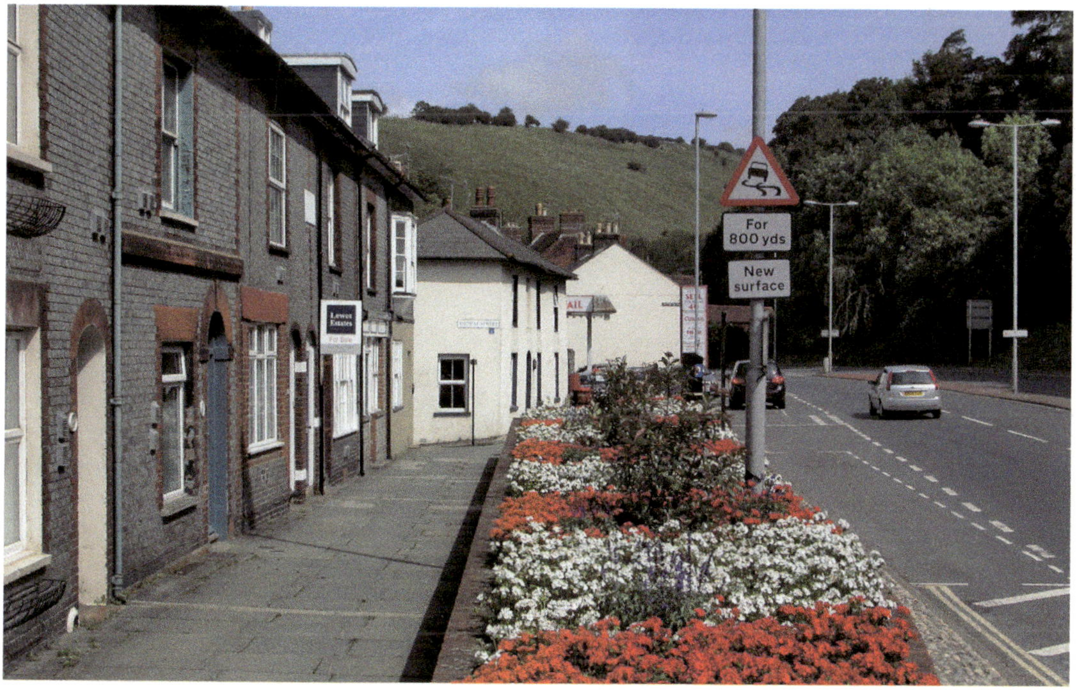

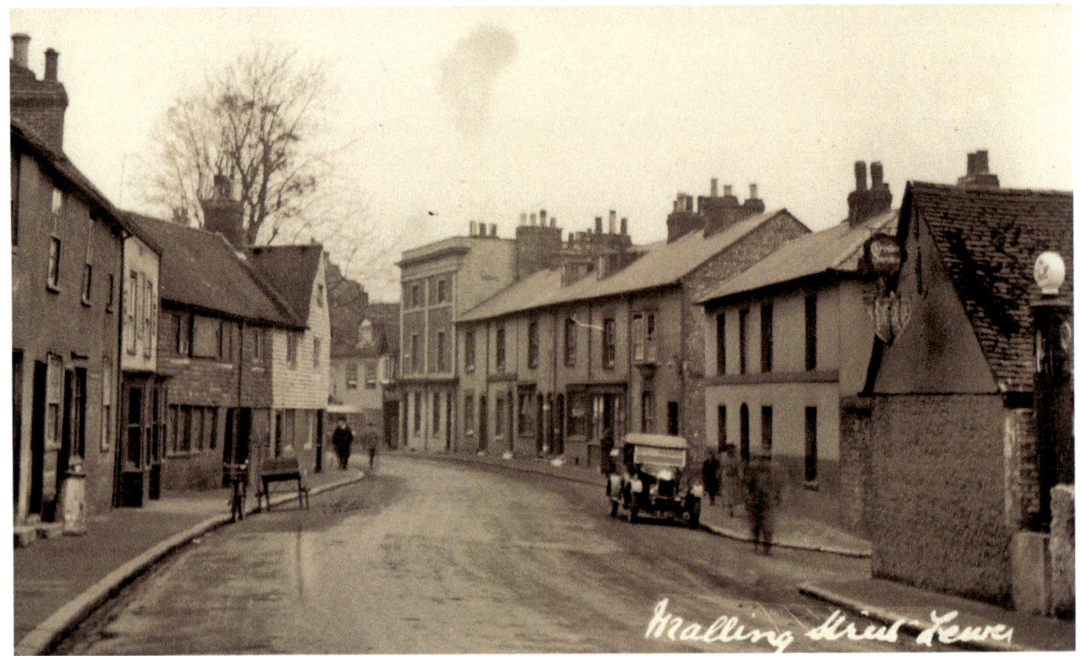

Brian the Snail

We turn around and the cottages are on the immediate right. All the buildings on the left were demolished for road widening. People appear in the postcard as blurs because of the slow shutter speed. The Phoenix Causeway into town follows the line of Soap Factory Lane, which ran to the river's edge. The roundabout sculpture is of an ammonite but was quickly christened Brian the Snail.

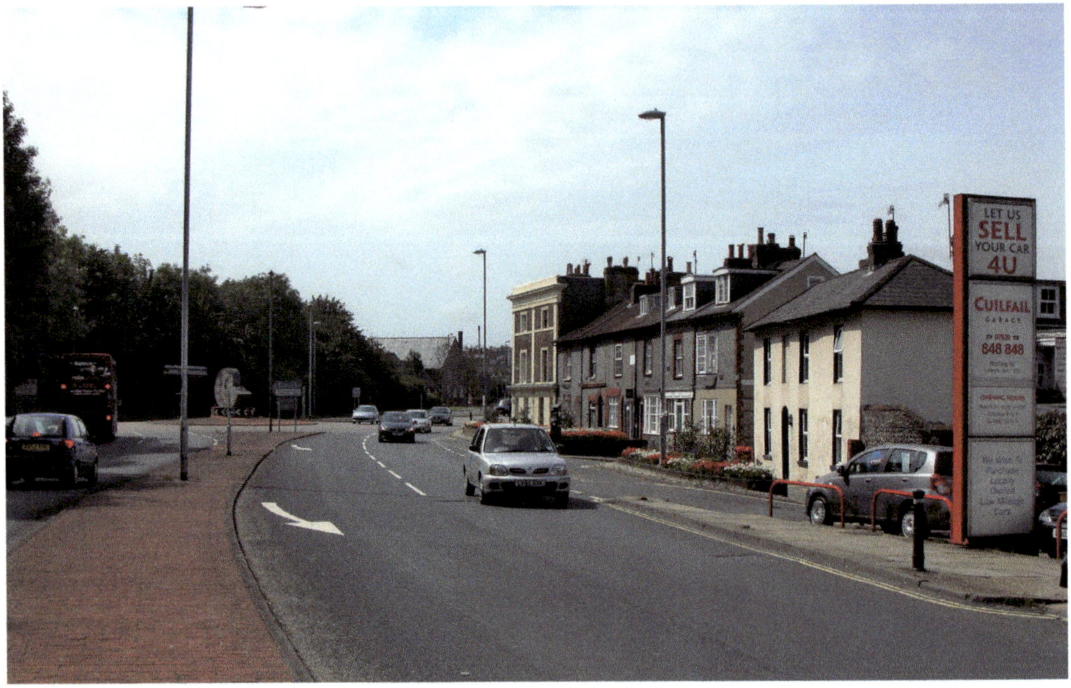

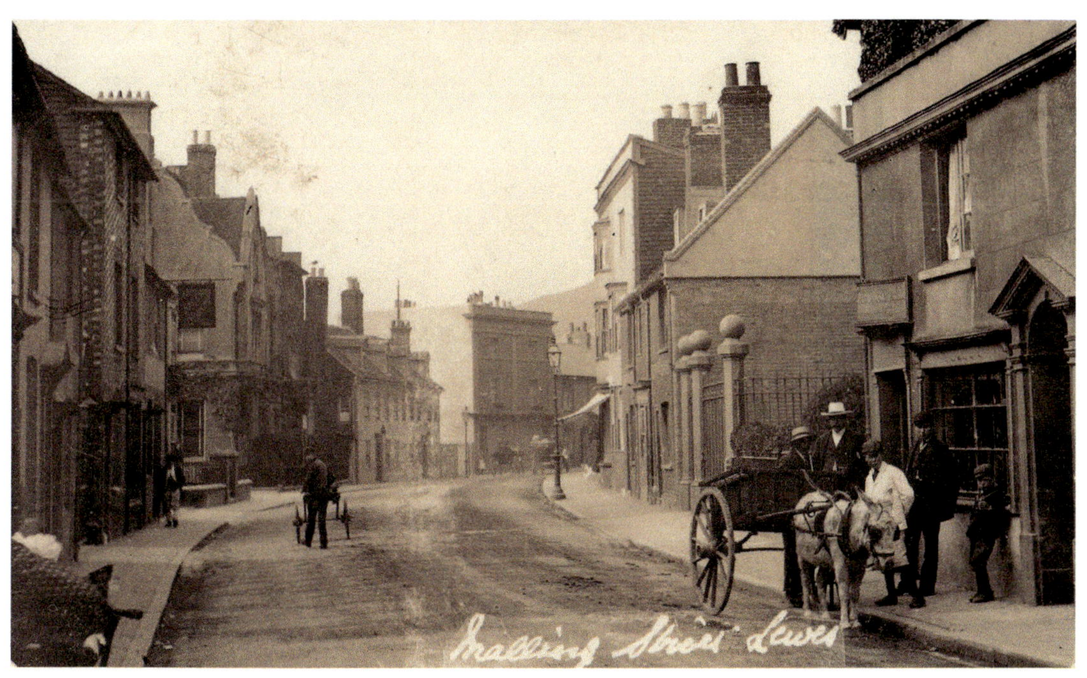

Even Lower Malling Street

Here we see the biggest change, with the near-annihilation of lower Malling Street. The only building which survived the demolition for constructing the Cuilfail Tunnel and the Phoenix Causeway is in the centre of the postcard and now has only Brian the Snail for company. Spot the Forester's Arms at 30 and the Hare and Hounds at 40, just along from today's Dorset Arms.

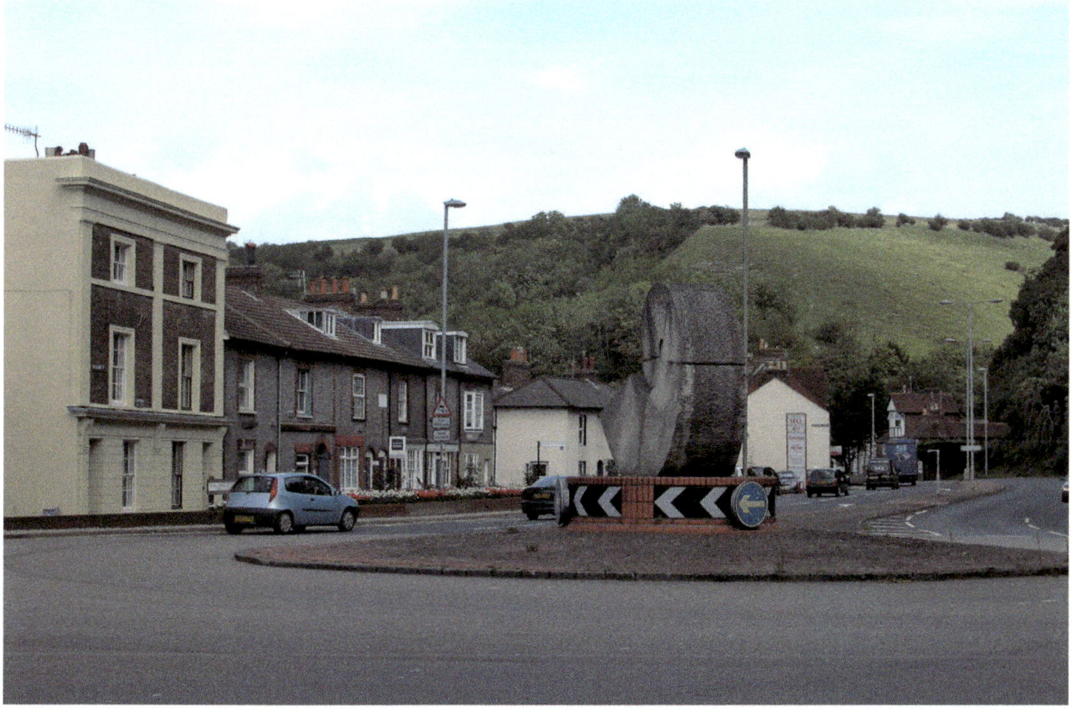

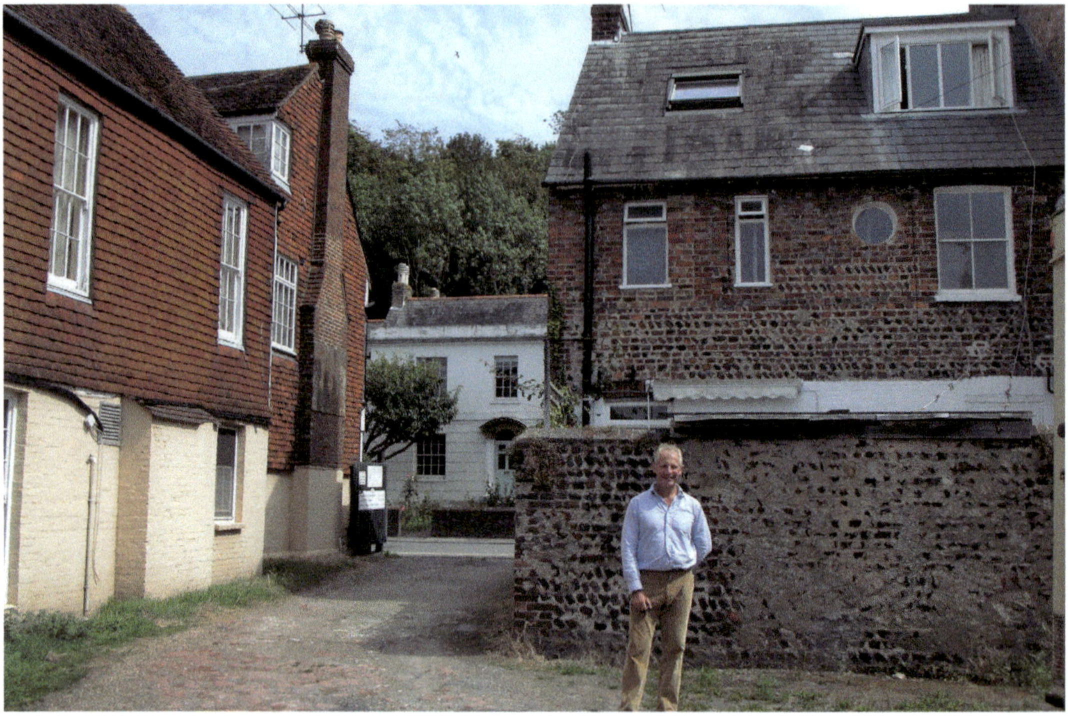

Cliffe Bonfire Society

We are in the territory of Cliffe Bonfire Society, which has taken an independent and traditional approach to Guy Fawkes Night for over 150 years. This group pose in the yard used by George Gardiner, the blacksmith, with a new banner presented by the ladies. The Dorset Arms is to the left. Steve Luker now runs his upholstery business here. He is a Cliffe bonfire boy and helped re-form the Seaford Bonfire Society.

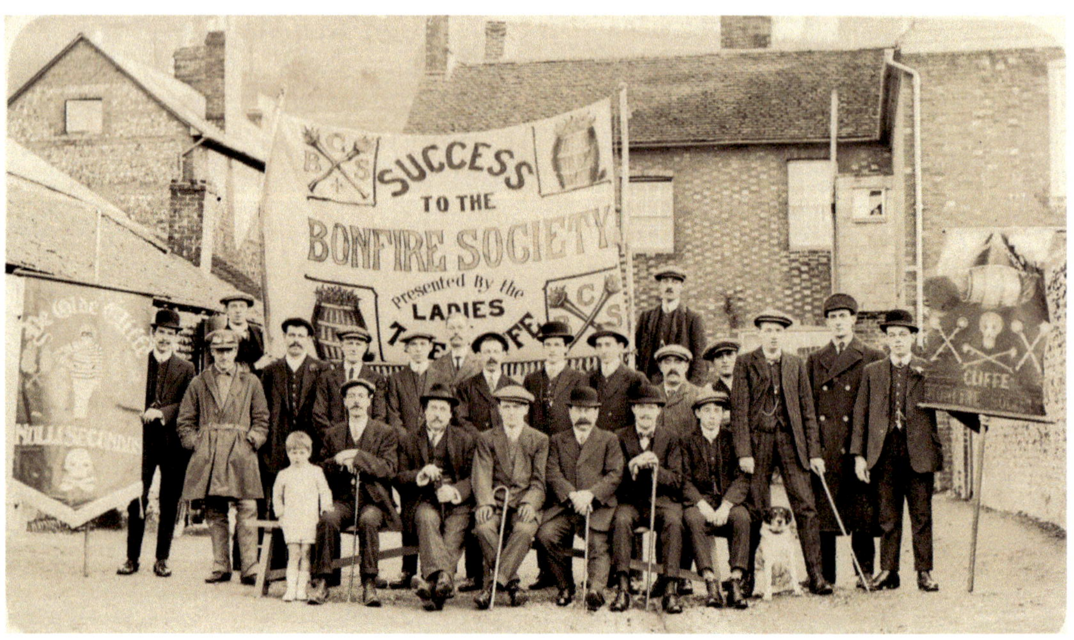

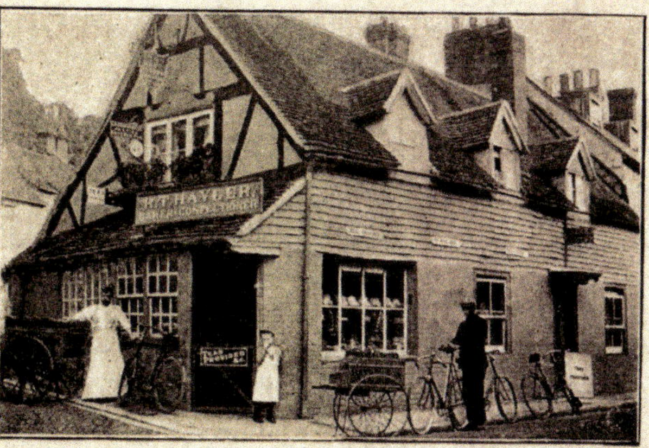

Hayler the Baker

On the corner of Chapel Hill, formerly East Street, which leads to the golf club, was the thriving shop of Mr Hayler the baker. He was a keen member of the South Street Juveniles' Bonfire Society. This wonderful advertising card of 1917 illustrates the versatility of his business and I particularly like the use of the piano. He is posing on the left as now does Gavin Teasdale, the owner of Bags of Books with Anna Morgan, who runs an equally vibrant business.

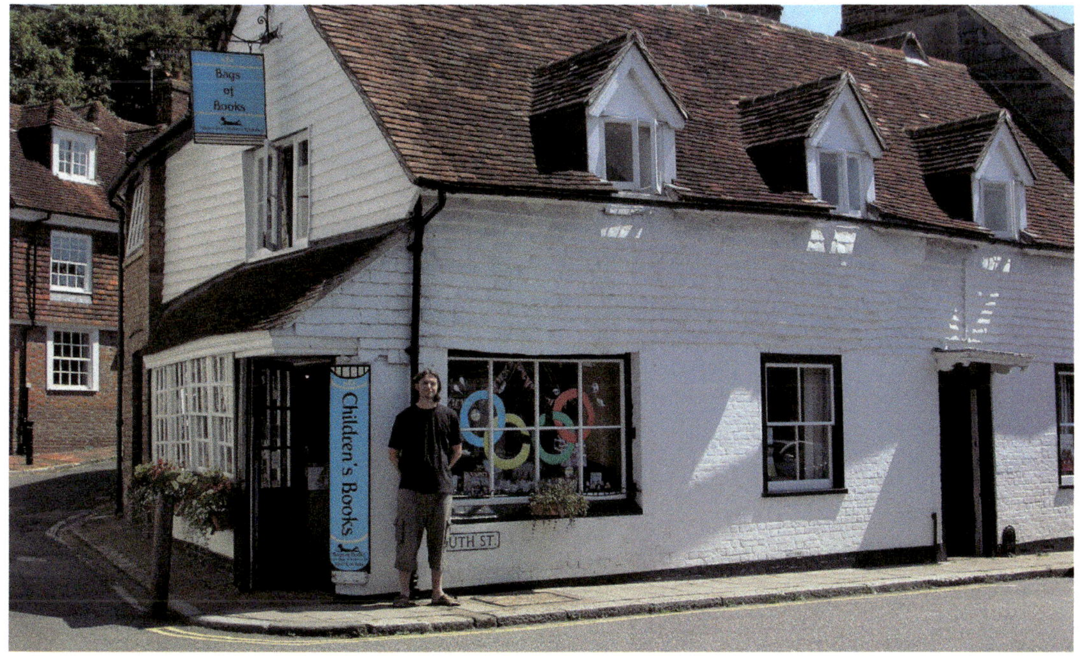

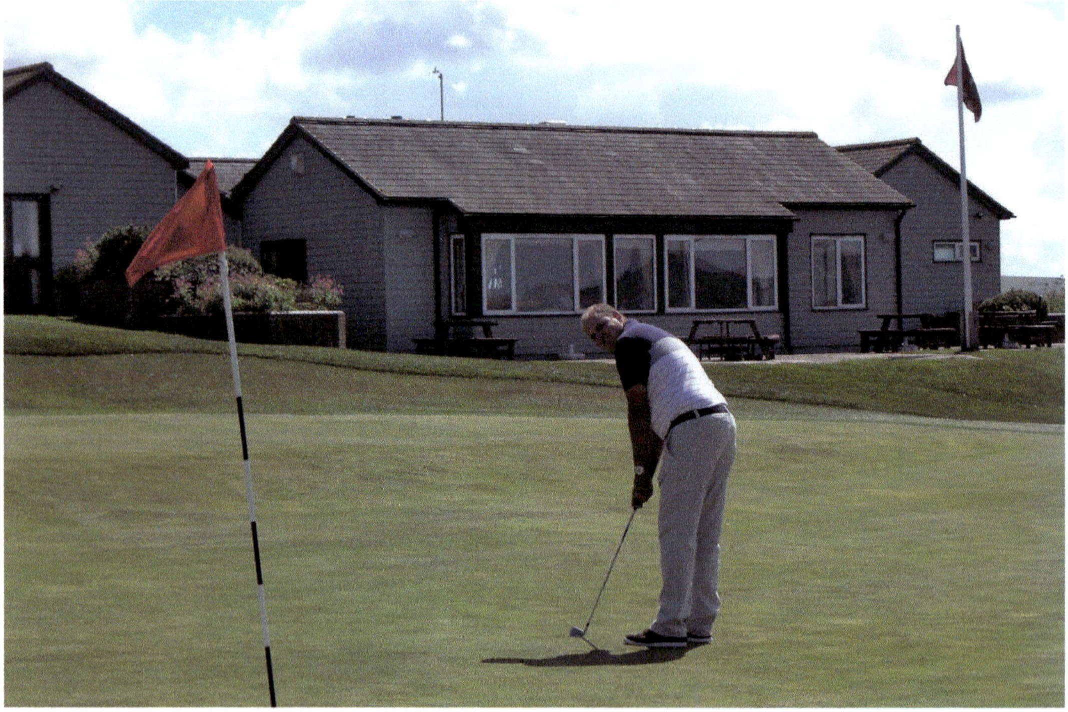

Lewes Golf Club

At the top of Chapel Hill is the town's golf course, part of which includes the earliest cricket ground. Lewes Golf Club was founded in 1896 by a group of local gentlemen although Graham White, in his fine history of the club, found evidence that the game was played there much earlier. The original clubhouse remains in use but has been greatly extended and improved, as has this fine downland course. Tom Hilton, the club professional, practices his putting with a 5-iron!

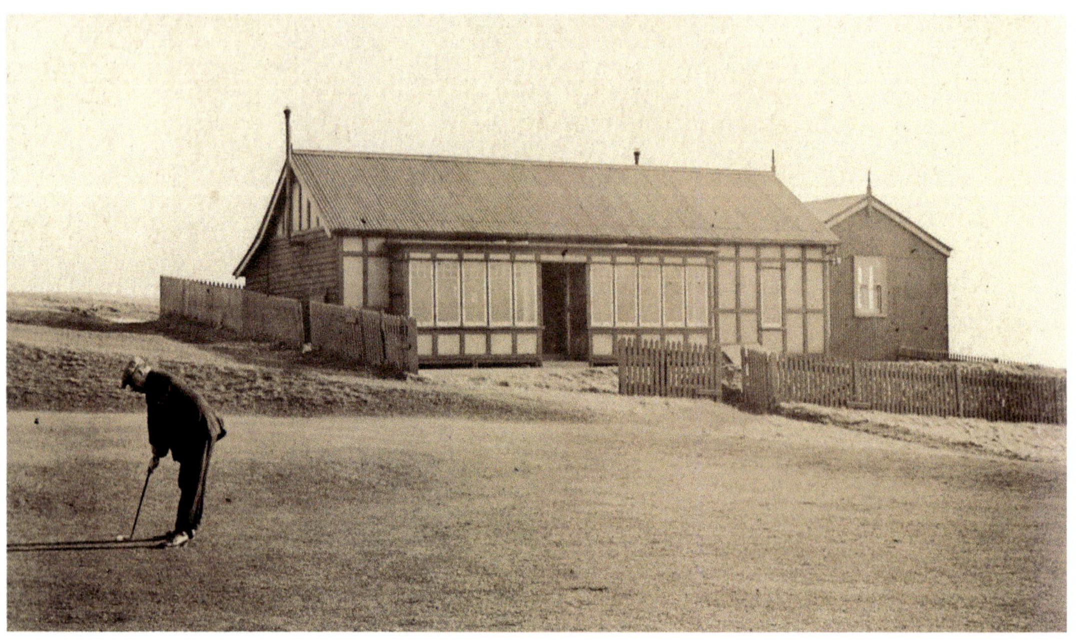

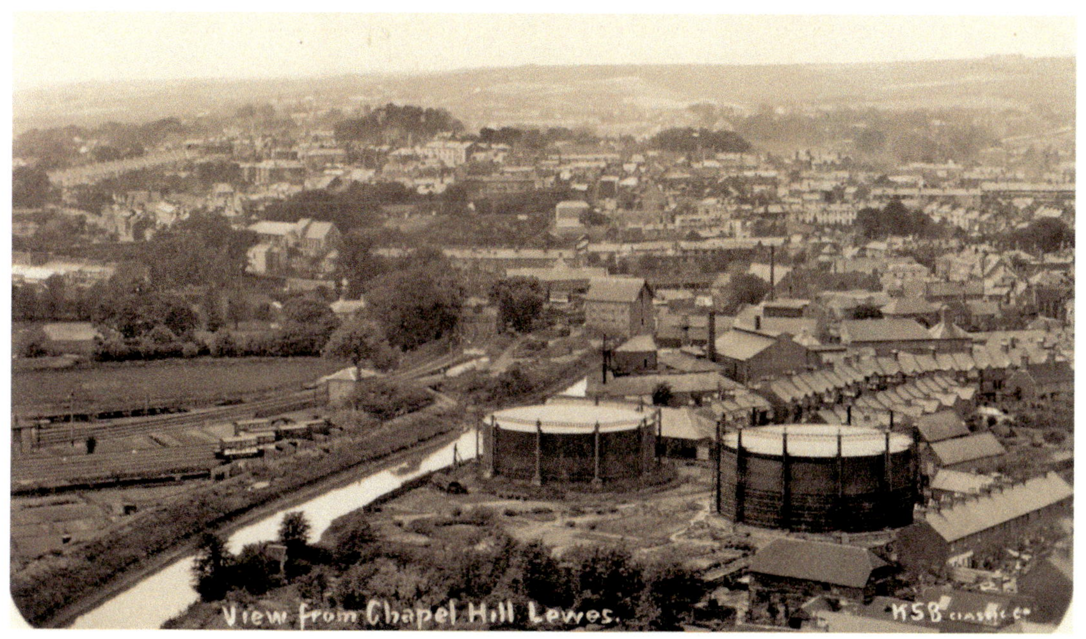

The Gasometers

From the golf course we look down on the town. The old gasometers were prominent until being demolished in the 1960s and stood just off Foundry Lane. The gas company was established in 1822. To the left were the extensive railway marshalling yards which developed along the original route of the Hastings line. This area, together with the expansive grounds of Leighside, now forms the Railway Land Nature Reserve.

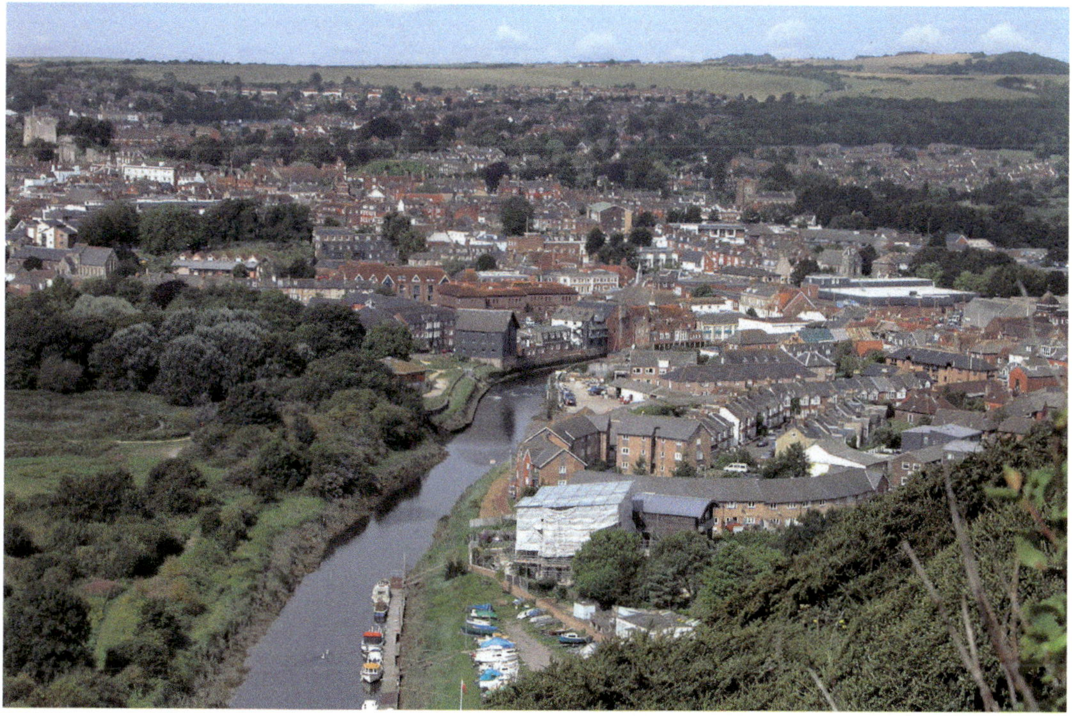

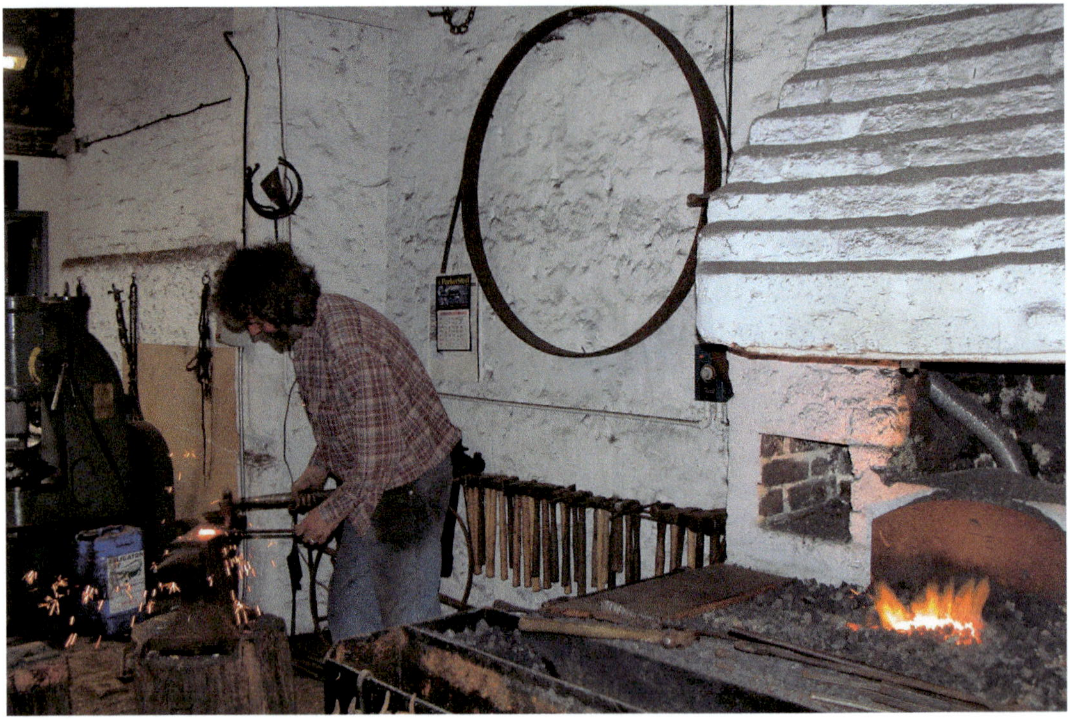

South Street Blacksmith

A busy blacksmith's business operated in South Street and was one of a dozen in the town in 1910. The premises later became a garage. The soldiers either side of the smithy employees could have been Lewes Territorials but more likely were visiting troops. The farms surrounding the town were popular campsites for Territorials and Reservists between the Boer War and 1914. The only surviving blacksmith is Ben Autie at the Star Forge in Fisher Street – a master craftsman and sculptor. The forge has probably been in continuous use for over 300 years.

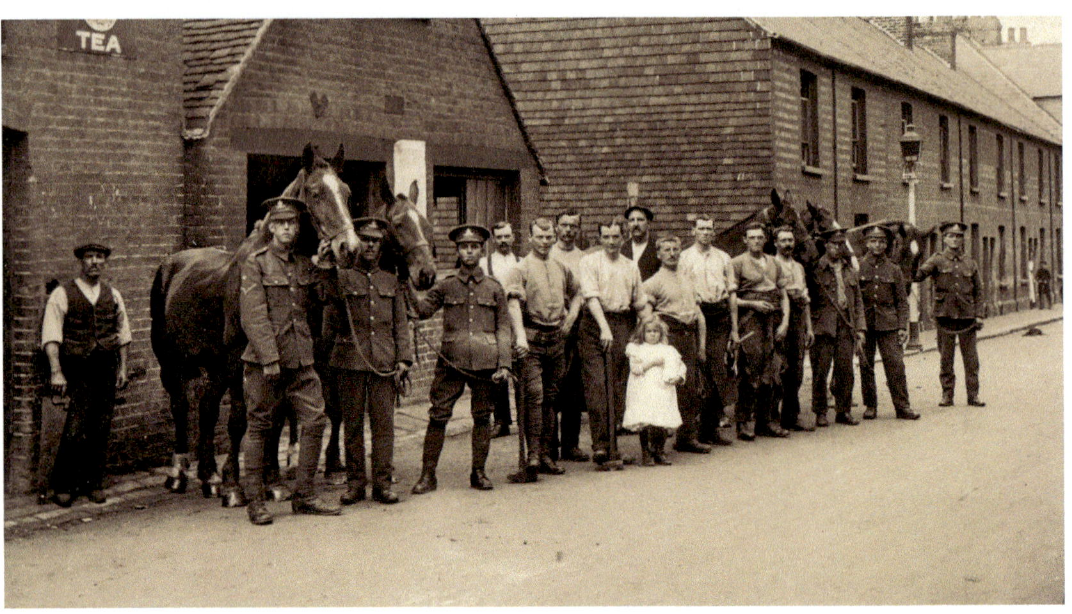

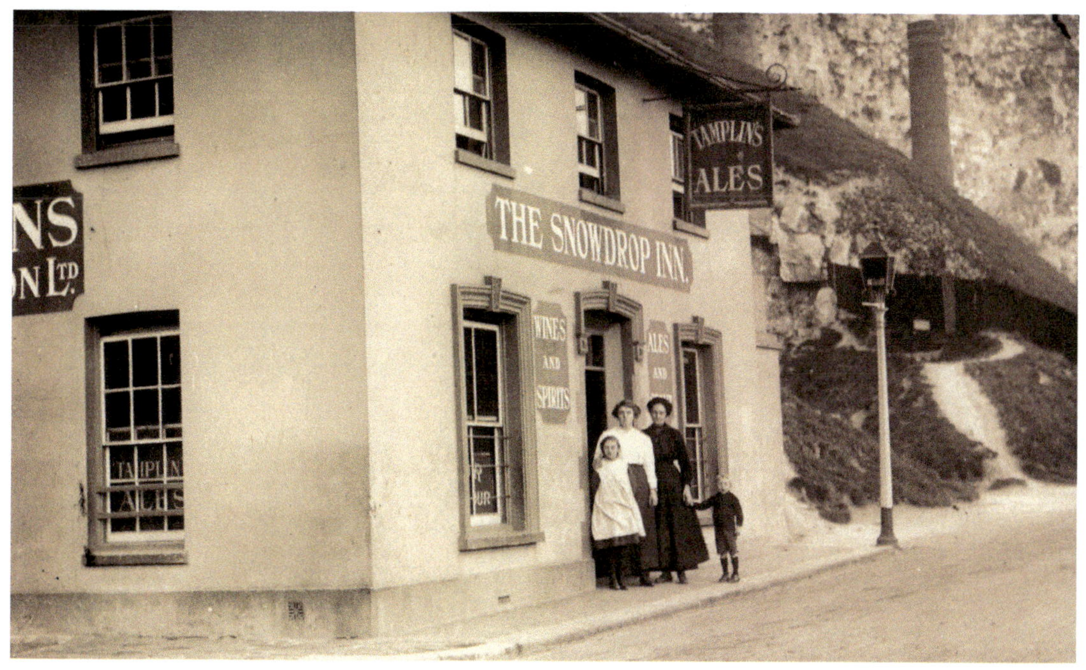

The Snowdrop South Street

The pub's name commemorates one of the worst disasters to hit Lewes. It stands on the site of Boulders Row, the Malling poorhouse, which was buried by an avalanche on 27 December 1836, killing eight of its occupants. The pub has been owned since 2009 by Dominic McCartan and Tony Leonard, who have won awards for their excellent food and wide range of ales

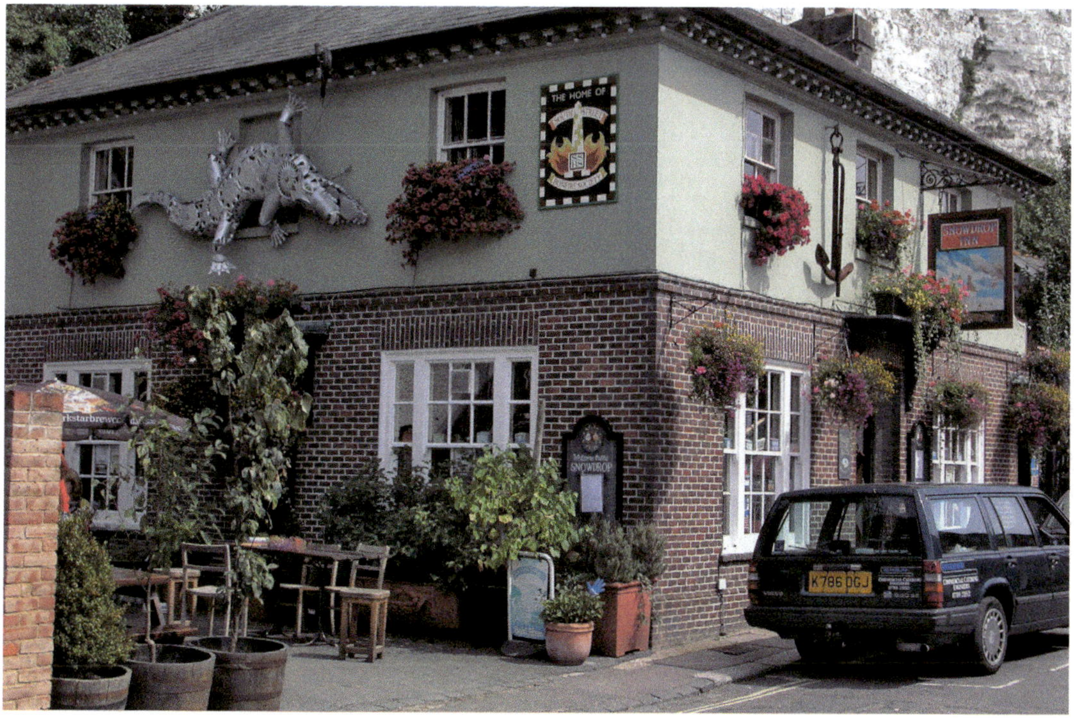

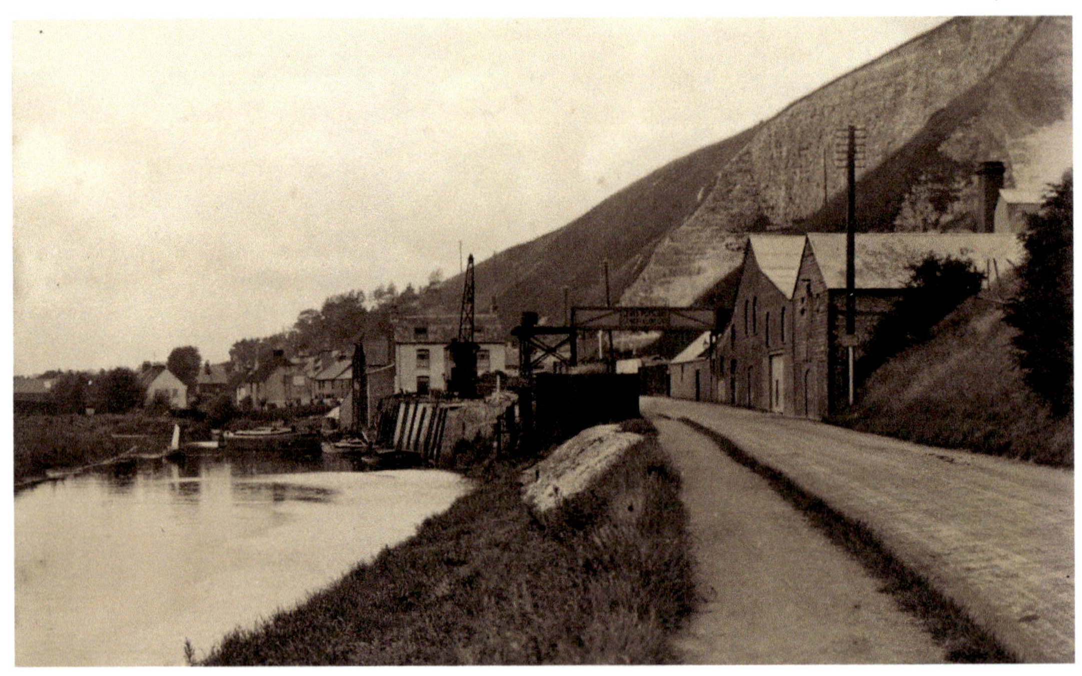

Tunnel Vision

It is difficult to remember life before the bypass and Cuilfail Tunnel. The eastern entrance at the end of South Street shows the buildings and wharf of the Portland Cement Company, which was one of two cement works on the road towards Southerham. The lay-by in the photograph was its approximate position.

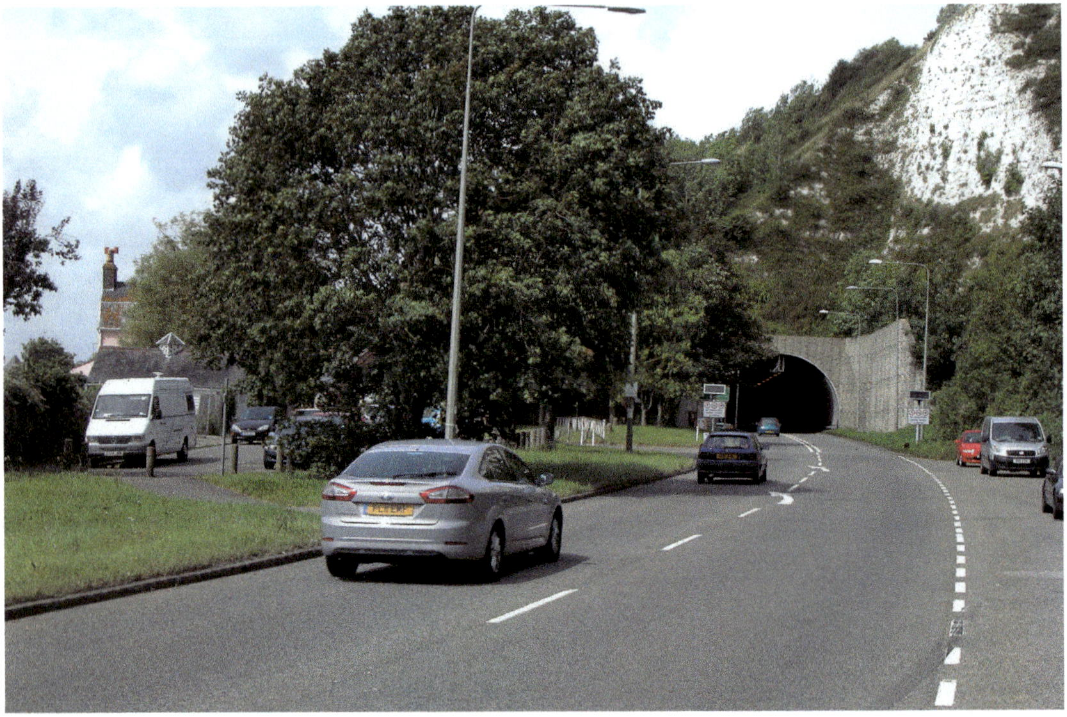

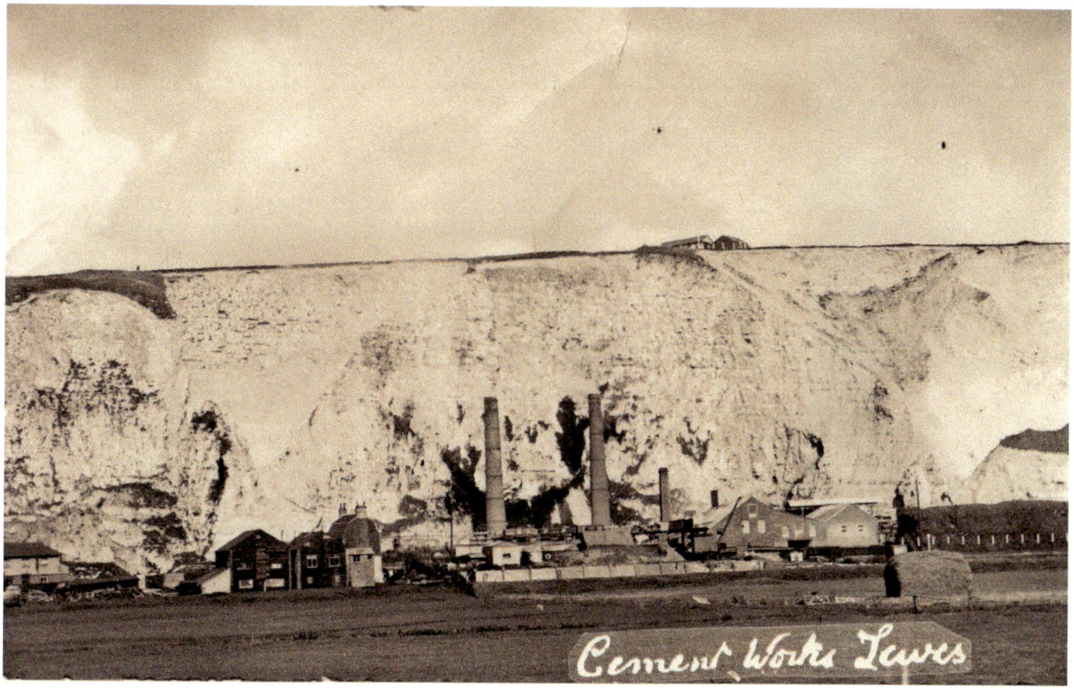

Portland Cement Works

Both images were taken from the opposite side of the river. Notice the golf club buildings directly above. Many of the adjacent riverside buildings remain but South Street is now closed off to through traffic.

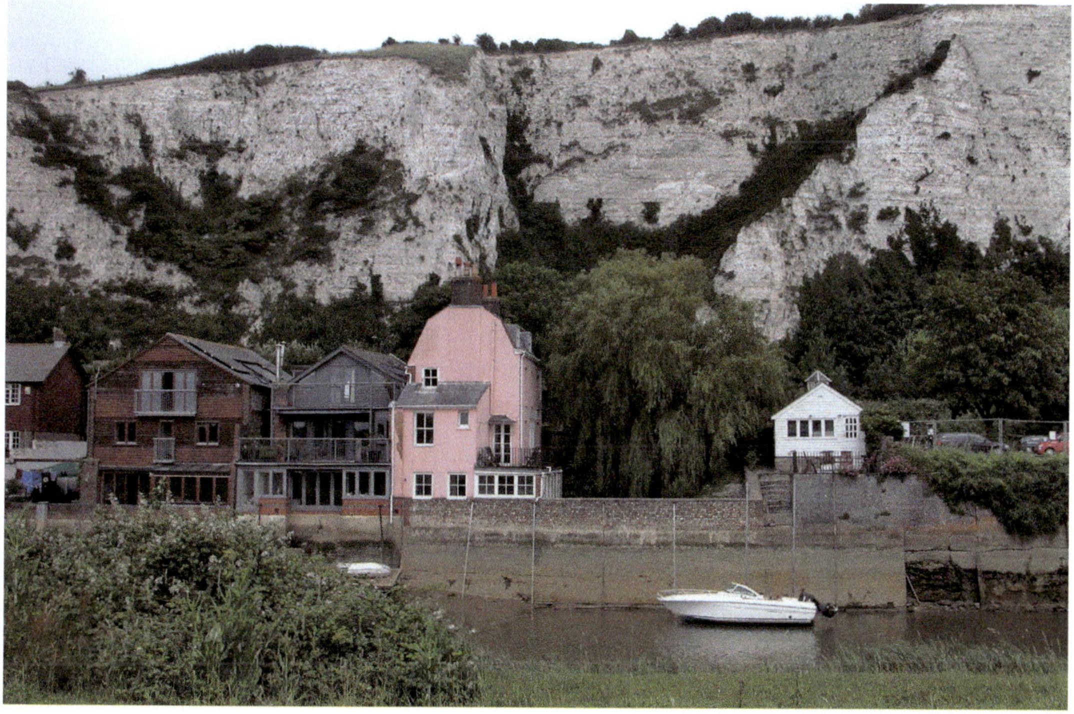

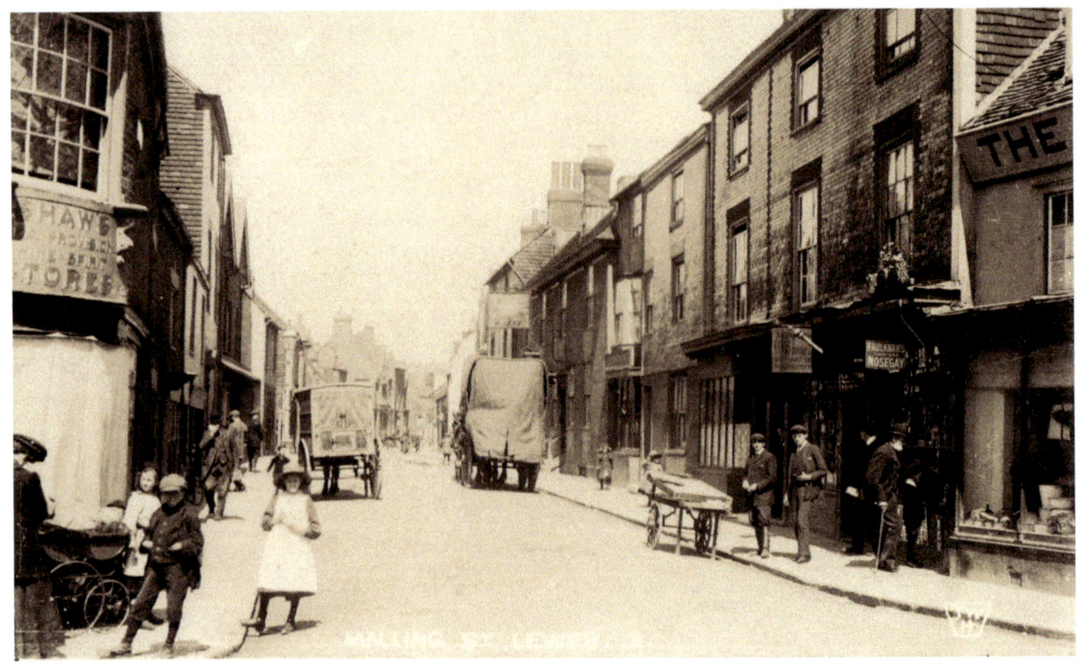

Cliffe Crossroad

We're at the crossroads of Malling Street, South Street, Cliffe High Street and Chapel Hill. It was a leading commercial centre that has largely disappeared. The sign of the Dorset Arms at No. 22 can be seen on the left and almost opposite that of The Swan. The latter closed in 1910 to become a laundry and then an Electricity Board depot. The houses beyond the Dorset Arms were demolished in the 1960s to facilitate a new access road to Cuilfail and the tunnel. Shaw's Stores on the corner became yet another car park.

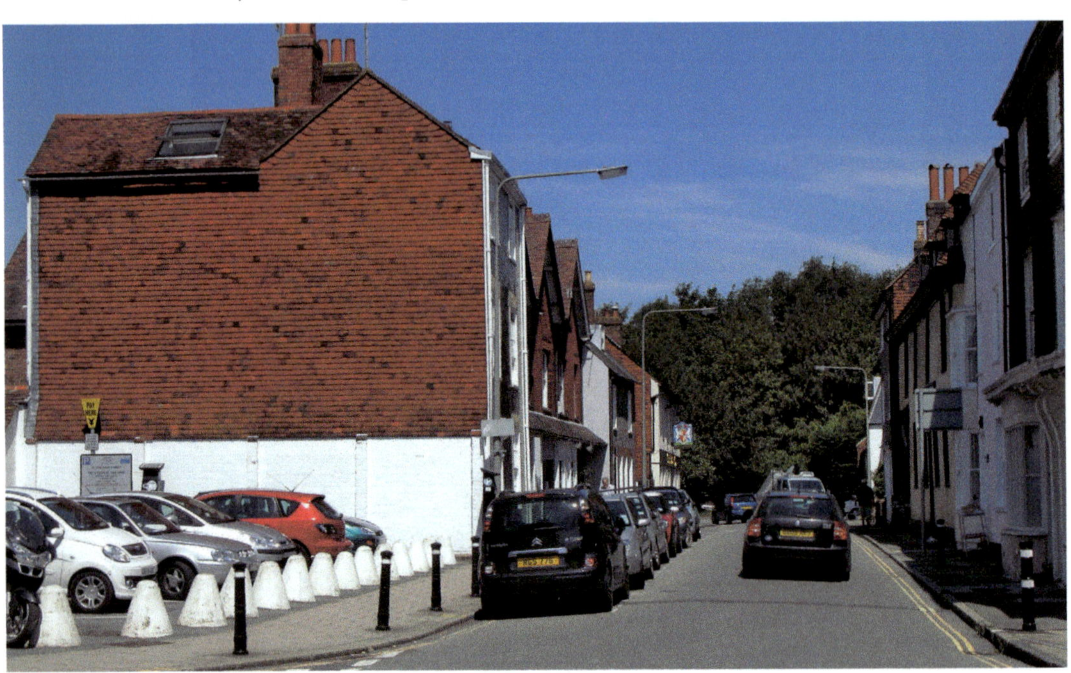

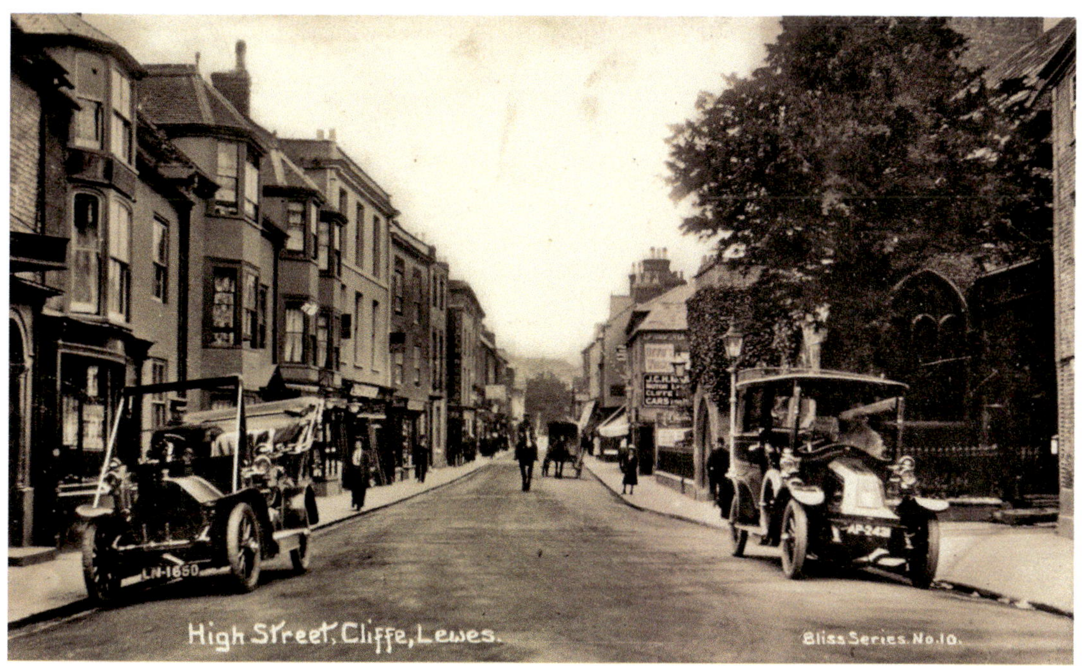

Cliffe High Street

Until the mid-1960s, all traffic from the east and north-east of Lewes would have travelled in and out of town through here. Quiet enough in 1910, with motorised transport still a rarity. Fifty years later the streets were clogged and polluted. Our view is from the junction with Malling Street and South Street and the pedestrian area is now keeping most, but not enough, traffic out. The buildings immediately on the left replaced the Odeon Cinema.

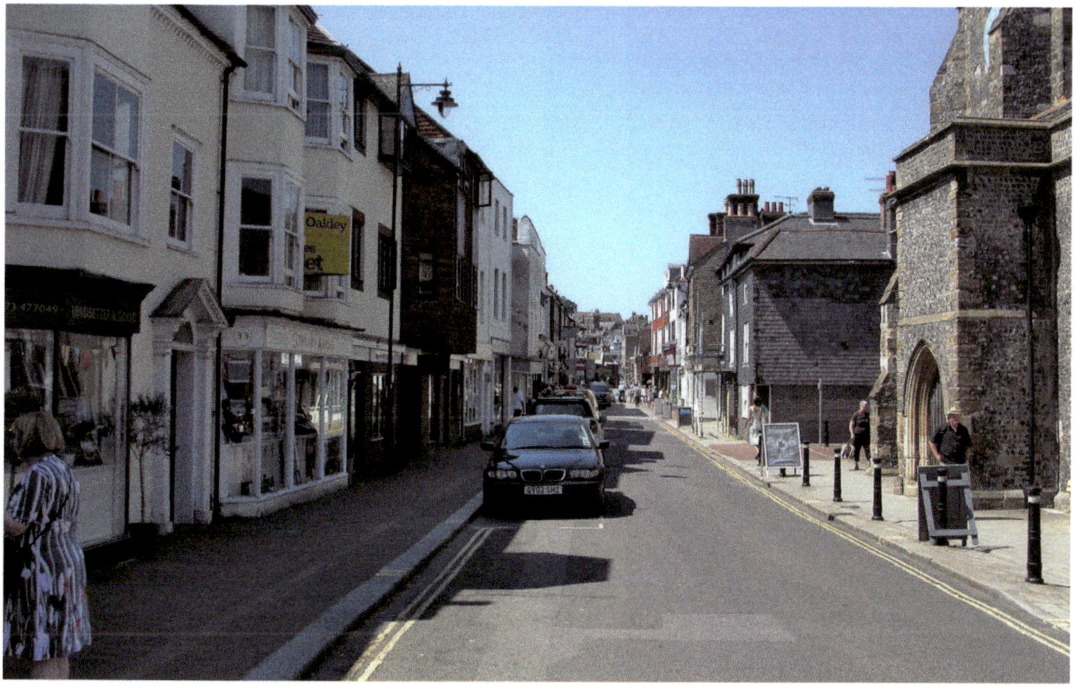

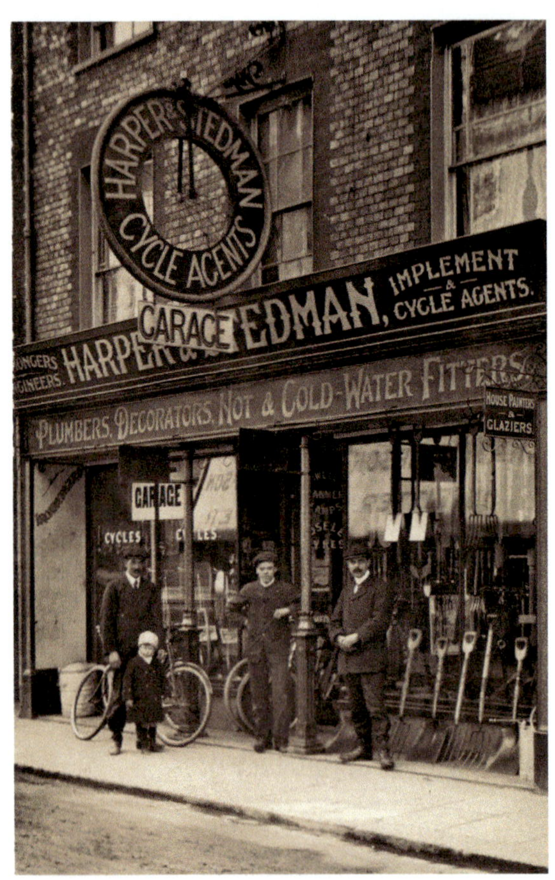

Harper & Stedman

For over 100 years until the 1980s, No. 44 Cliffe High Street had been the Lewes base of Harper & Eede, formerly Harper & Stedman. The business relocated to Ringmer in the 1980s where it still thrives as part of Ernest Doe & Sons Ltd. Its versatility appears to have been behind its success and Lansdowne Health Foods, now in occupancy, offer as big a variety of delicious foods. Susan Dobell, standing at the doorway, was the only staff member not to be photo-phobic!

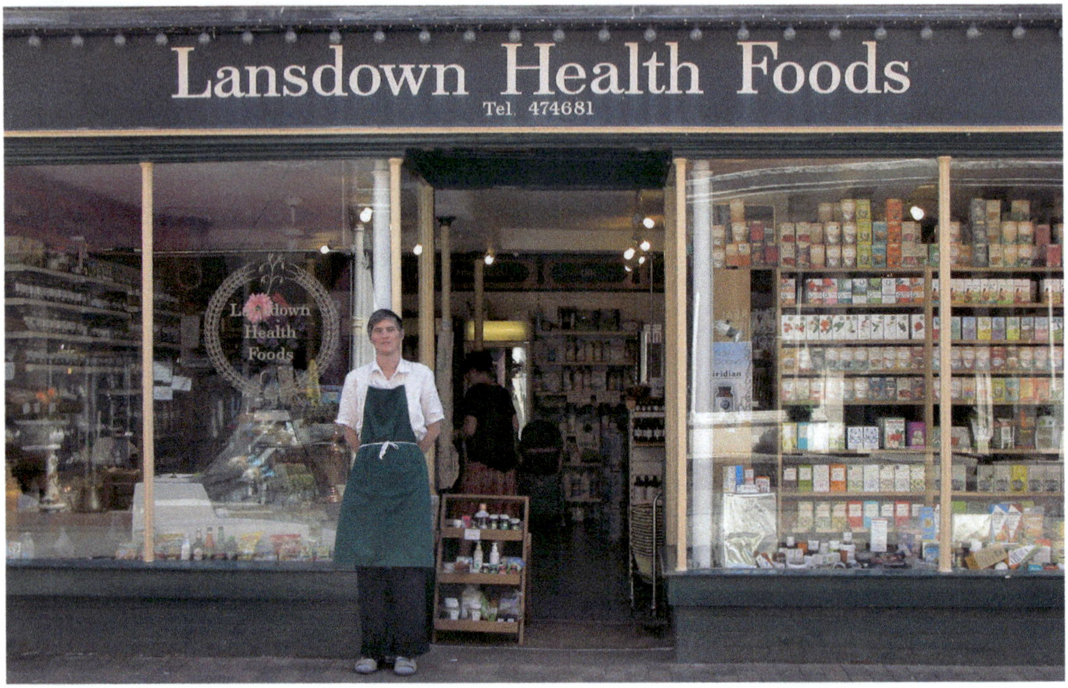

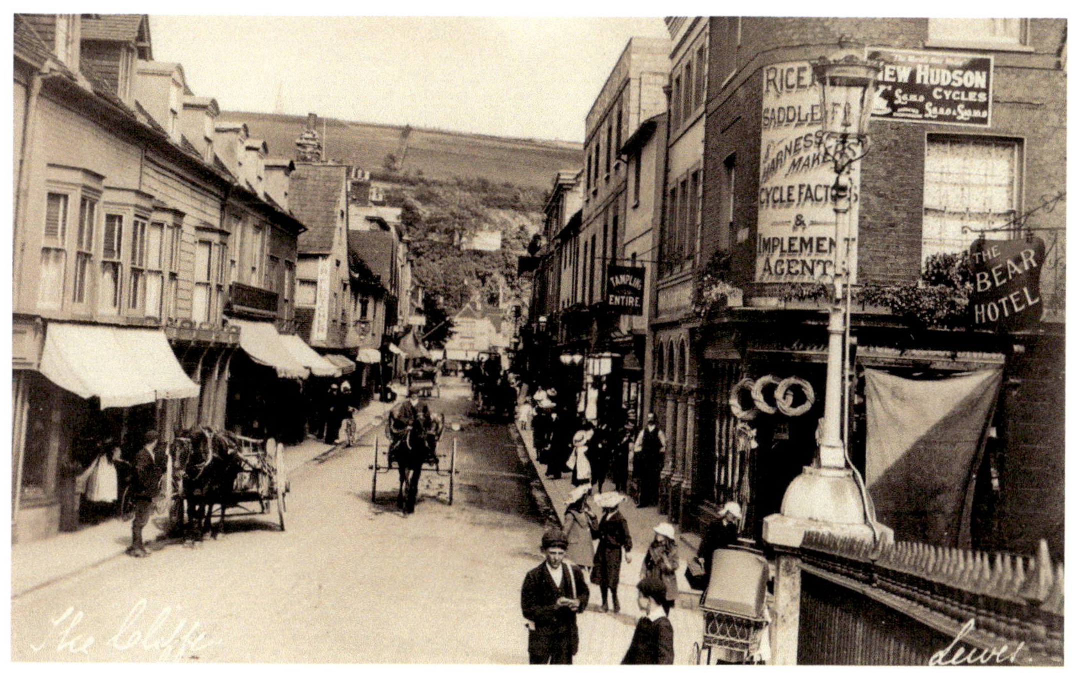

Cliffe Bridge

From Cliffe Bridge we get a better idea of this busy area, which was a separate community until being incorporated into Lewes in 1881. Even now Cliffe retains a lively independence. The river was the divide and the bridge the only crossing until the building of the Phoenix Causeway in 1968. The Cuilfail Estate development is now largely lost in the trees. Bill's original store dominates the corner shop formerly occupied by Rice & Sons.

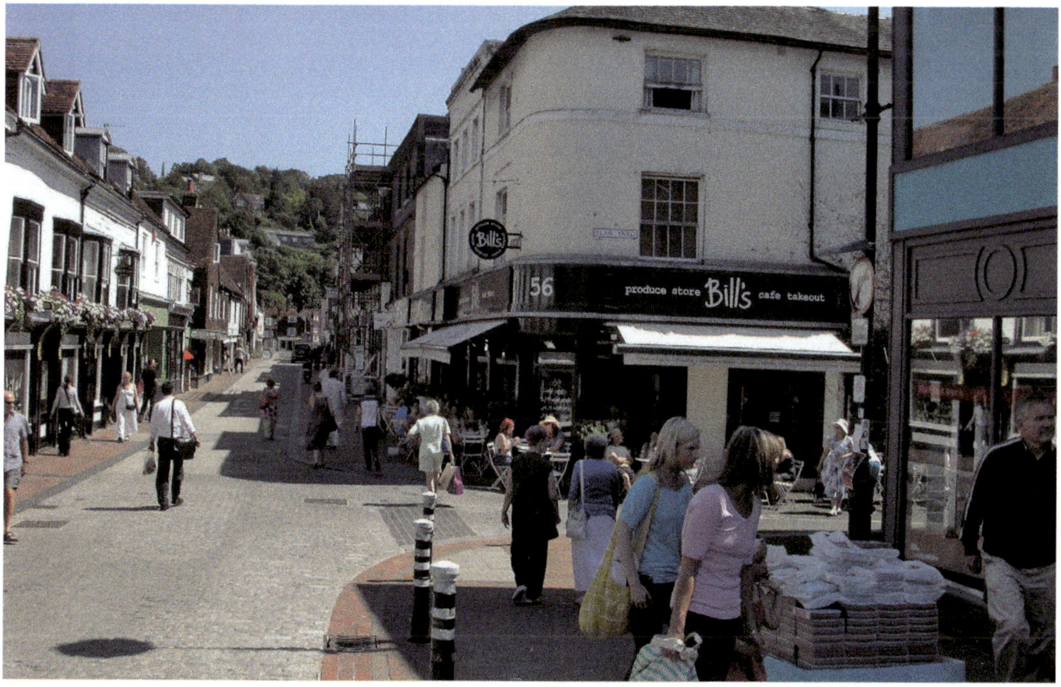

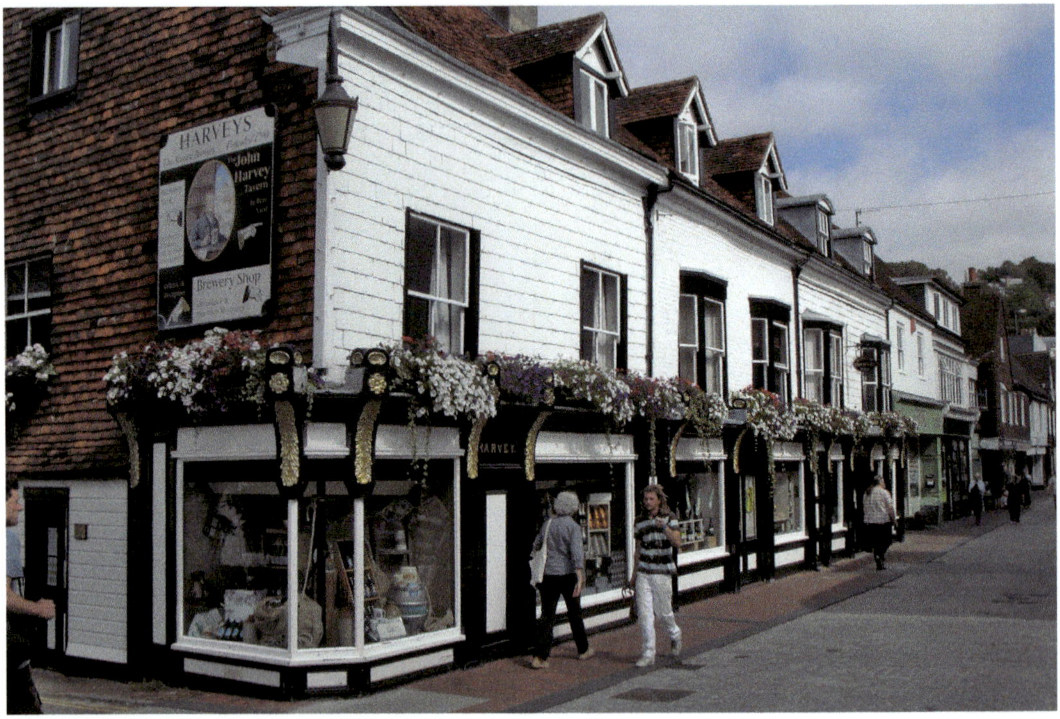

Small Beer and Large Beer in Cliffe

The Cliffe Bazaar looks a strange little shop and sold a wide range of new and second-hand goods. I have not identified the worried-looking owner. Its prominent corner site is now incorporated into the wonderful Harvey's Brewery shop. Harvey's is the last of nine breweries that have operated in Lewes and I love that special aroma of hops which pervades the town on brewing days. I wish I could have provided a scratch-and-sniff patch!

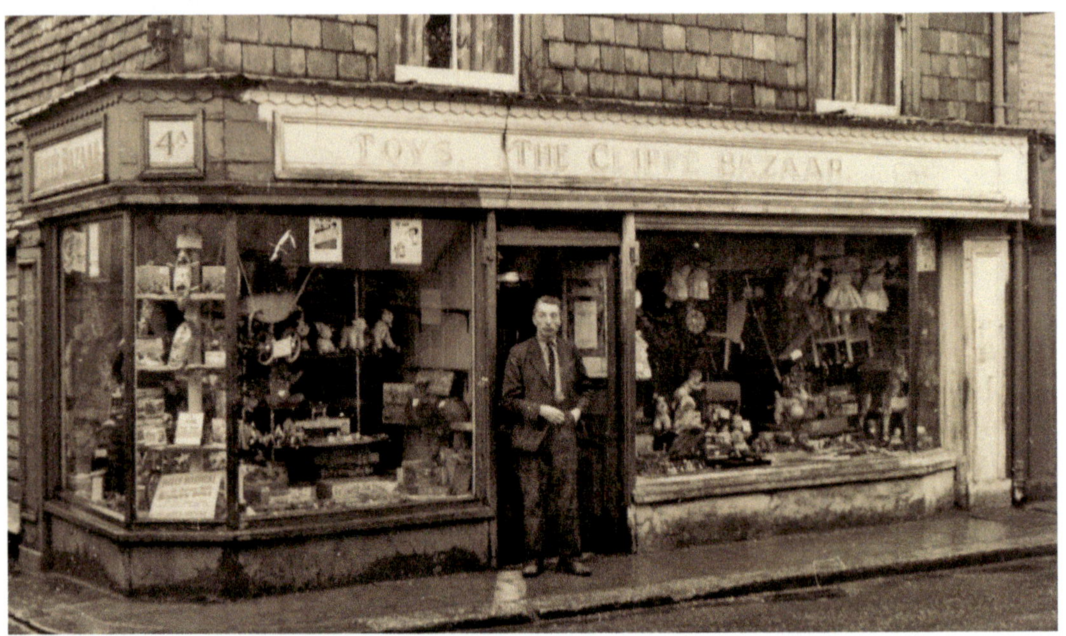

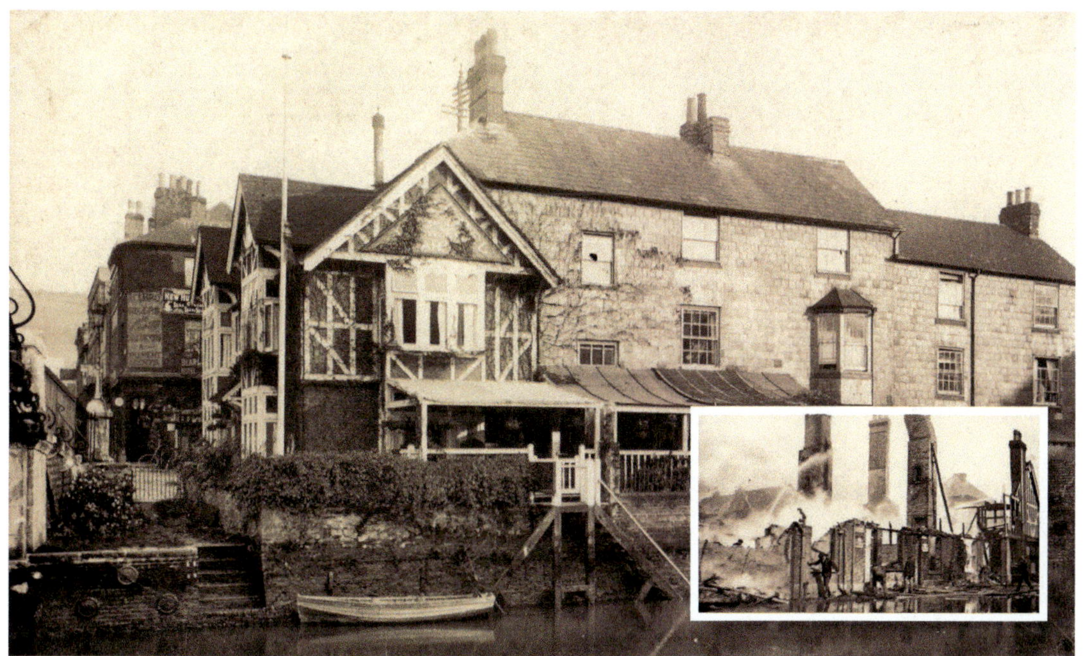

Bear Hotel

This provided the focus for Cliffe business, especially the wool trade, local administration and social activity. It stood by Cliffe Bridge for more than three centuries until burning down in 1918. The fire was devastating and the inset postcard shows the side view in Bear Lane. There was stabling at the rear for up to eighty horses. Further stables on the other side of the lane are now the John Harvey Tavern, run by Lisa Martin and Peter Riches. It is noted for its food and is the Cliffe Bonfire headquarters.

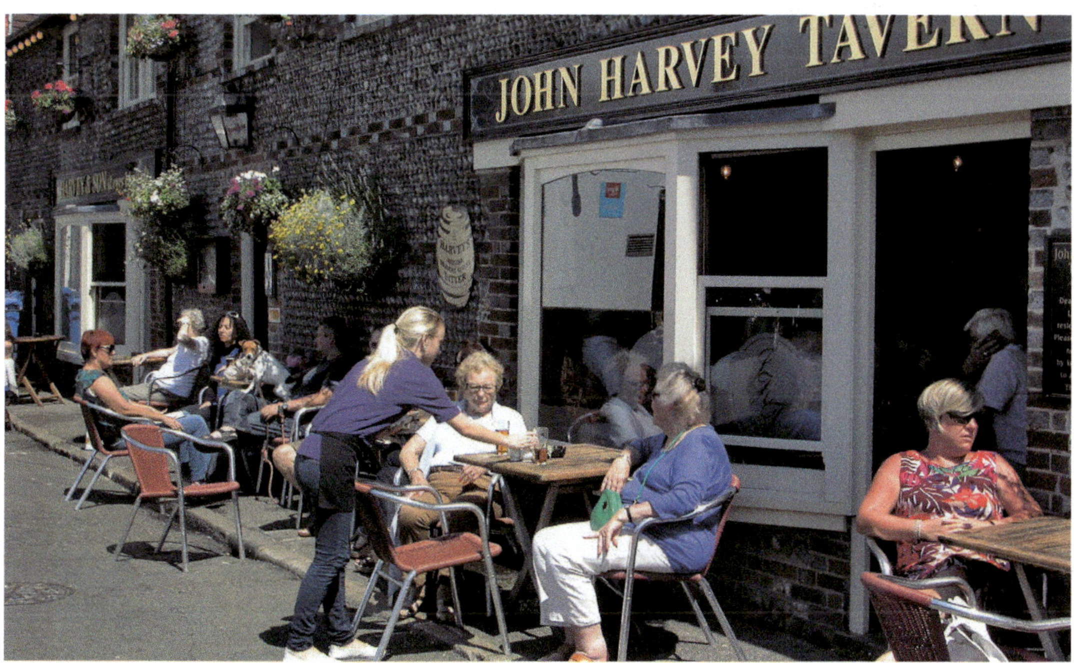

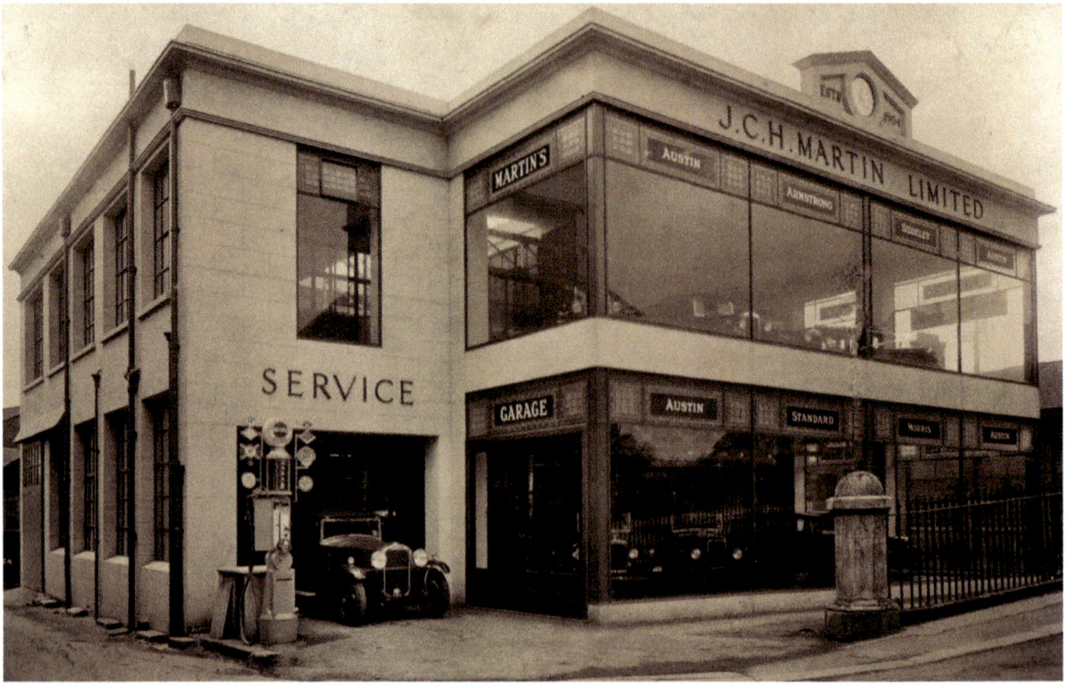

Martin's New Garage

The Bear site was quickly cleared but stood empty until Martin moved across the river in about 1930. In the 1960s it became a FADS store and latterly Argos. It is a rare and striking Art Deco building – possibly the only one in Lewes.

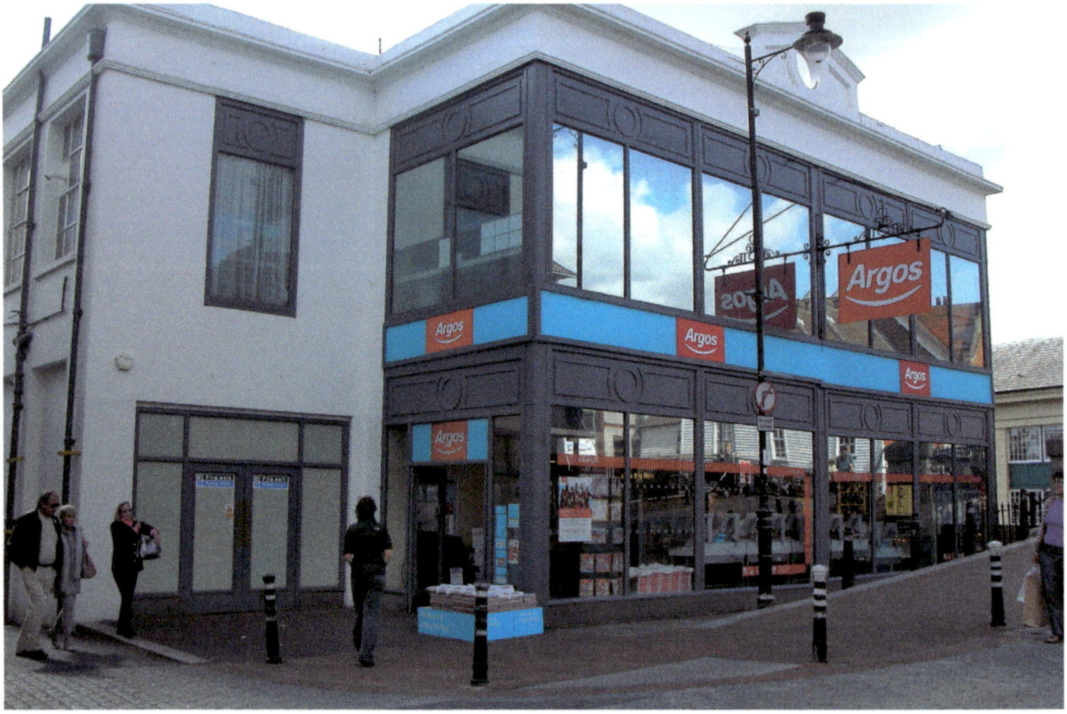

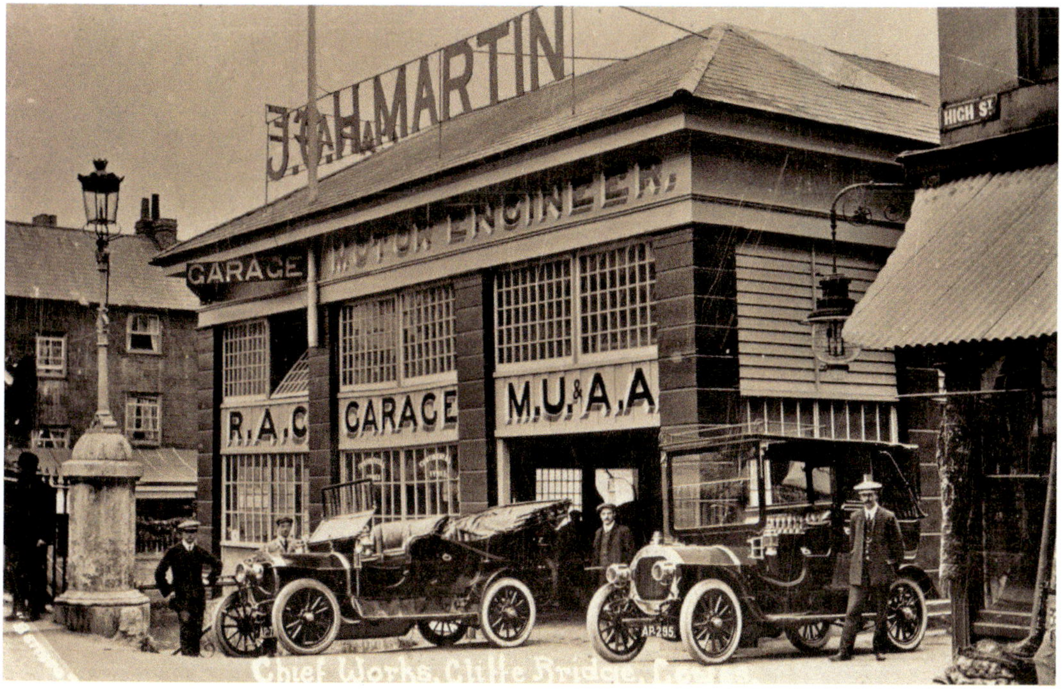

Martin's Original Garage

This occupied the riverside building before relocating 30 yards to the other side of the river. It was used by other businesses, notably as a factory for Russell & Bromley in the nineteenth century and by Beck's Taxis twenty years ago. It gradually fell into disrepair but was luckily saved from demolition and became the lively Riverside Centre.

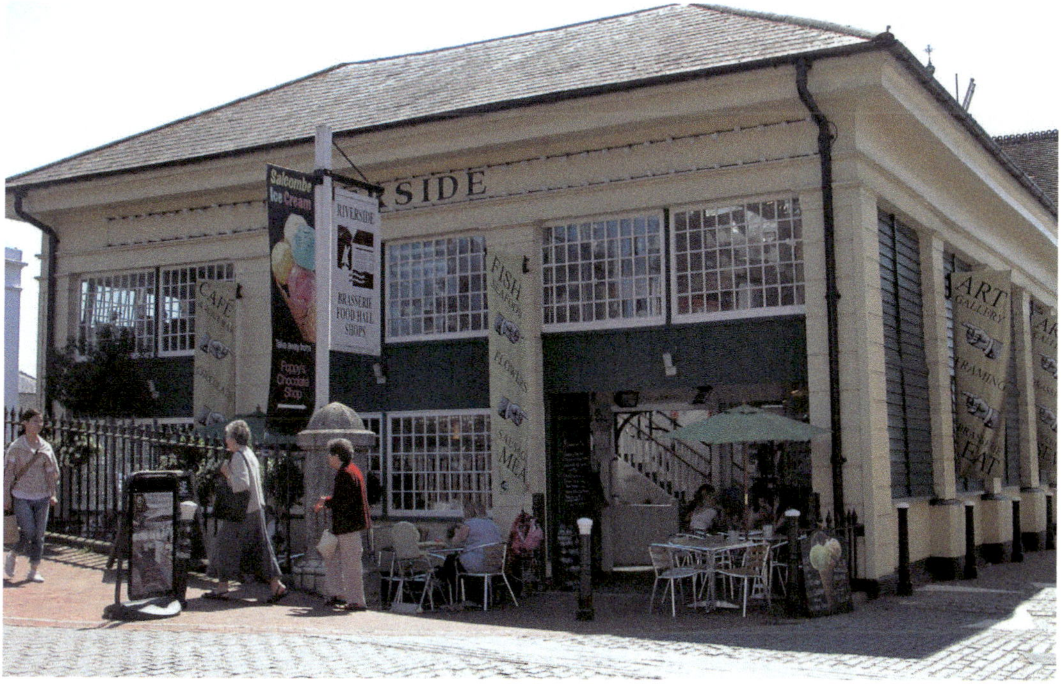

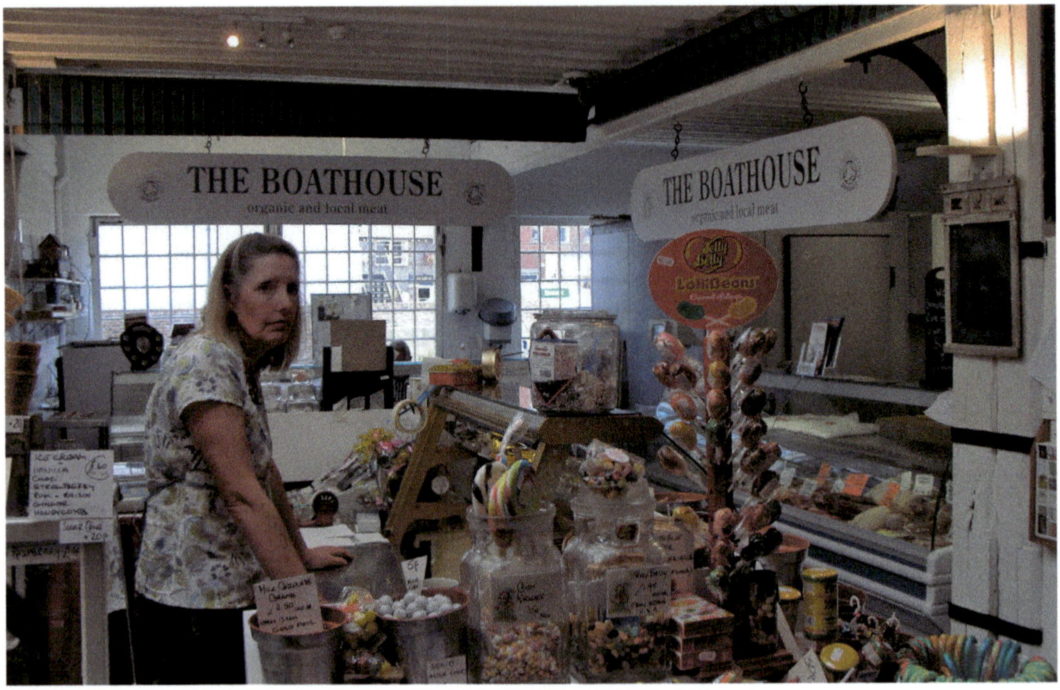

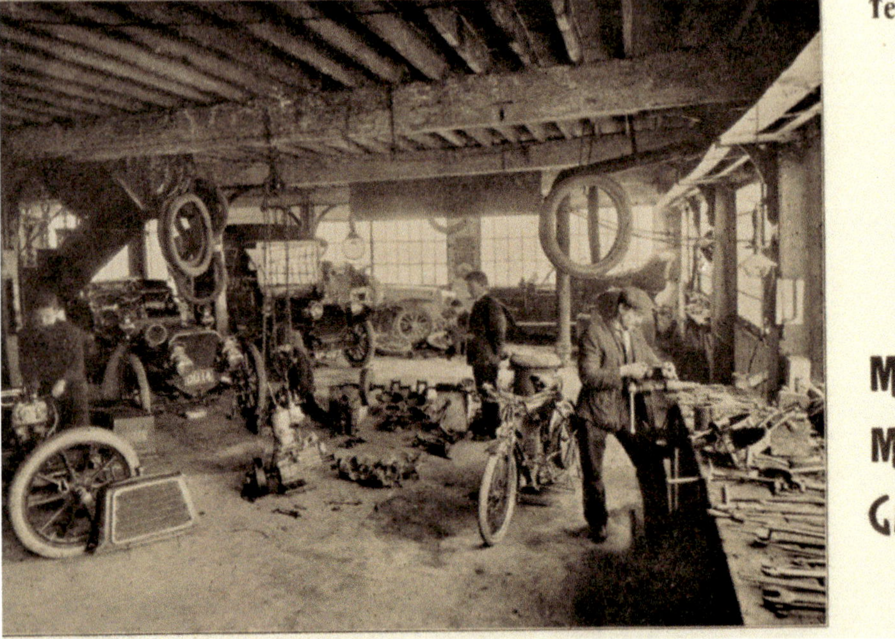

Inside Martin's Garage

This rare interior view shows the garage employees hard at work on motorcycles and cars. The tools and processes look primitive compared with today but most garages developed from being blacksmiths and wheelwrights. Martin sold out to Caffyn's in the 1950s. My photograph looks across the stall of Poppy's of Lewes, run by Sue Shultz, to the Boathouse stall and river view beyond. How did you ring Lewes 45a?

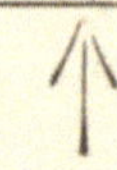

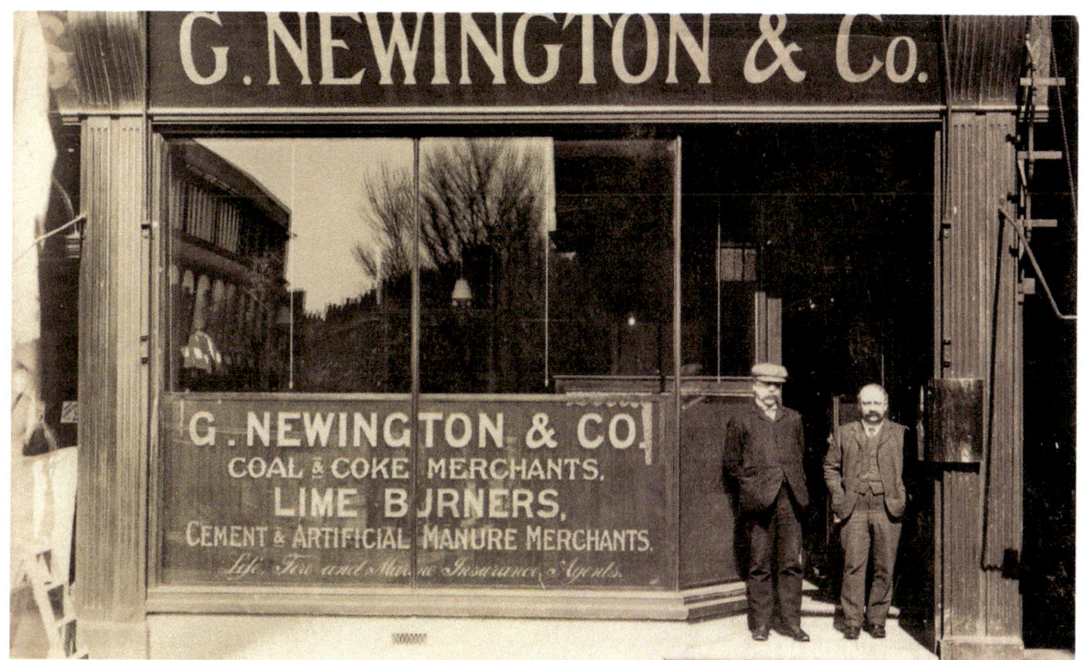

Newington & Co. Lime Burners

This was one of the many local businesses that thrived on the back of the two cement works. They were next to Hepworth's, as shown on the following page, and occupied part of the Seveirg Buildings which were demolished in the 1960s to develop the town square area. Costa Coffee is now on this site.

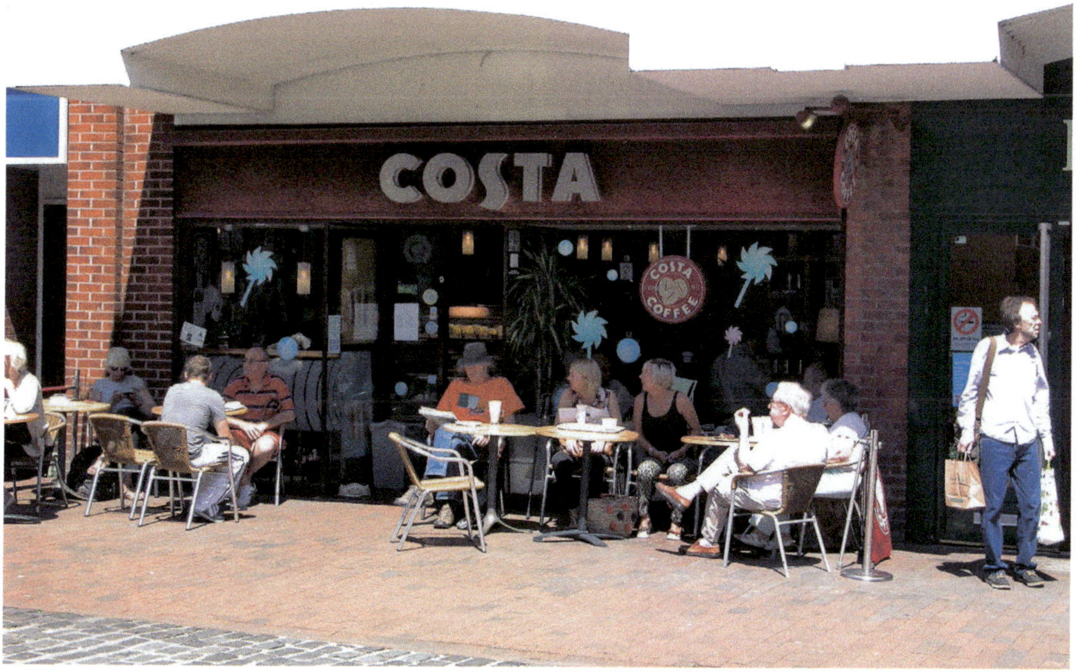

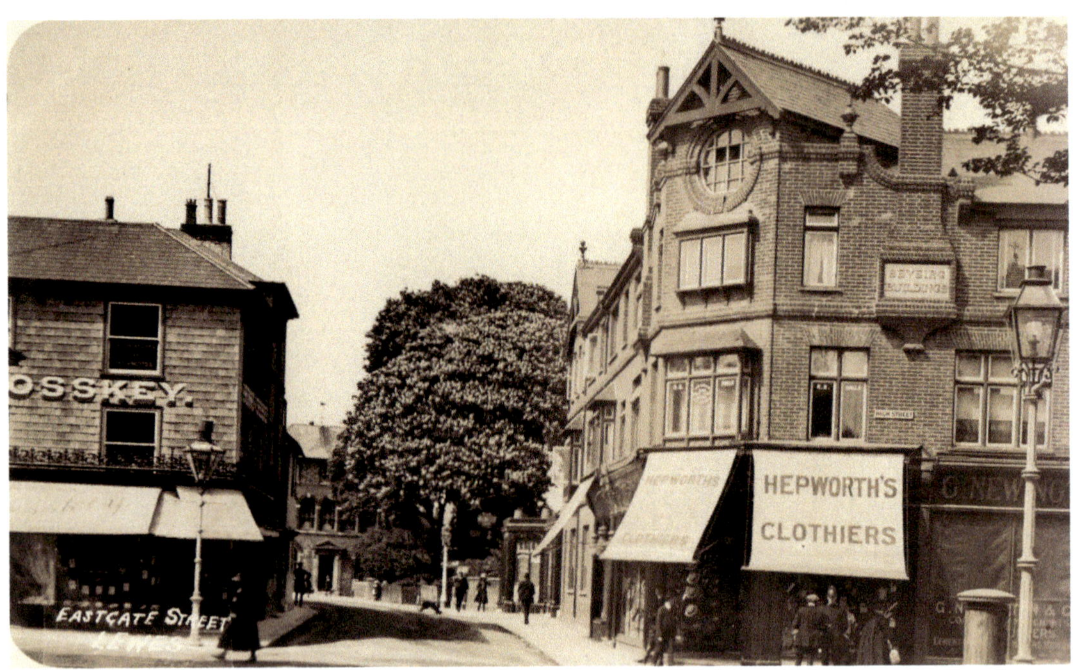

Eastgate Street

This quiet scene looking into Eastgate Street reminds us of the eclectic business of Browne & Crosskey, built on the site of the Holy Trinity church, and of the fine-looking Seveirg (the owner's name backwards) Buildings on the opposite corner. All tranquillity is now gone, with traffic rushing in from the Phoenix Causeway, and it is best not to comment on the ghastly Boots store. Nearby was the medieval East Gate entrance into the town.

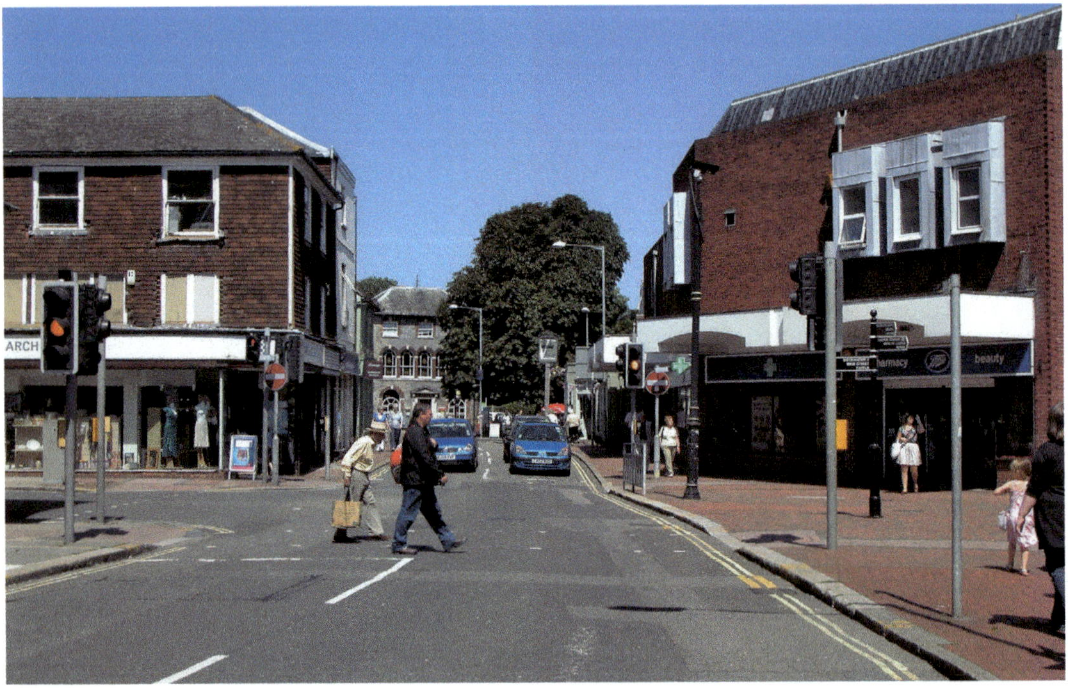

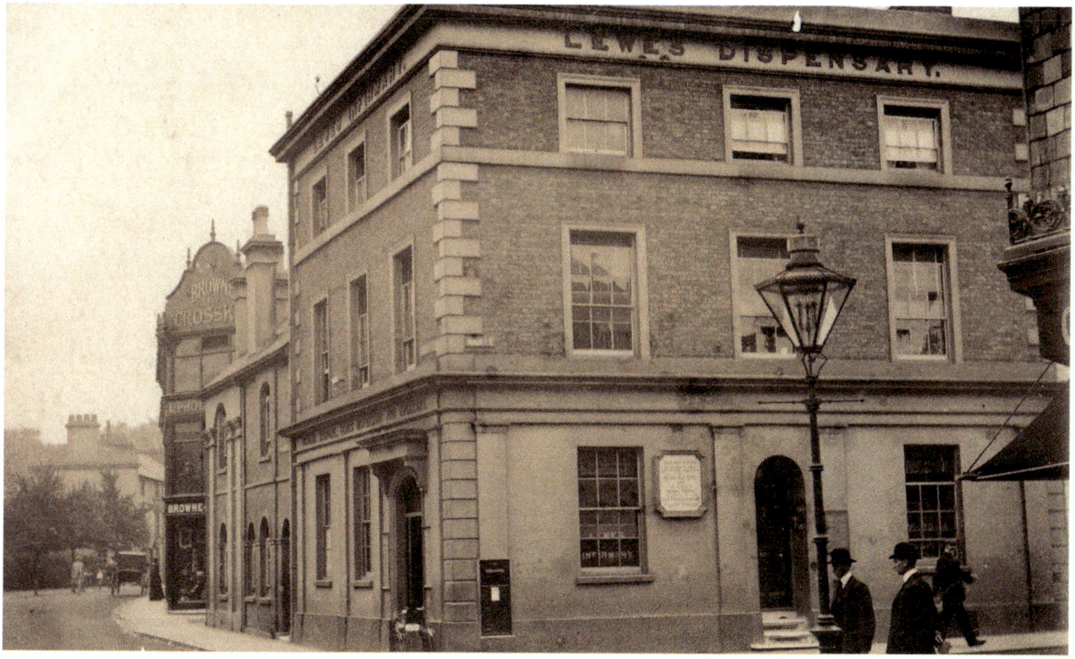

Lewes Infirmary

Looking in the opposite direction we see the Lewes Hospital, Infirmary & Dispensary and, beyond, Browne & Crosskey's furniture store. The infirmary provided for those unable to pay for medical care but not receiving poor relief. Payments were made by an employer or patron subscribing half a guinea (55p) a year. It was replaced by the Victoria Hospital in 1910 and the building became the Lewes, and then Sussex County, Building Society and is now the National Westminster Bank. The Sussex Ambulance Service Headquarters are on the furniture store site.

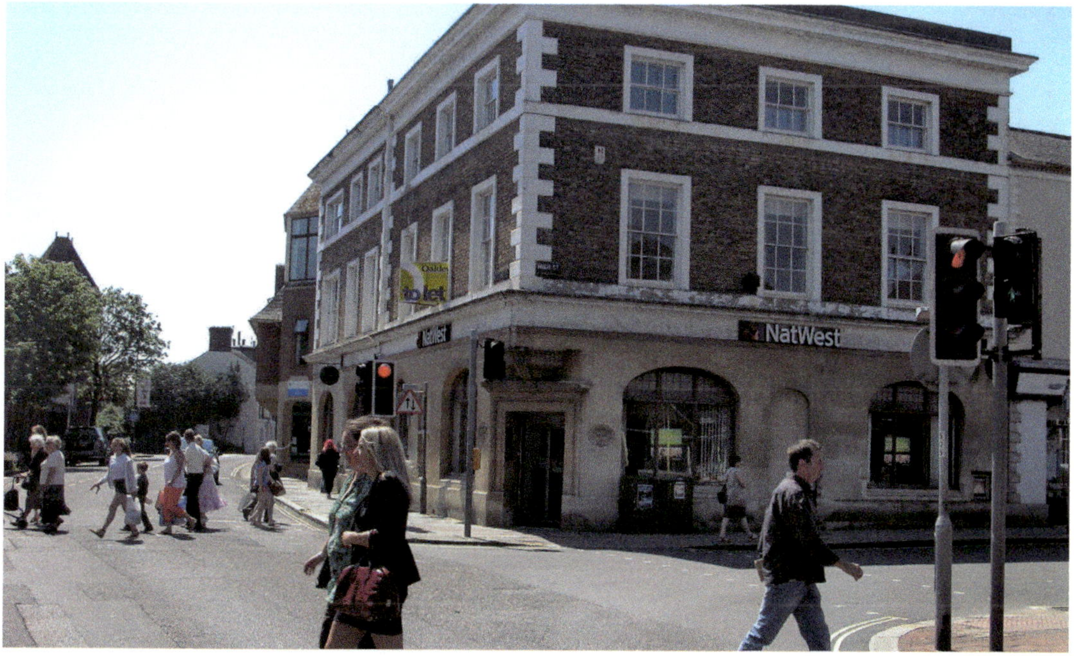

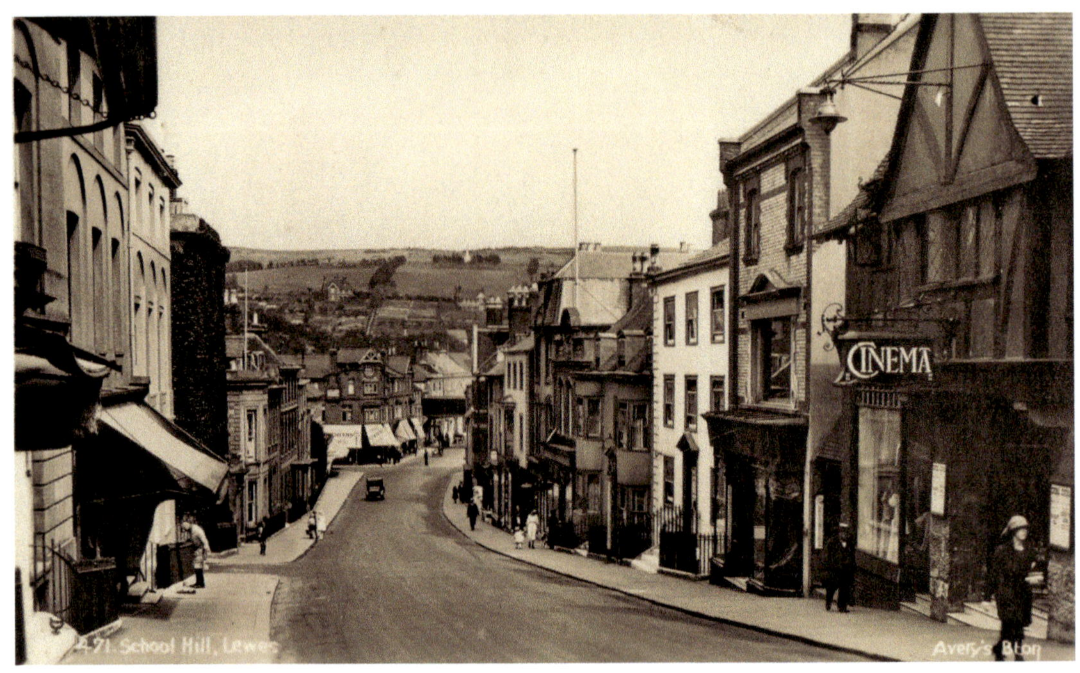

Cinema De Luxe, School Hill

We have climbed just above the junction with Albion Street. The Cinema De Luxe operated where now the *Sussex Express* building stands. Wickle, one of my favourite coffee stops, occupies the former Clothkits premises and is just as funky. It is typical of the shops here and on the High Street in being narrow and long (laid down on a Saxon plan of 10 by 100-feet plots according to John Houghton) and with interesting cellars.

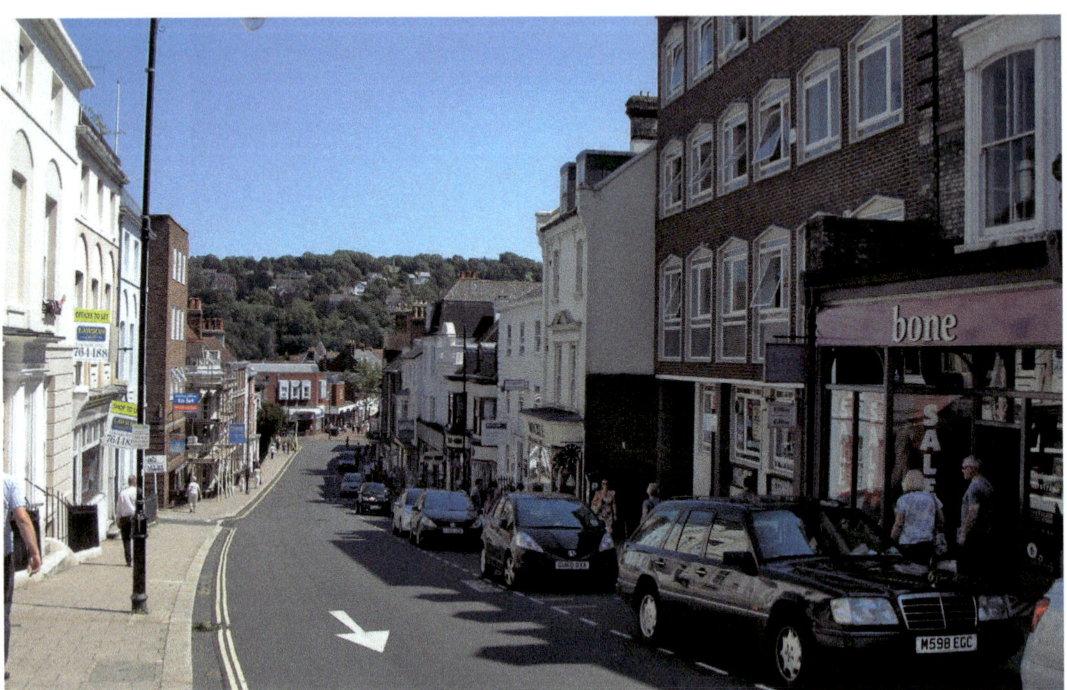

Market Street and the Crown inn

This is the junction of Market Street, formerly Aylward's Corner, and School Hill. Now the main road out of Lewes, it was quiet enough in 1907 for the girls to stand unconcerned in the middle of the road. The Crown Inn has had a chequered past but survives after 300 years, while Addison's opposite is now an estate agents. The Market Tower, next to The Crown, was built in 1792 and houses Gabriel, the town bell, removed from the church of St Nicholas, which occupied the nearby war memorial site.

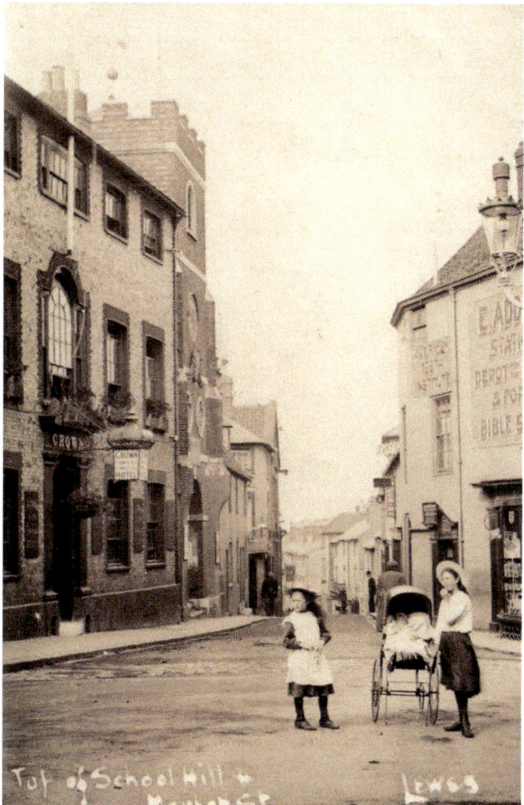

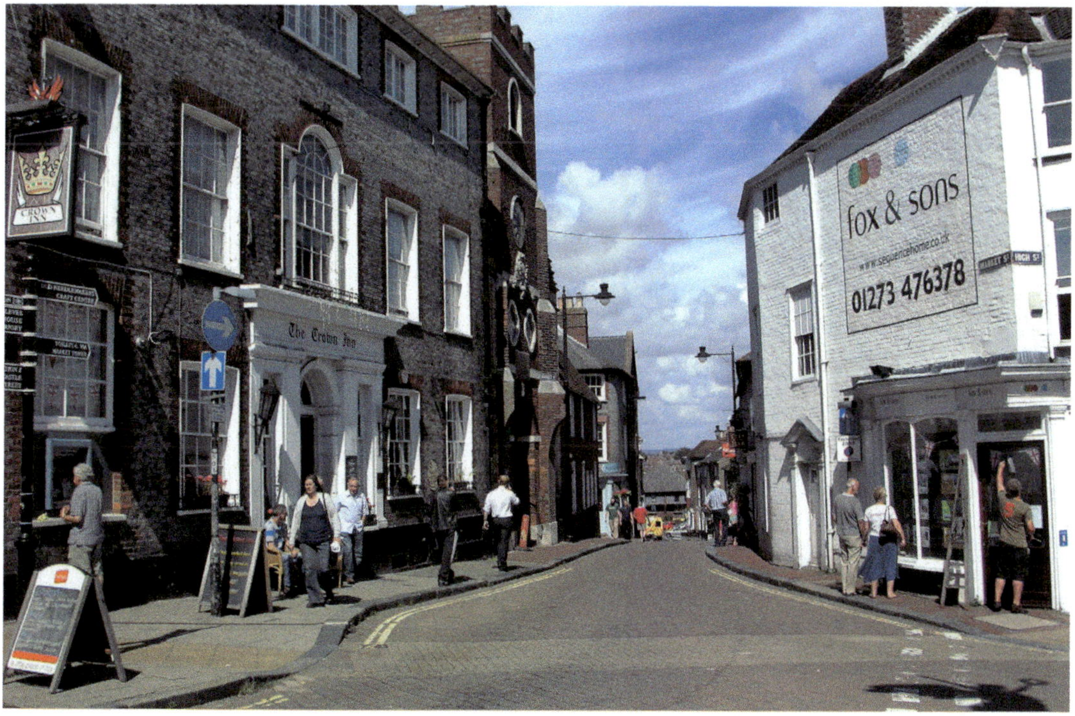

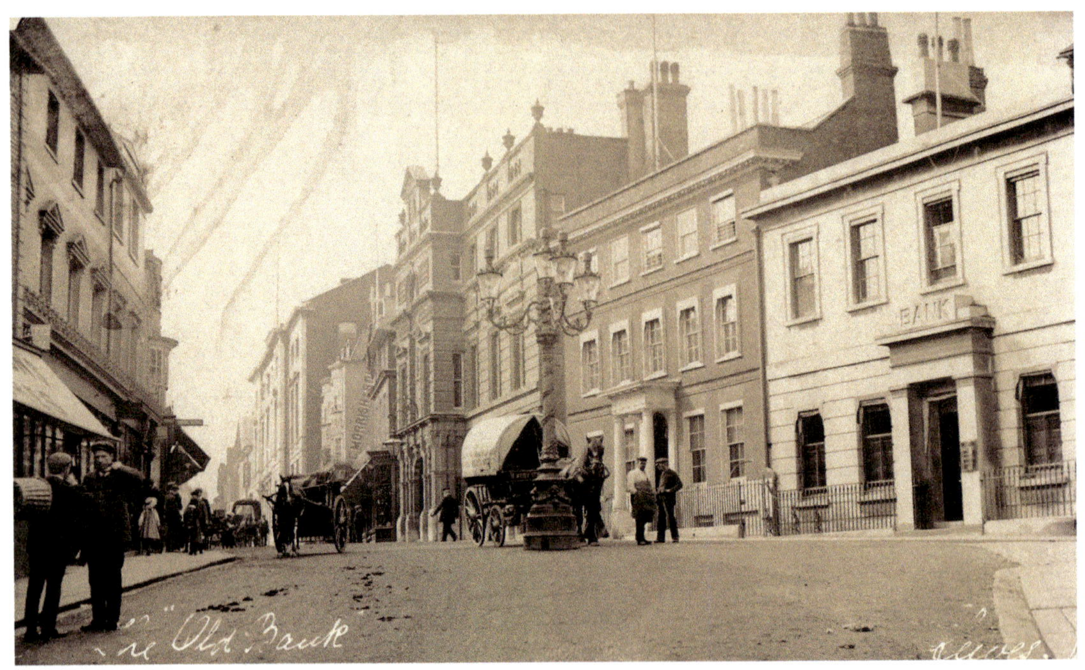

Before the War Memorial

The top of School Hill appears more spacious without the war memorial, which replaced the ornate lamp standard in 1922. To the left, the fine brick Town Hall was built on the site of The Star coaching inn in 1893 and outside of which the Protestant martyrs were burnt in 1555–58. Next, the grand town house of Mr Whitfield adjoins Lewes Old Bank, of which he was a director. It became part of Barclays but retained its name.

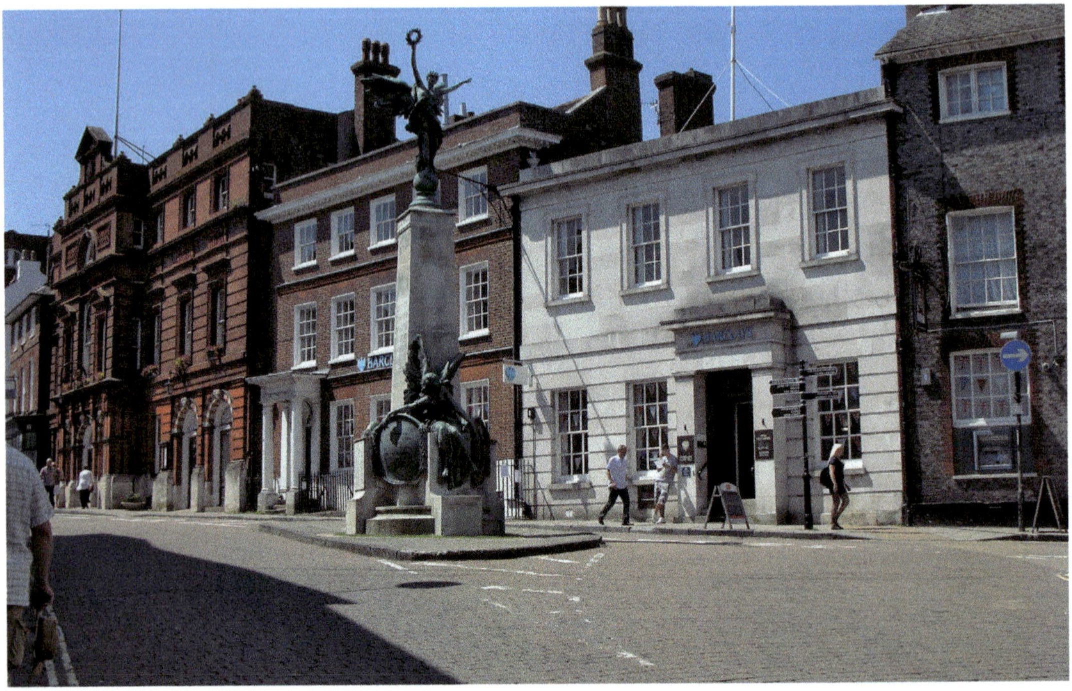

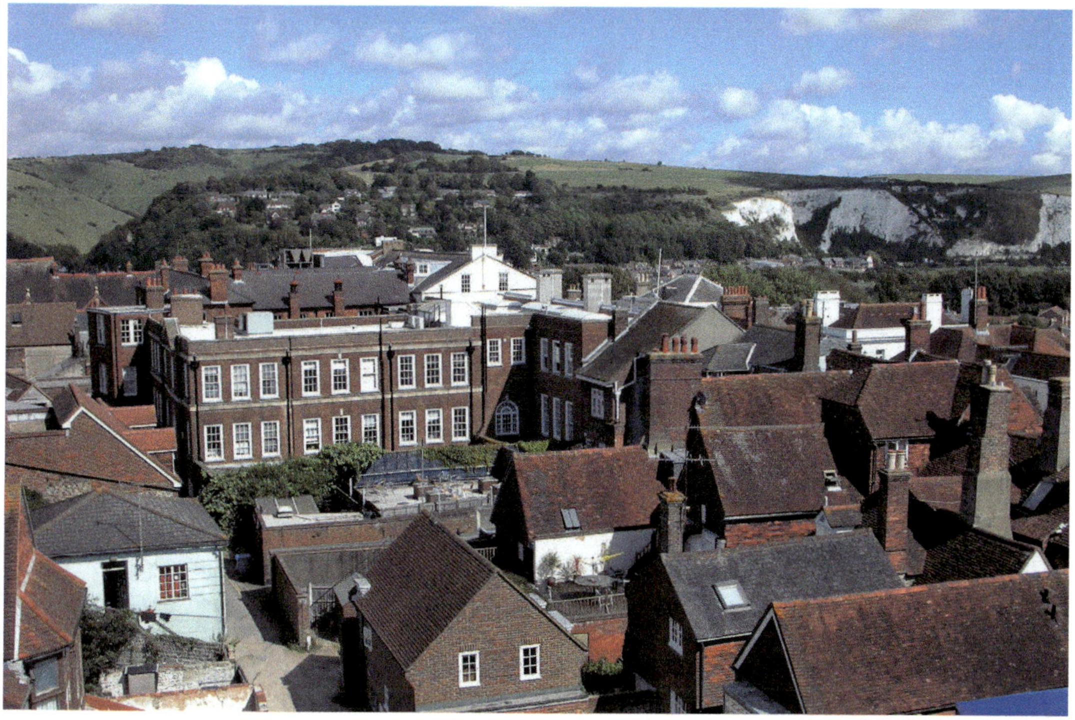

East from the Castle Tower

This view has changed little in 100 years. The County Hall and the long-time Assizes, now the County Court, have been extended to the rear and abut Castle Ditch Lane. Trees and development have covered Cuilfail in the background so that the Martyrs' Memorial is lost from sight.

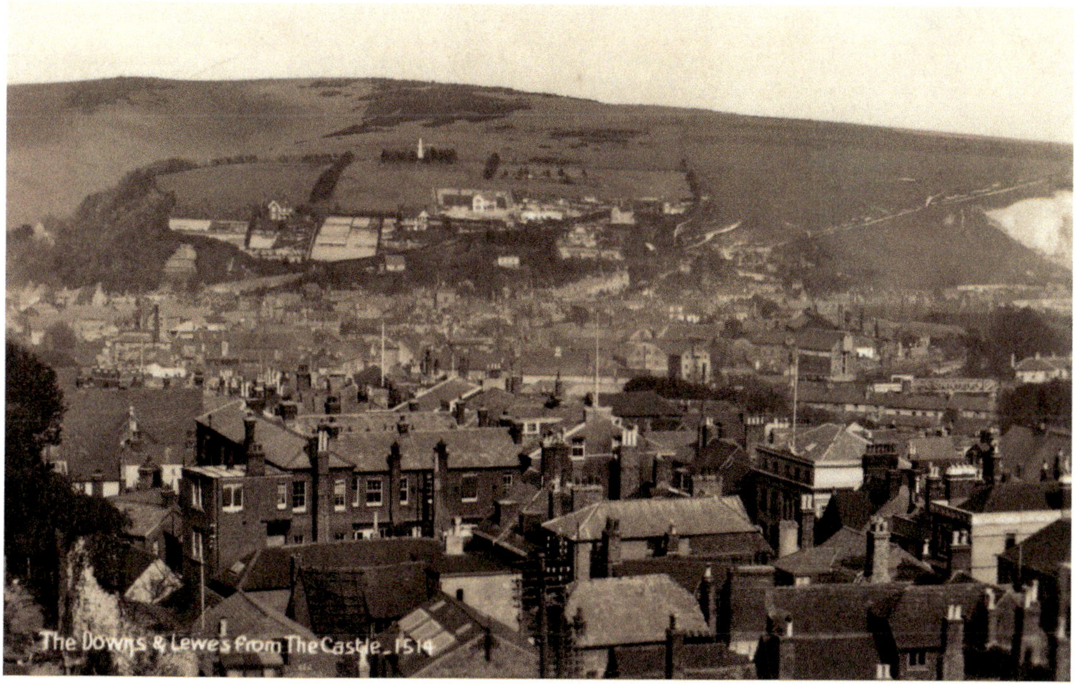

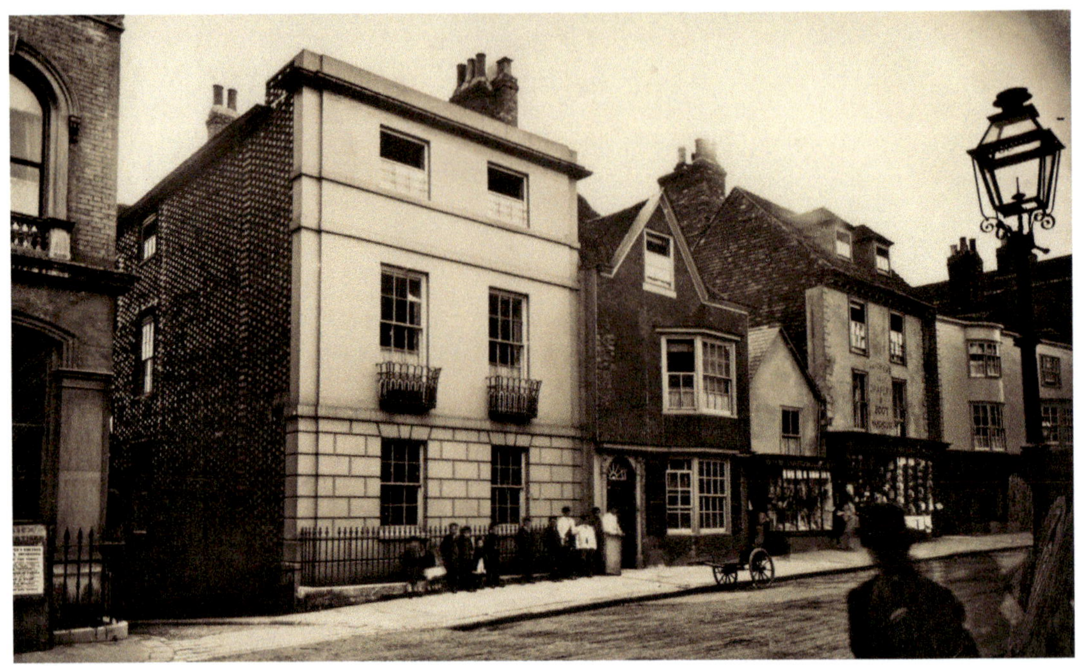

Post Office

Like many Lewes buildings, the post office is little changed in its upper stories. At the end of the nineteenth century it became a private boarding school for Quaker girls after moving from Dial House. It was run with twenty-five boarders by Mrs Rachel Special and sisters Mary and Katherine Trussed. Religious instruction was given at the Meeting House in Friars Walk on Wednesdays and Sundays. I'll give you a tip; always look up at buildings from the opposite side of the road.

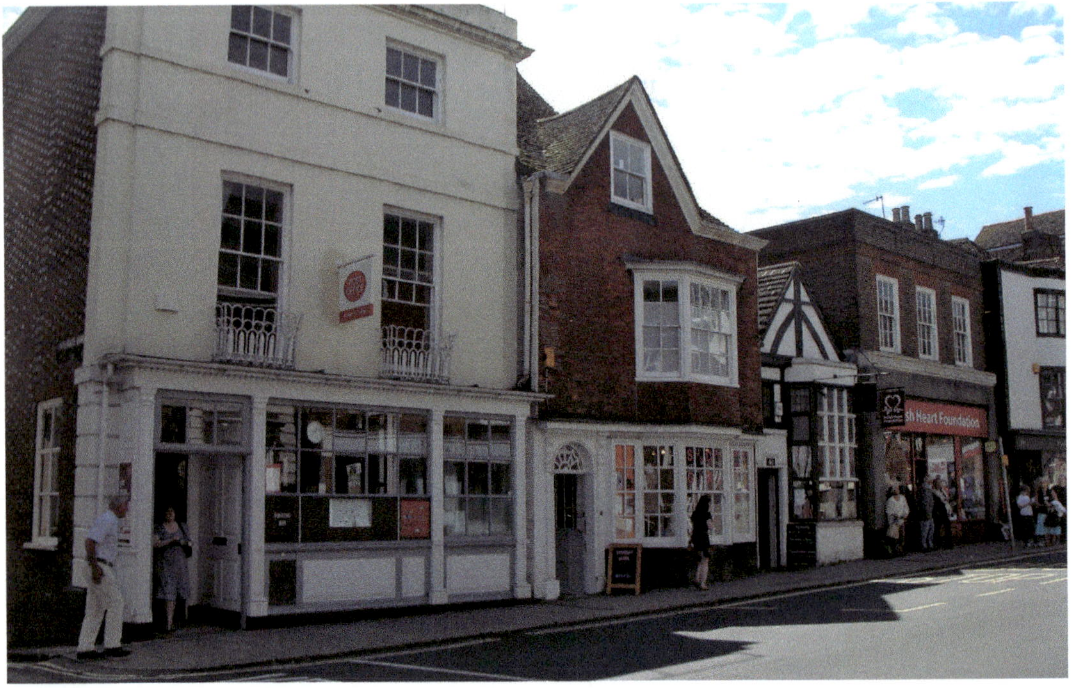

County Theatre, Watergate Lane

By the side of the post office we cut into Watergate Lane, which leads down to a former watergate in the town wall. Near the top of the lane on the east side was Lewes' little-known third cinema, the County Theatre; obviously a grand place judging by the well-dressed commissioners. It was demolished in the late 1920s to allow the County Council to add a council chamber to Pelham House, which it had purchased in 1922. Pelham House was used as the County Council headquarters until 2004, when a new chamber was created at County Hall. The Lewes Little Theatre in Lancaster Street now provides our high culture, as does the Lewes Operatic Society.

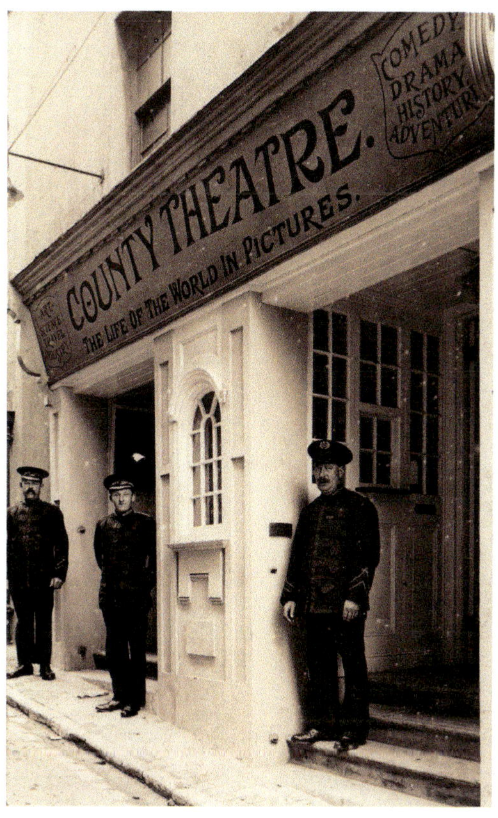

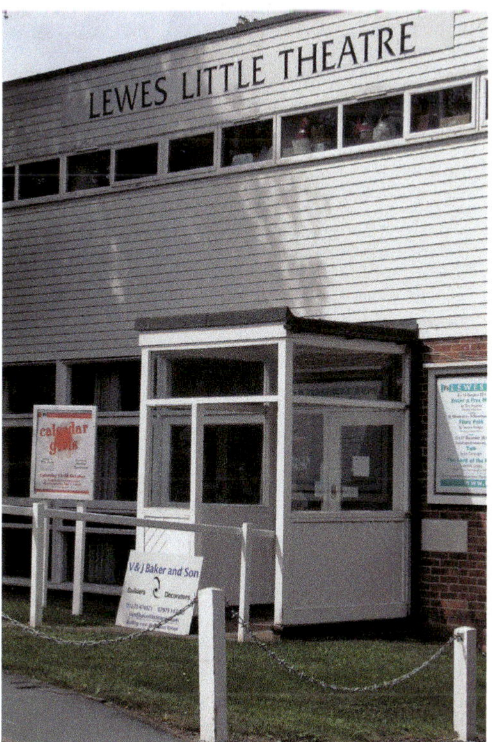

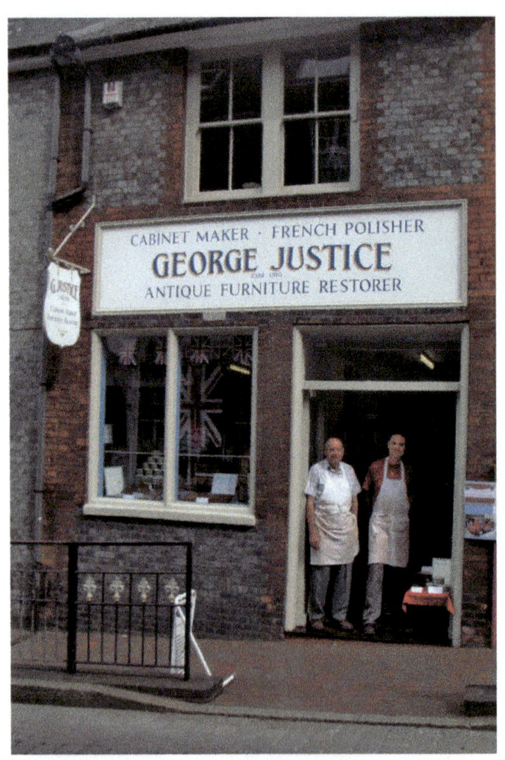

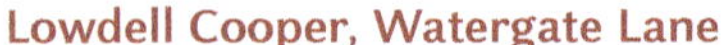

Lowdell Cooper, Watergate Lane

The ironmongery workshops of Lowdell Cooper, were, I believe, adjacent to the old drill hall further down on the west side and a couple of town houses are now on the site. The company was founded in 1812 and had its shop and offices at 61/62 High Street. Once a common sight, craftsmen are now rarely seen in town. However, here are Colin Tompsett (left) and his son Jonathan outside their wonderfully preserved workshop in Market Street, where they keep alive the old skills of furniture restoration and French polishing. George Justice Ltd, established in 1910, moved into this former smithy in 1919.

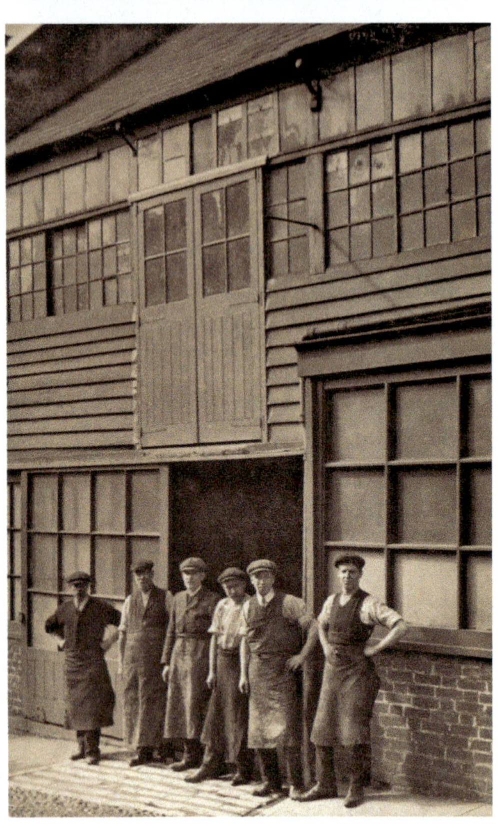

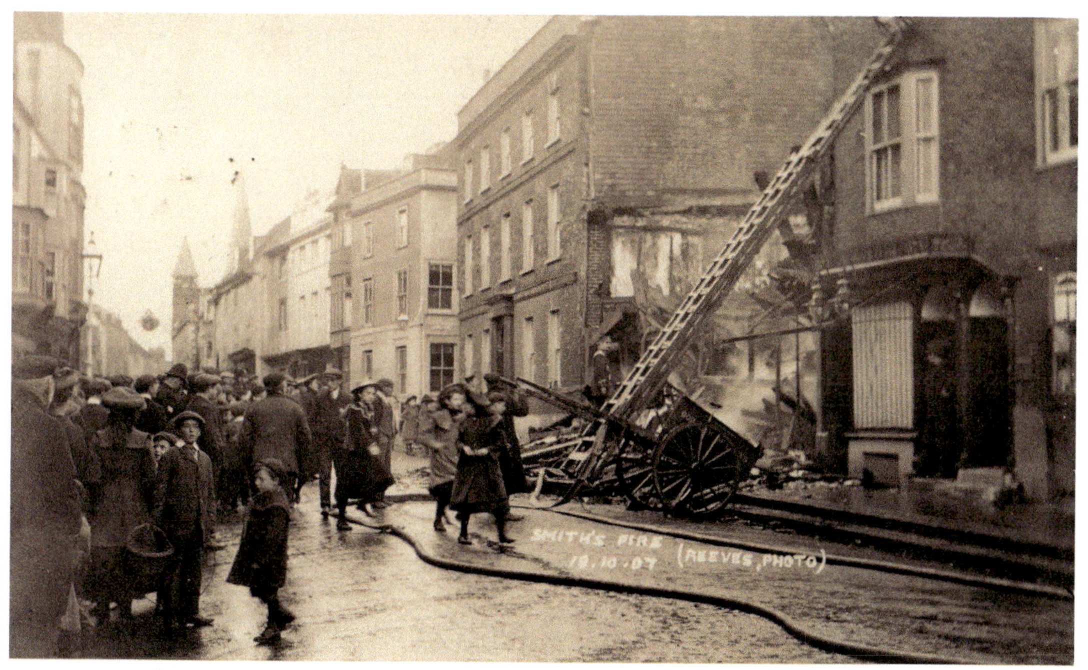

Upper High Street

Back on the High Street we look towards St Michael's church and see the aftermath of the Smith's Fire on 19 October 1907. Mr Smith, a general furnisher and photographer, was lucky to be rescued by a passing policeman who spotted the fire while patrolling in Castle Ditch Lane at the rear. The fine house with the gable and balcony was built the following year. Barbican House beyond, on Castlegate corner, houses the Sussex Archaeological Society and its museum. Its eighteenth-century façade hides an earlier oak frame and roof.

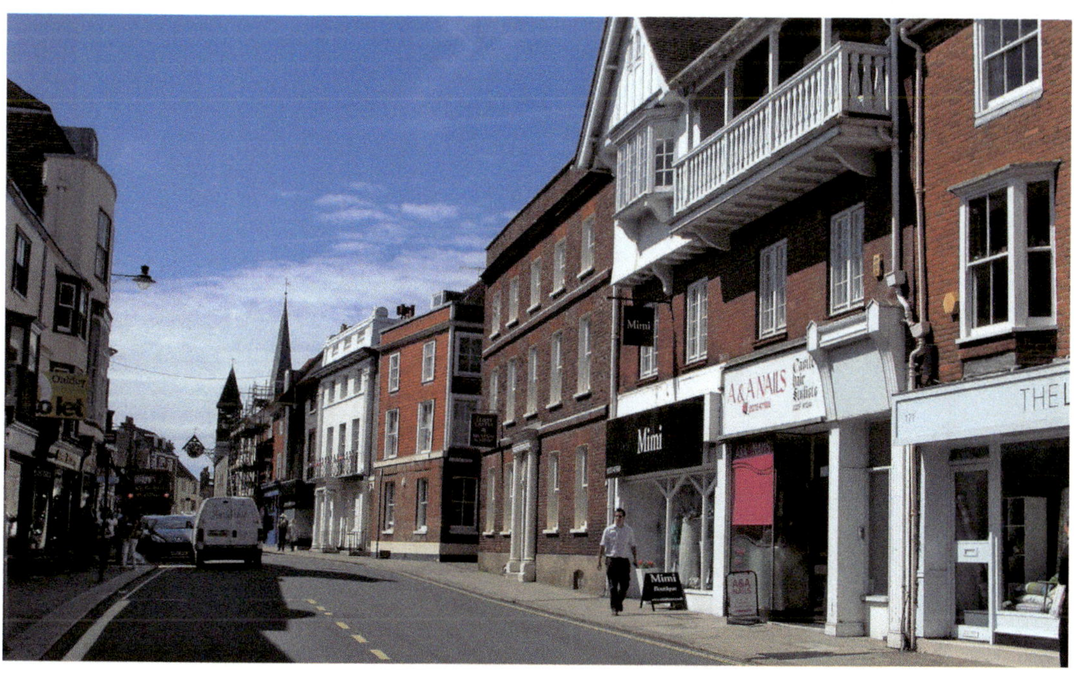

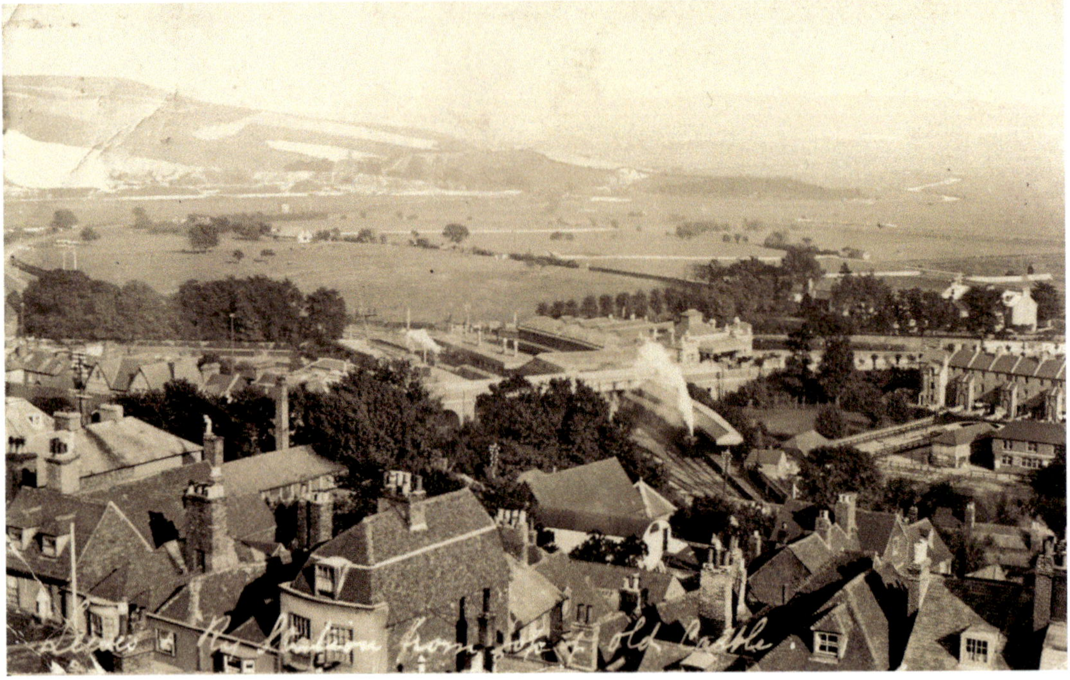

South from the Castle Tower

Another panoramic view, this time looking south towards Caburn and Firle Beacon. The High Street is reassuringly little changed but we can see the spread of Lewes beyond the railway station, though still with a pleasing profusion of trees.

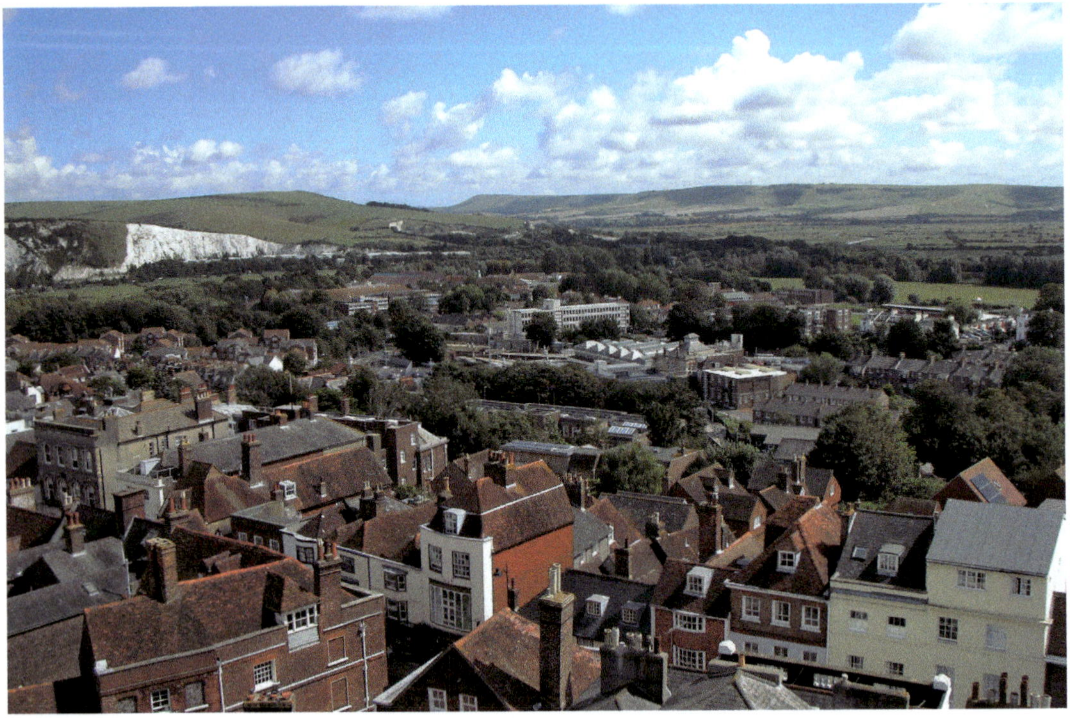

Barbican Gate

Built in the fourteenth century, some 200
years after the castle, the barbican has become
a Lewes icon on par with the castle. The
postcard, by another fine photographer,
F. Douglas Miller of Haywards Heath, shows it
from the High Street. My photograph is taken
from the castle steps to the west.

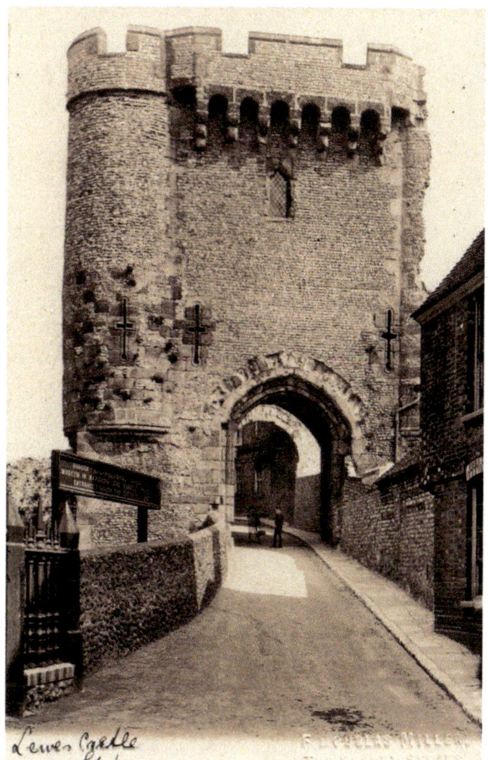

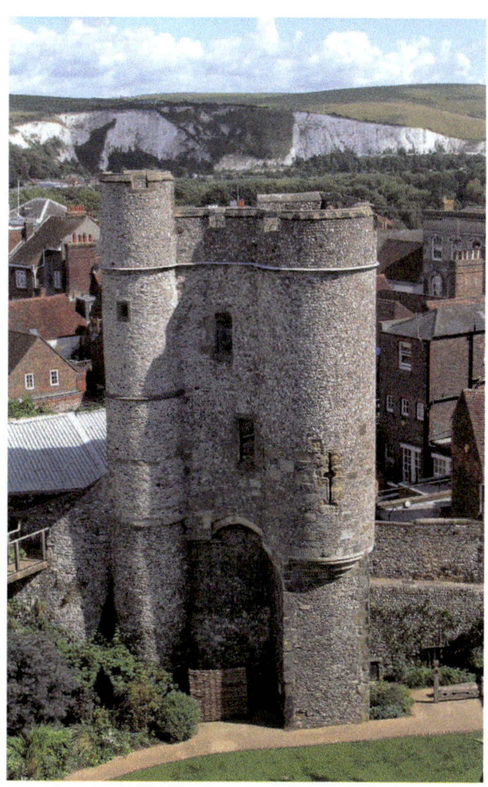

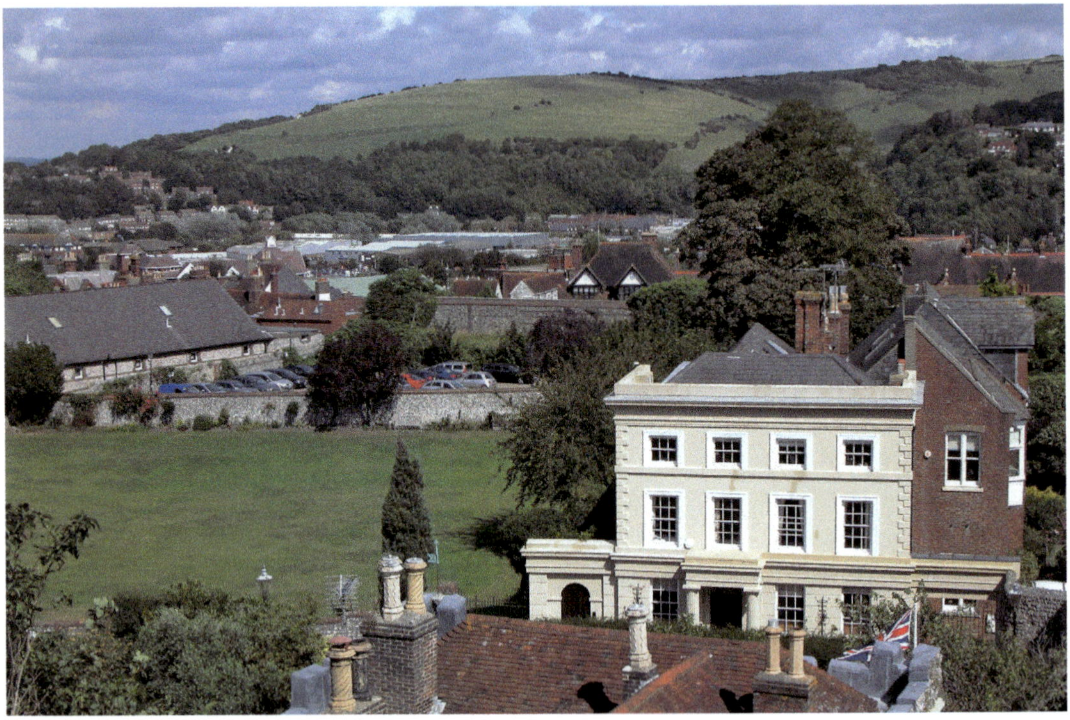

From the Castle Steps

We look down on Castlegate House (*c.* 1860), in whose garden was the Castle Brewery. The Tilting Green became the bumpy home to the Lewes Bowling Society, whose members use 200-year-old, wooden, cheese-shaped bowls. The Maltings (*c.* 1855) belonged to Beard's Star Brewery and houses the County Record Office until it moves to purpose-built premises, The Keep, at Falmer next year.

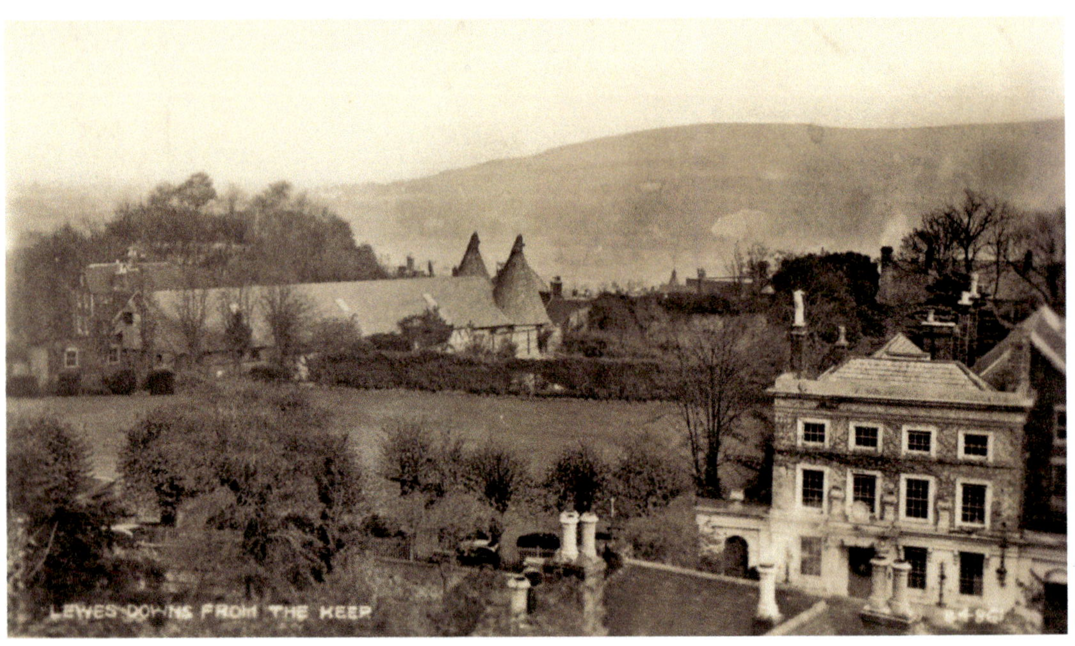

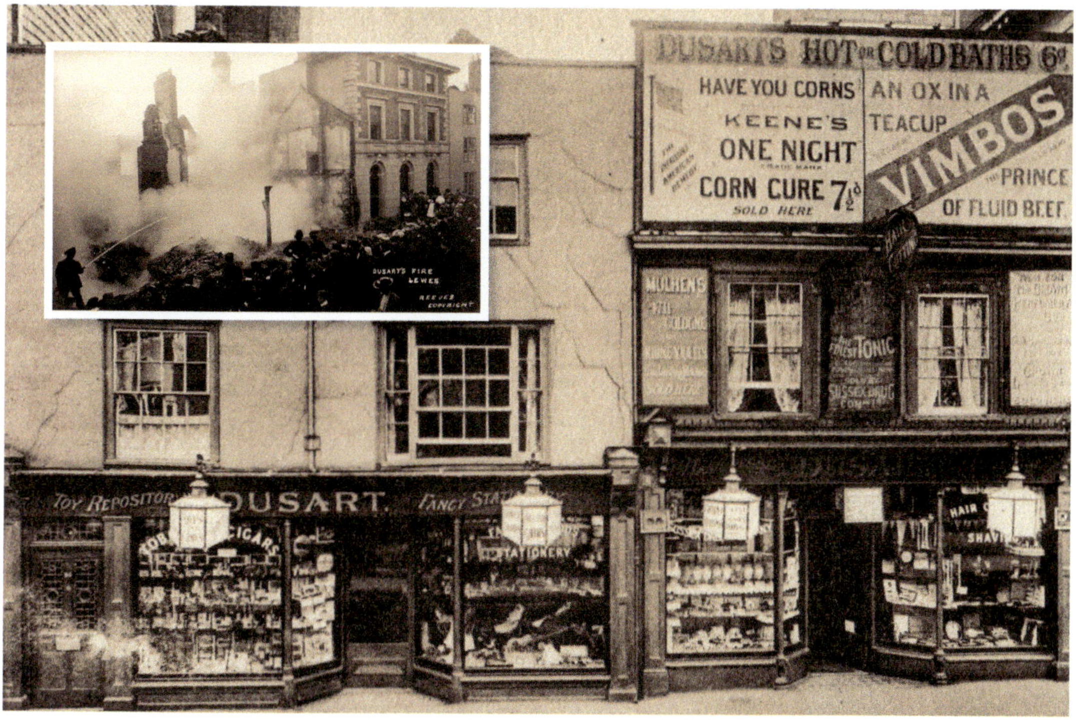

The Great Fire of Lewes

The most famous Lewes fire is that of the Dusart's premises on 4 October 1904. This double-fronted business in the High Street was a tobacconist, stationer, toy shop, hairdresser, and hot and cold baths. It was a total loss and major damage was caused to adjoining buildings. The response of the town's antiquated fire service was woeful and, in consequence, the Borough decided on a major reorganisation and re-equipping. In 1907 a new fire station was built at the bottom of North Street.

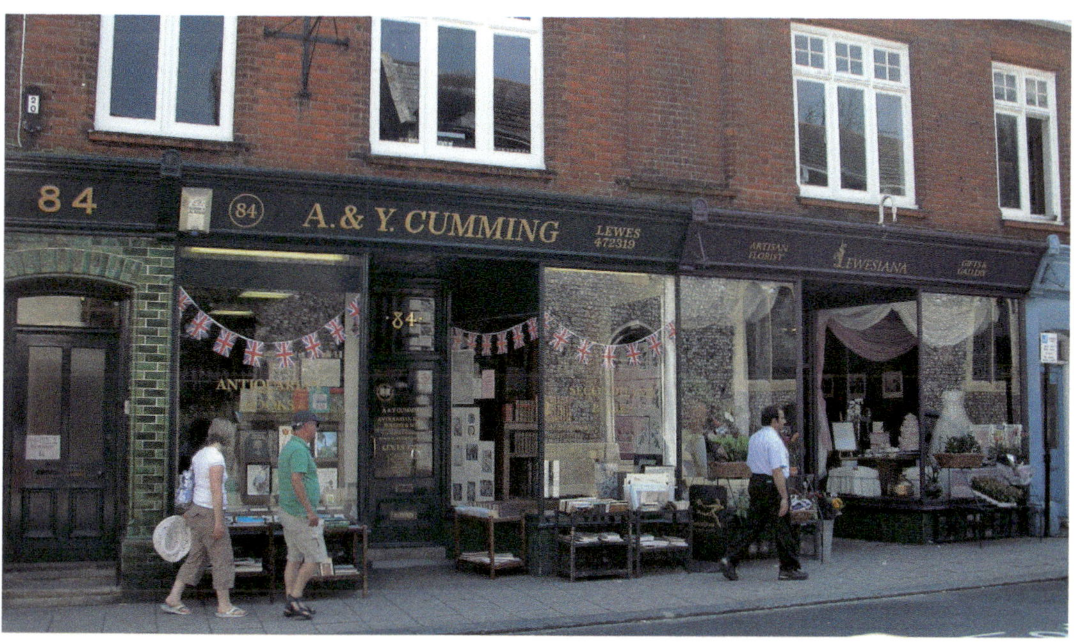

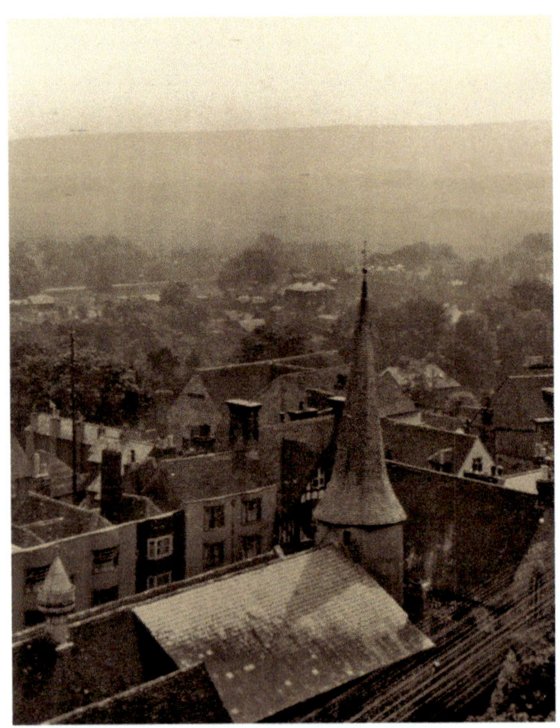

From the Castle Tower we have this unusual view of St Michael's church and the upper High Street. The rare, round flint tower is probably a twelfth-century survivor, with the church's Gothic façade being designed by Joseph Daw in the mid-eighteenth century.

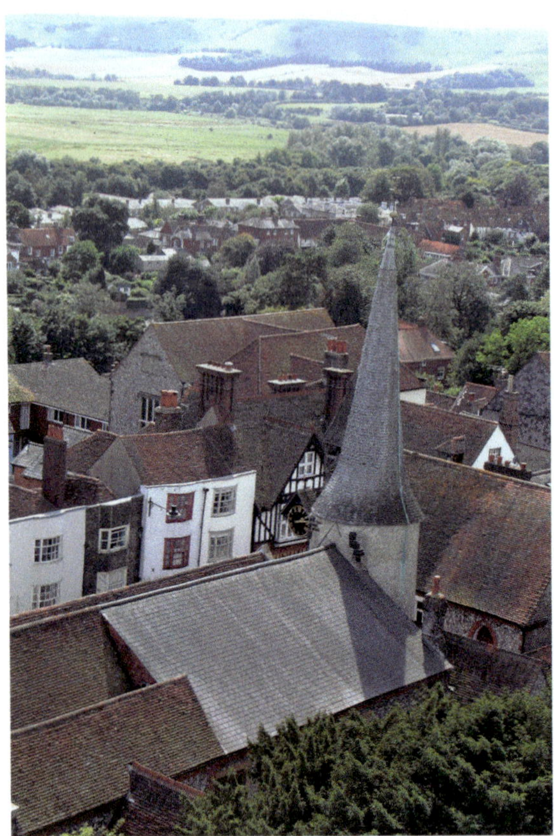

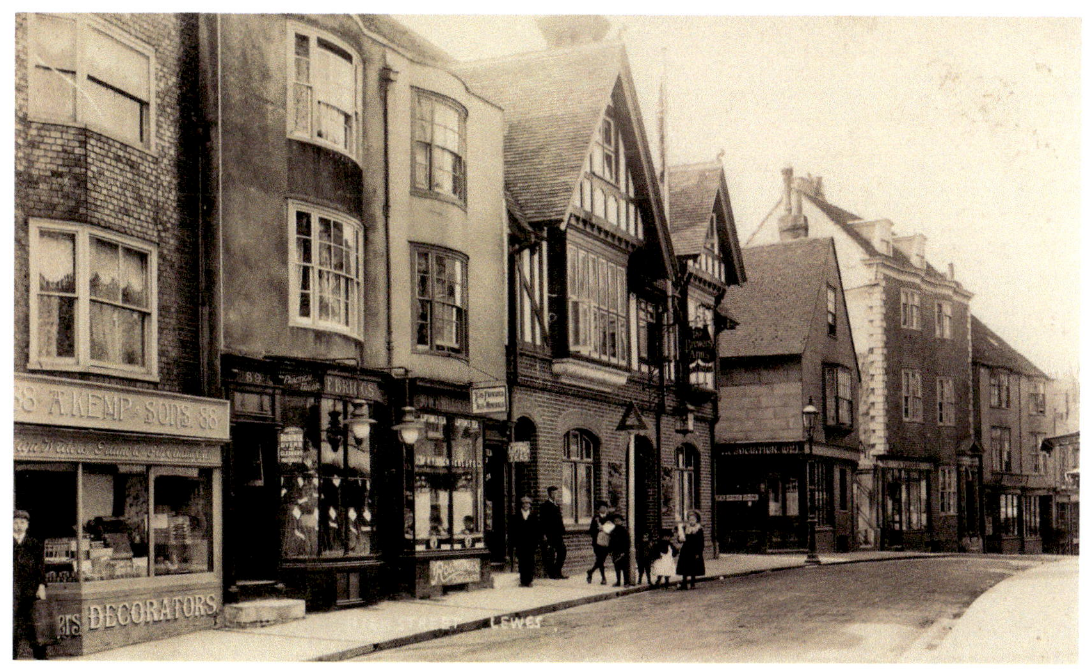

Bottleneck from the East

As we approach the 'bottleneck' it is good to see another area of Lewes where small local businesses continue to flourish. The Brewer's Arms, in the centre, had not long been rebuilt when the postcard was published and in earlier times had been called The Ship. Bull House, beyond, with its Tom Paine associations, was then a reading room and later became a tea room.

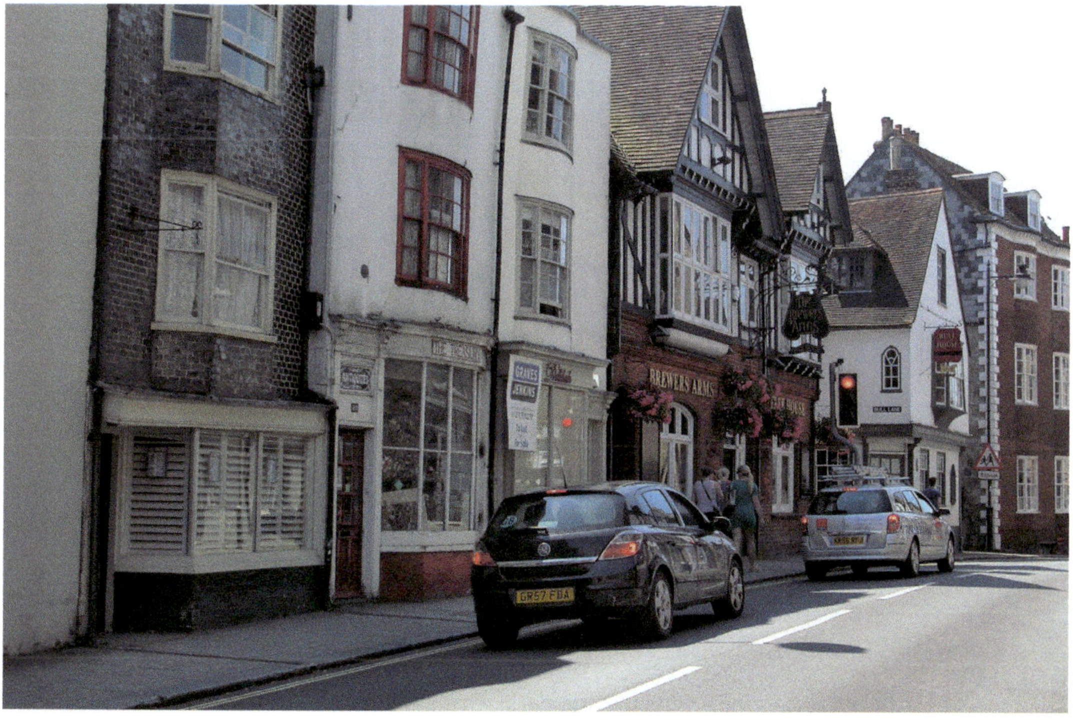

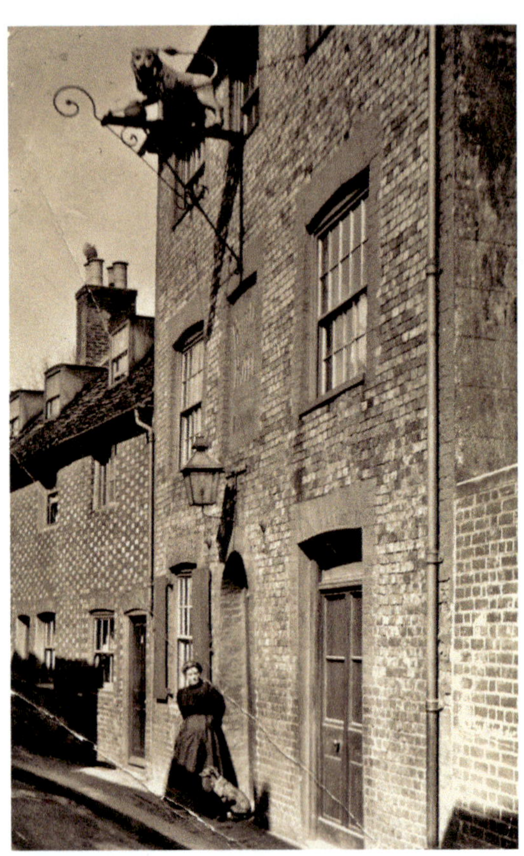

White Lion, Westgate Street

Turning right into Westgate Street we see The White Lion alehouse, which grandly called itself a hotel. The licensee, Mrs Fuller, is standing outside. It was demolished in 1937 under a slum clearance scheme and I was told that the owners, given their loss of livelihood, committed suicide. The original sign was rescued by the Friends of Lewes and placed near to the site. When I took the photograph in August 2012 it was missing, being refurbished again.

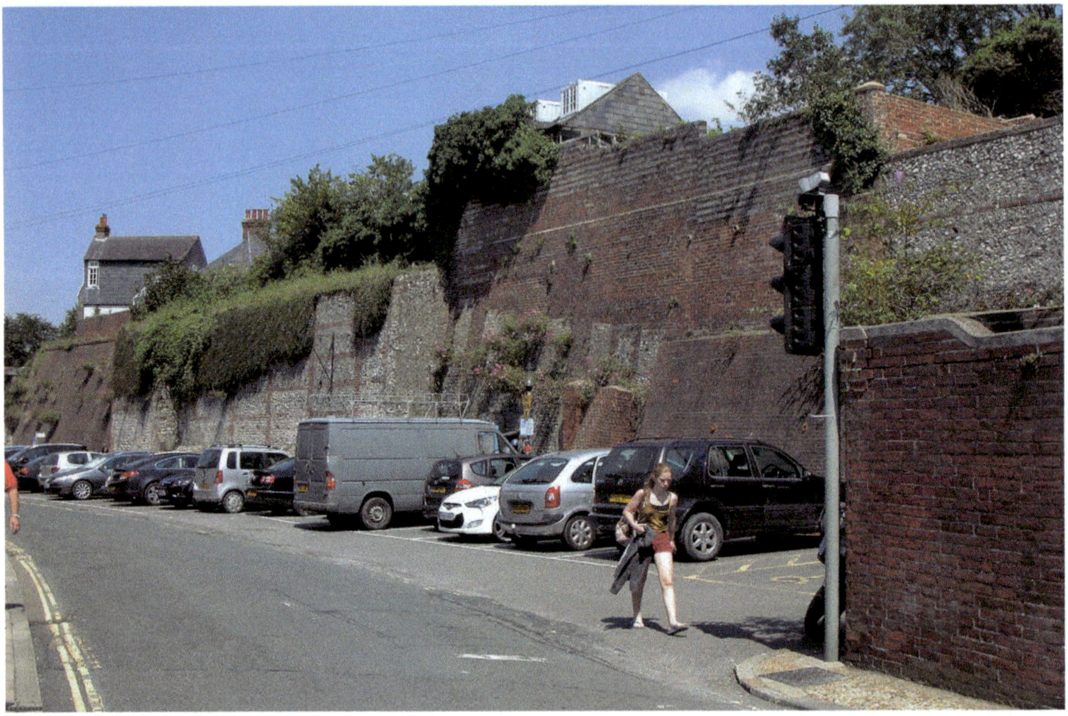

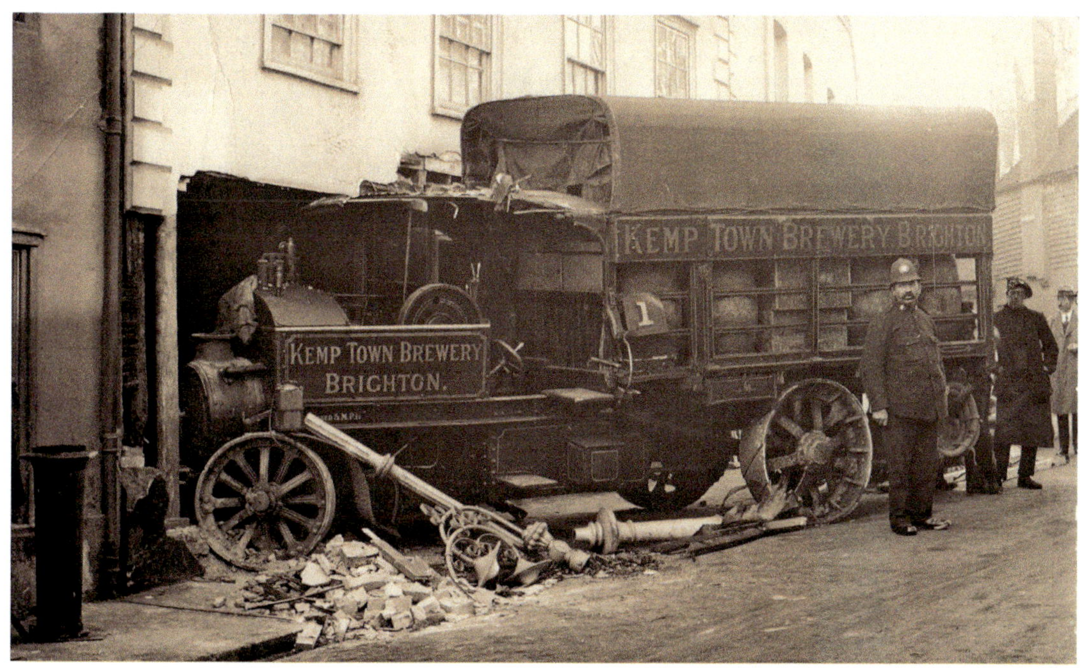

Beer Lorry Disaster

This happened in the bottleneck in 1915 when a lorry of the Kemp Town Brewery from Brighton lost the use of its brakes on St Anne's Hill and crashed into 103 High Street. The Foden demolished an ornate lamppost before scaring to death the Bentham family, who were taking tea in the front room on the other side of the front door. Luckily there were no injuries and the beer survived. It looks as if the house repairs continue!

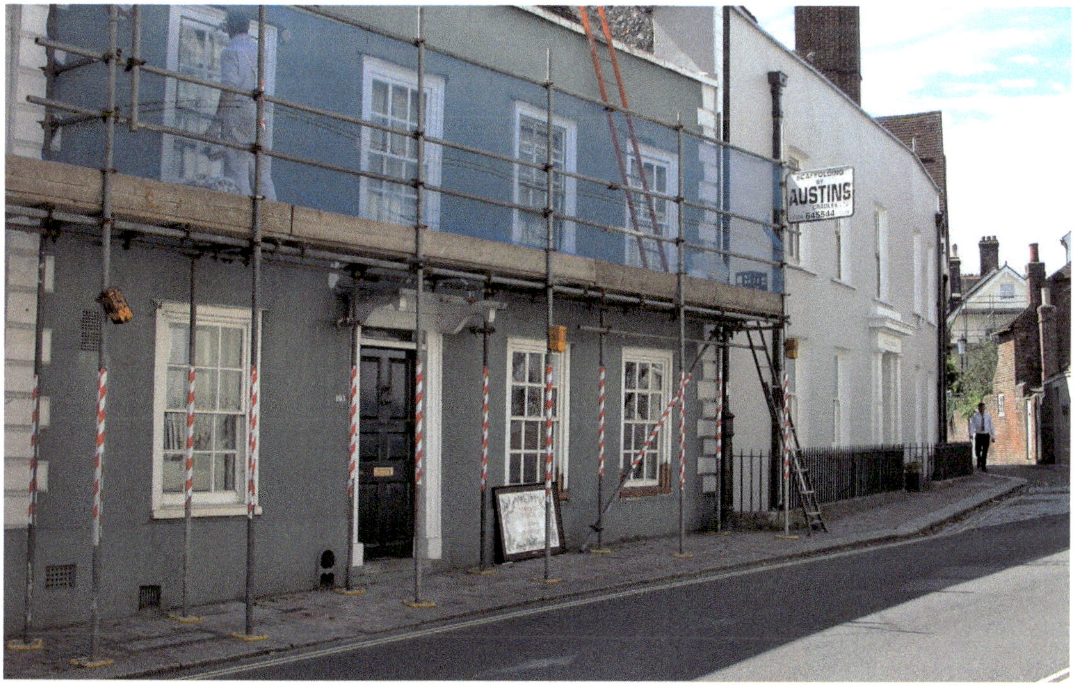

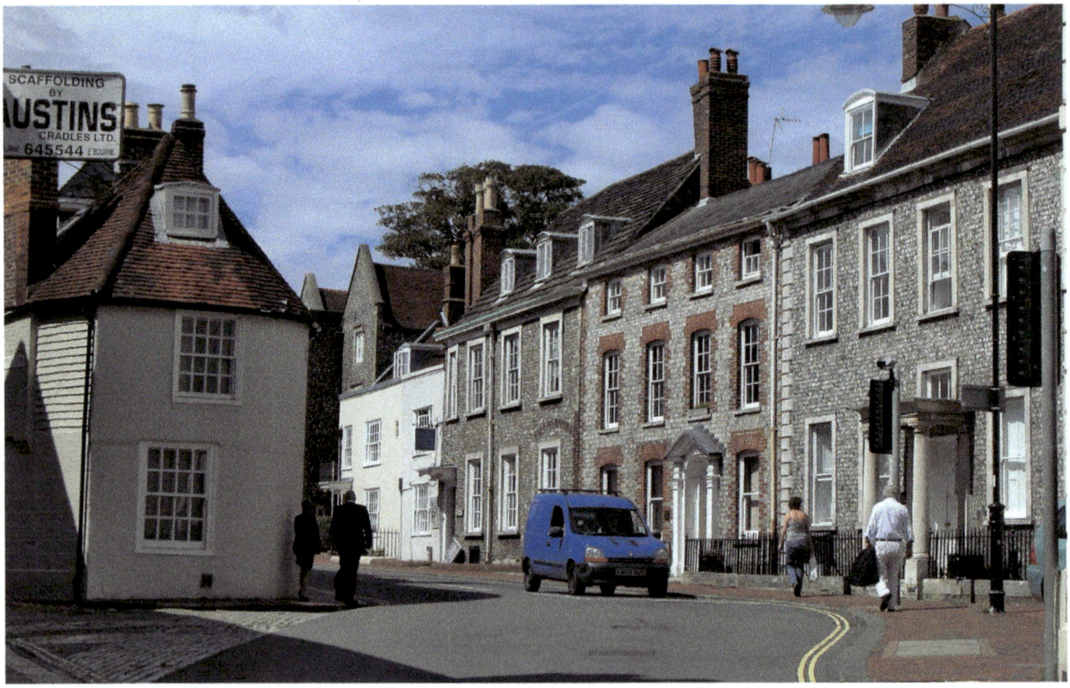

Lewes Old Grammar School

Through the 'bottleneck' and into the old parish of St Mary and St James Westout, now St Anne's, we have a good view of Lewes Old Grammar School, which celebrated its 500th anniversary in 2012. The building dates to 1851 and the school had previous homes. The removal of the ivy highlights the building's wonderful knapped flints. The quaint property on the left is called the Old Toll House and has been a shop.

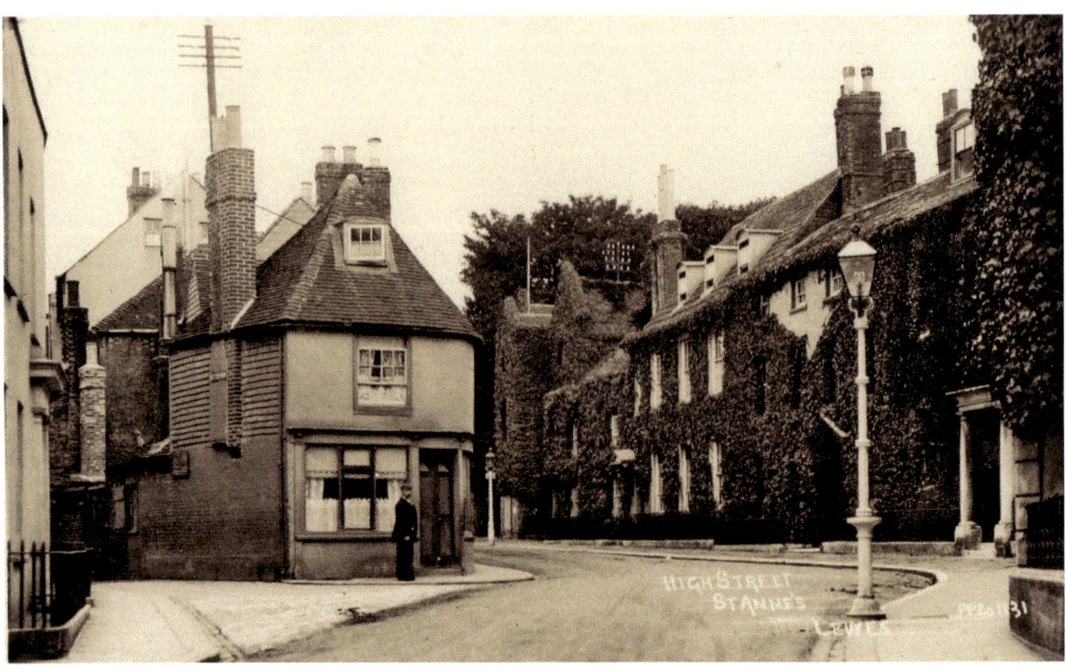

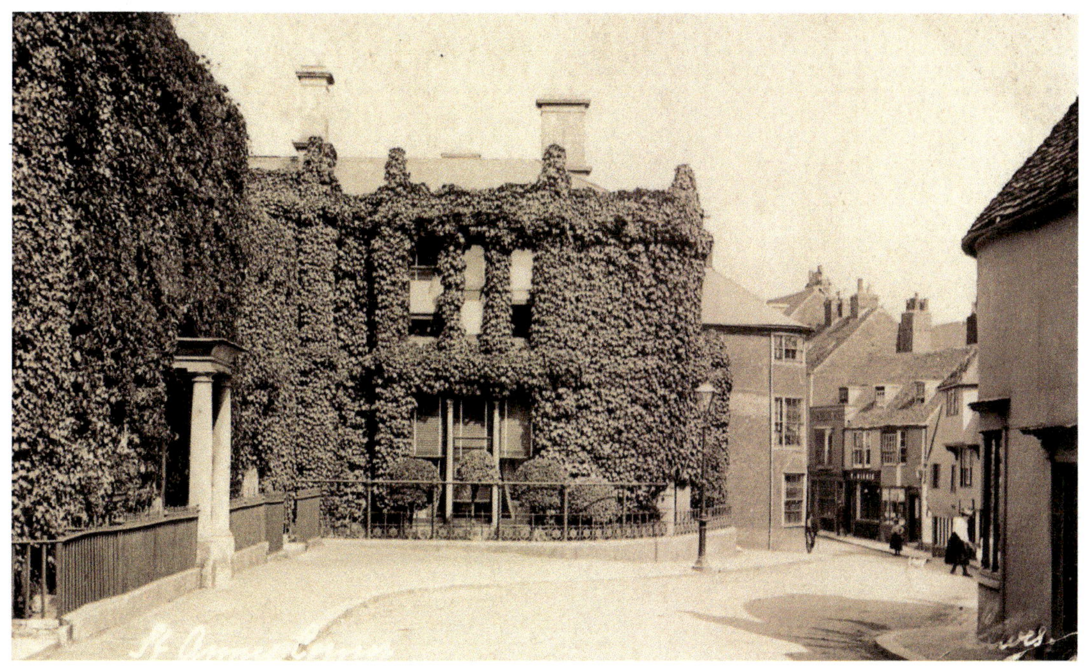

Bottleneck from the West

Looking back on the left is Tyne House next to St Anne's House, both cleared of ivy. In the middle of the bottleneck is the fifteenth-century bookshop. It is difficult to imagine that thirty years ago, before the bypass, all traffic from the A26 and A27 went through here in two lanes as it did up and down School Hill.

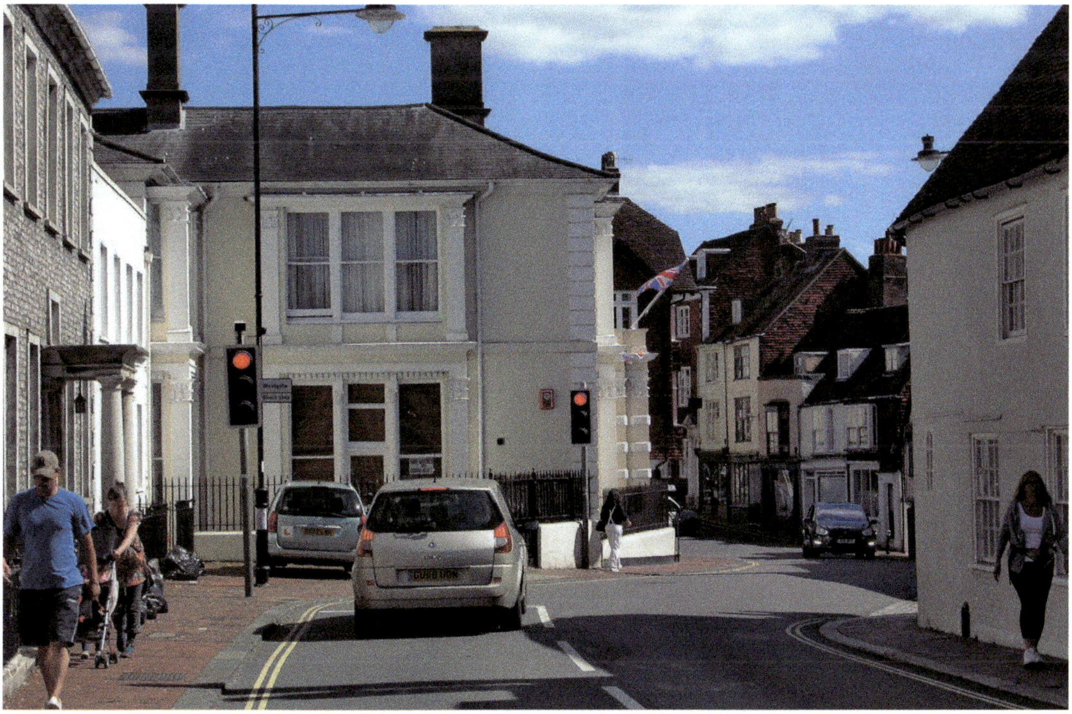

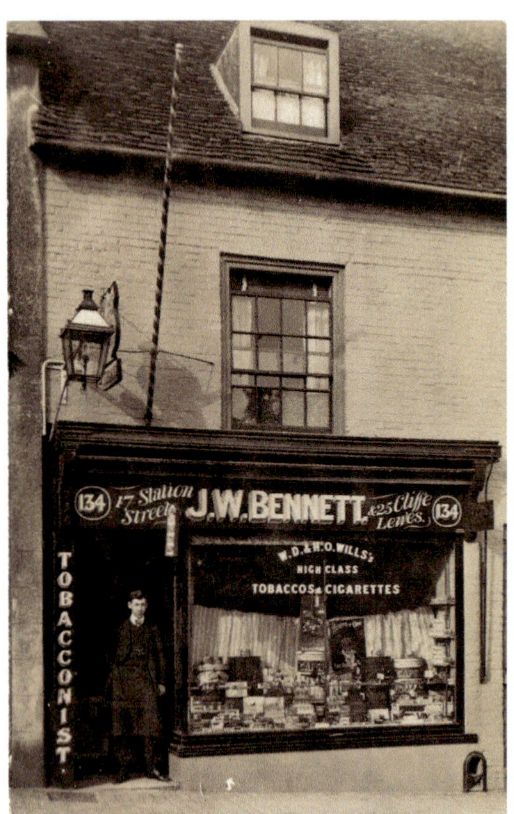

Bennett's, St Anne's Hill

This was one of three shops owned in the town by J. W. Bennett. In 1941 the property was named The Millers by its owners, the artistic St Frances Byng-Stamper and her sister Caroline Lucas, and used for exhibitions and recitals. In her waspish diary, wonderfully edited by Diana Crook, on 5 May that year Mrs Henry Dudeney notes, 'They now call their house in the High Street "Millers". A little too elegant and super-cultured for me...'

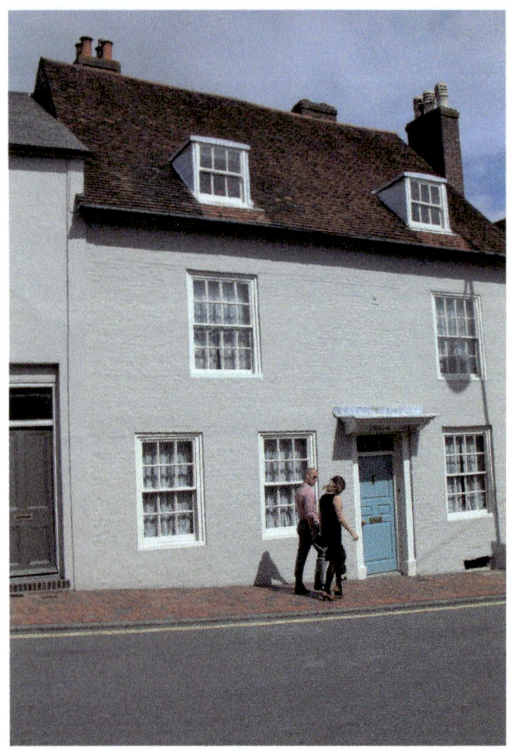

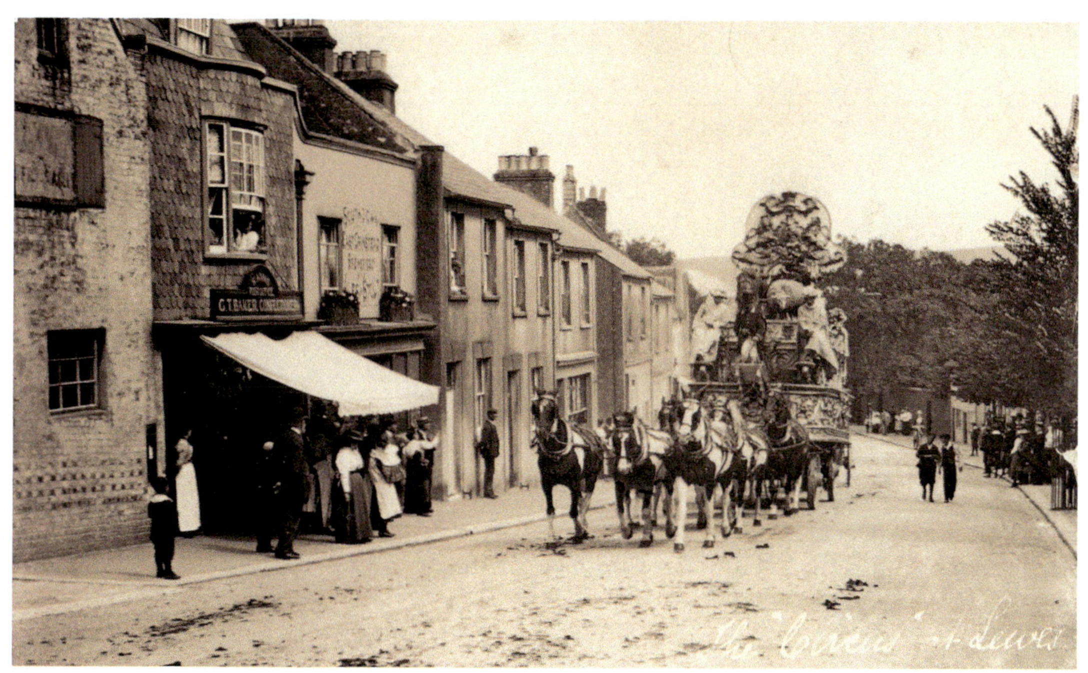

The Circus on St Anne's Hill

In 1907, the crowds lined St Anne's Hill to see Lord John Sanger's circus. The sub-post office and stores was run by Mr G. T. Baker who also owned, as I did, the baker's shop at 45 Western Road. Next door, The Morning Star public house became the Bow Windows bookshop. To the left are the stables of the Pelham Arms Hotel which became a garage and was then demolished and redeveloped as Well House Place.

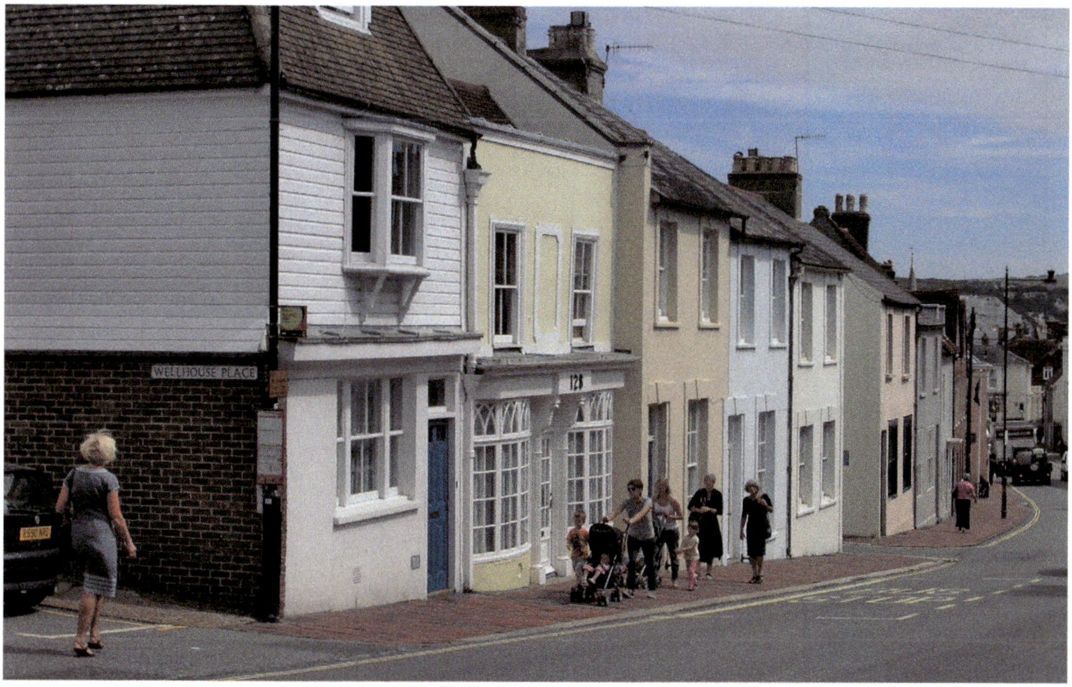

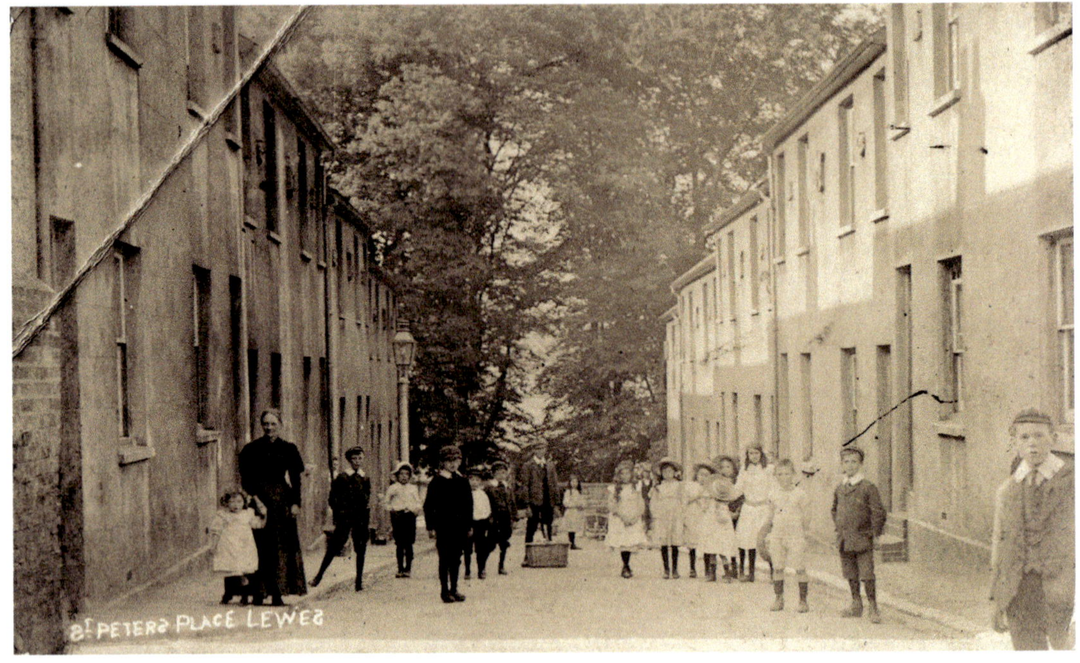

St Peter's Place

This little street sits quietly off St Anne's Hill. It was built for Lord Nevill in 1868 and carries his armorial emblems and motto. It became known as 'Tory terrace', as he made it clear that his tenants should vote Conservative. He never knew if they did; the public poll gave way to secret voting in 1870.

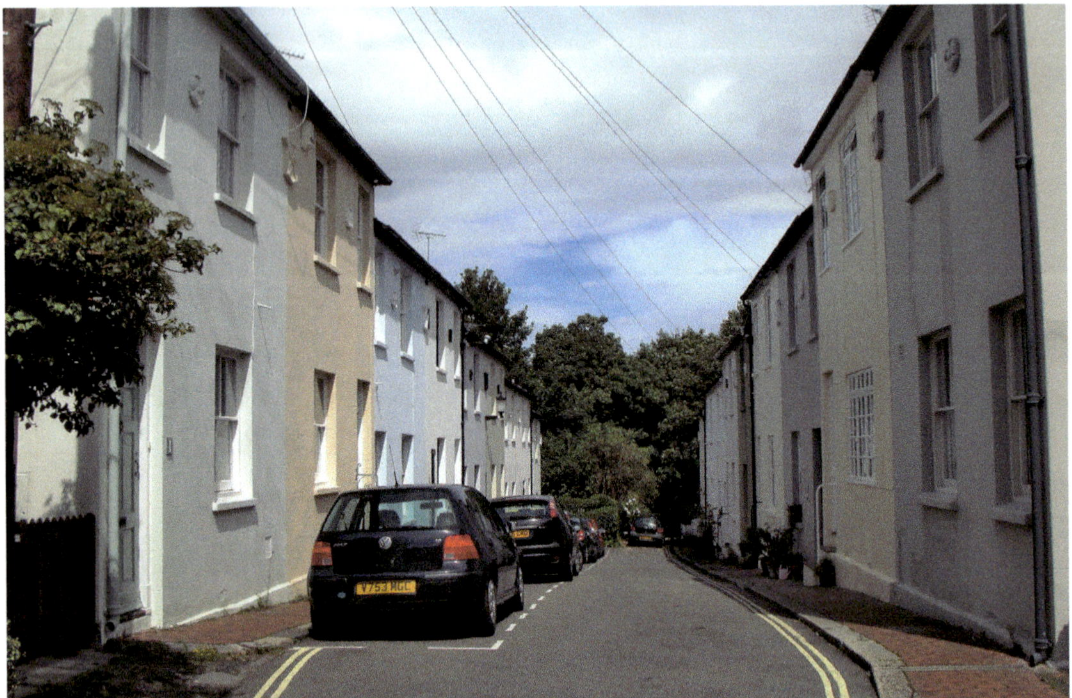

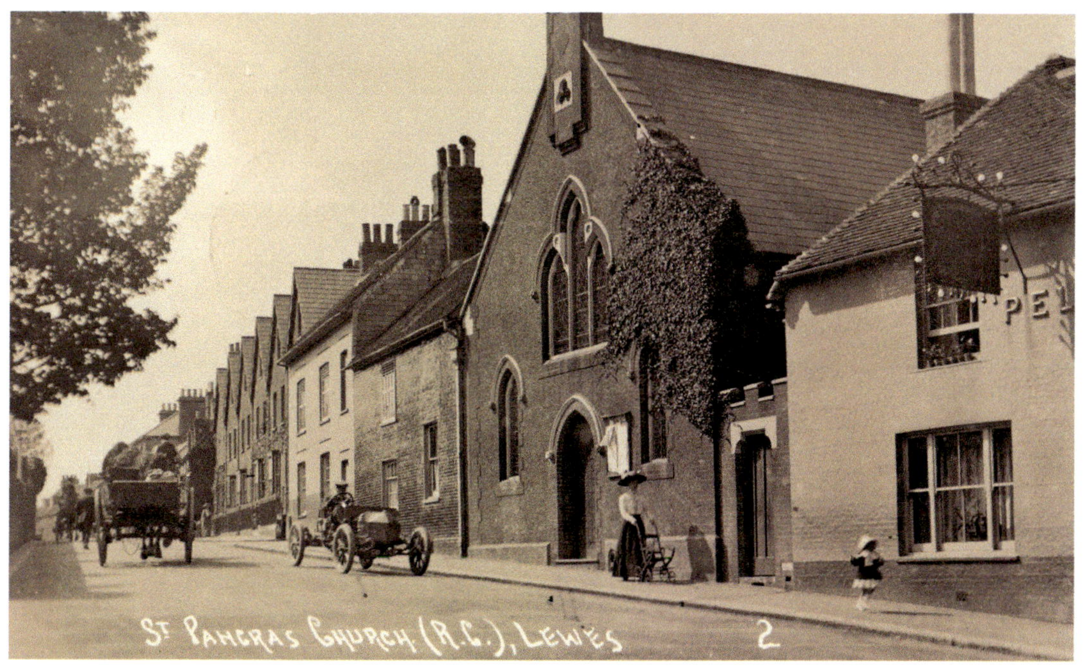

St Pancras Church

The fine brickwork of St Pancras Roman Catholic church dominates the picture and you will notice the changes made to the building. The cottages to the right were demolished to create the church's new entrance and car park in Irelands Lane. Beyond is the fine St Anne's Terrace while St Anne's church is lost behind the trees. The Pelham Arms butts in from the left and was first recorded under this name in 1758, having previously been The Rose and then The Dog.

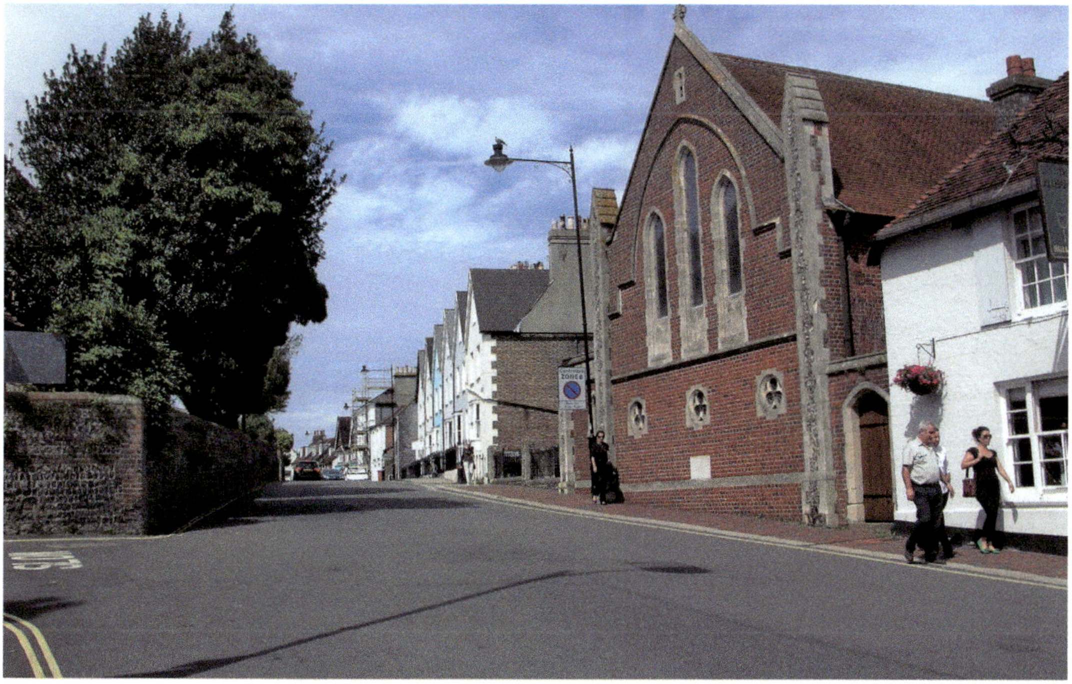

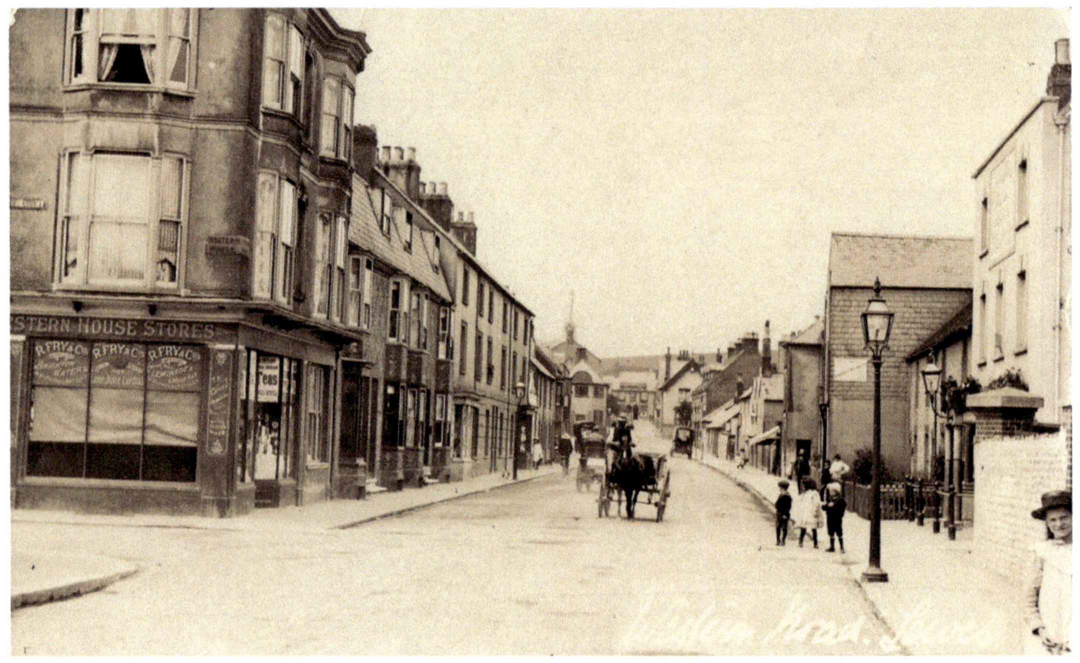

Western Road

We're at its junction with St Anne's Crescent. The buildings are little changed, but on the right the old stables of The Black Horse were demolished in the 1960s to build offices for the Department of Employment. My photograph was taken in a quiet moment before the County Hall staff burst out of their daily captivity.

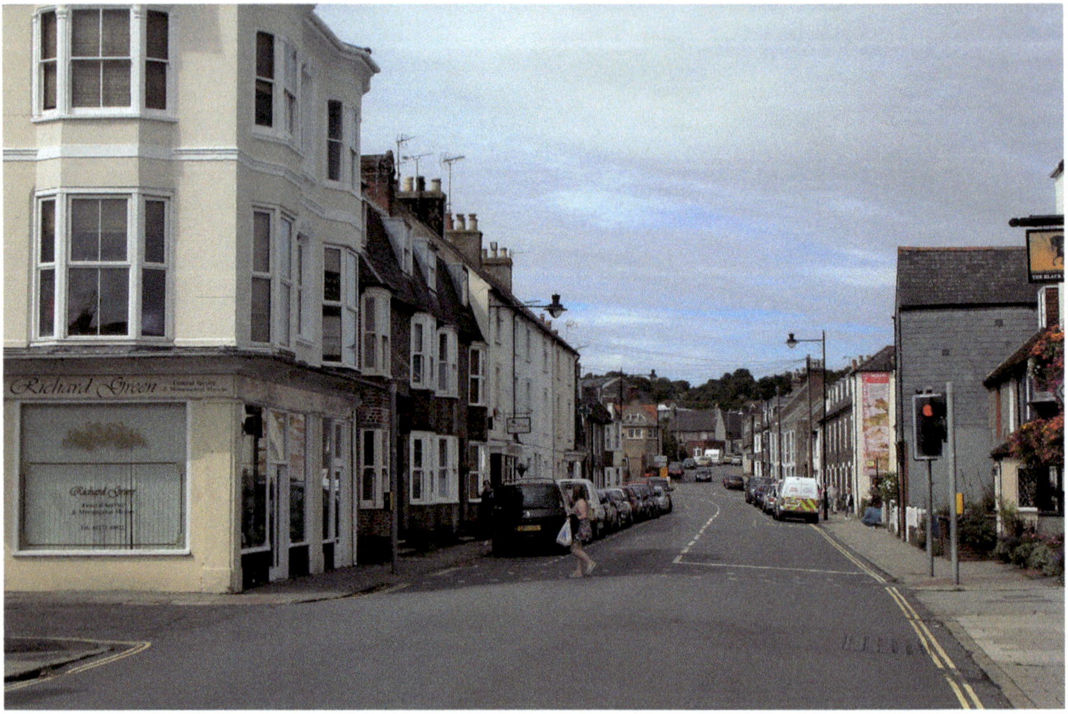

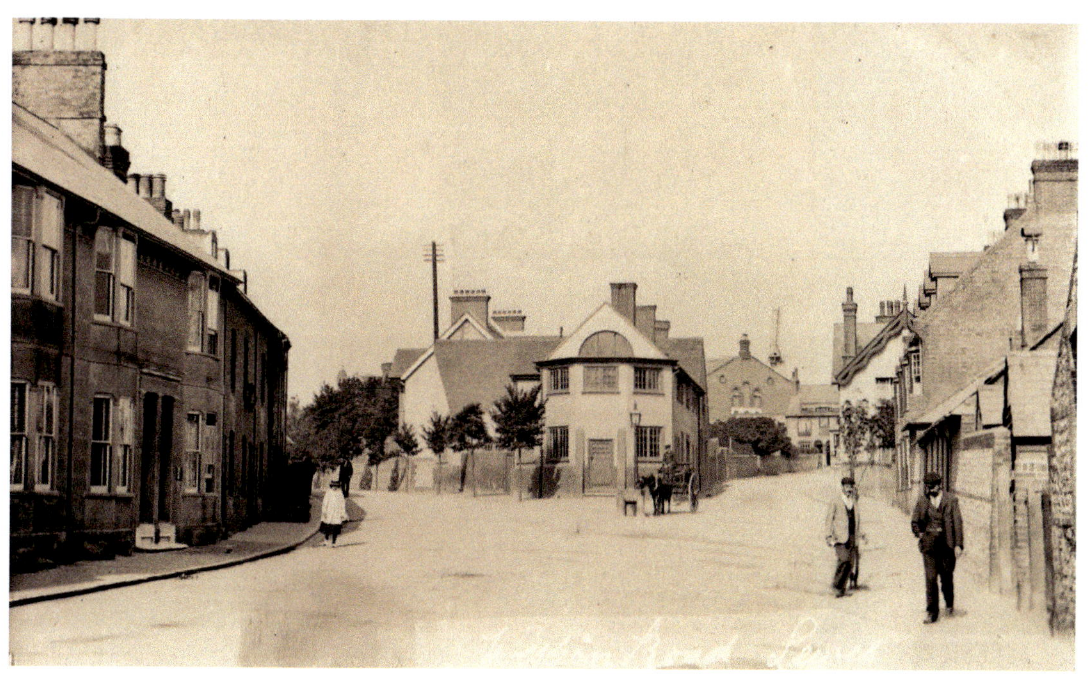

Canon O'Donnell Centre

Still in Western Road, which continues to the prison, we are looking at the decaying Canon O'Donnell Centre, with Spital Road off to the right. Beyond are the cottages converted from the remains of the St Nicholas leper hospital and demolished in 1933 to allow the school extension. Two pubs feature; in the background is The Windmill, with a sail of the prison mill beyond it, and to the right is The Rifleman, formerly The Hole in the Wall and latterly The Pewter Pot. It was demolished recently and a terrace of houses, almost in keeping, has appeared.

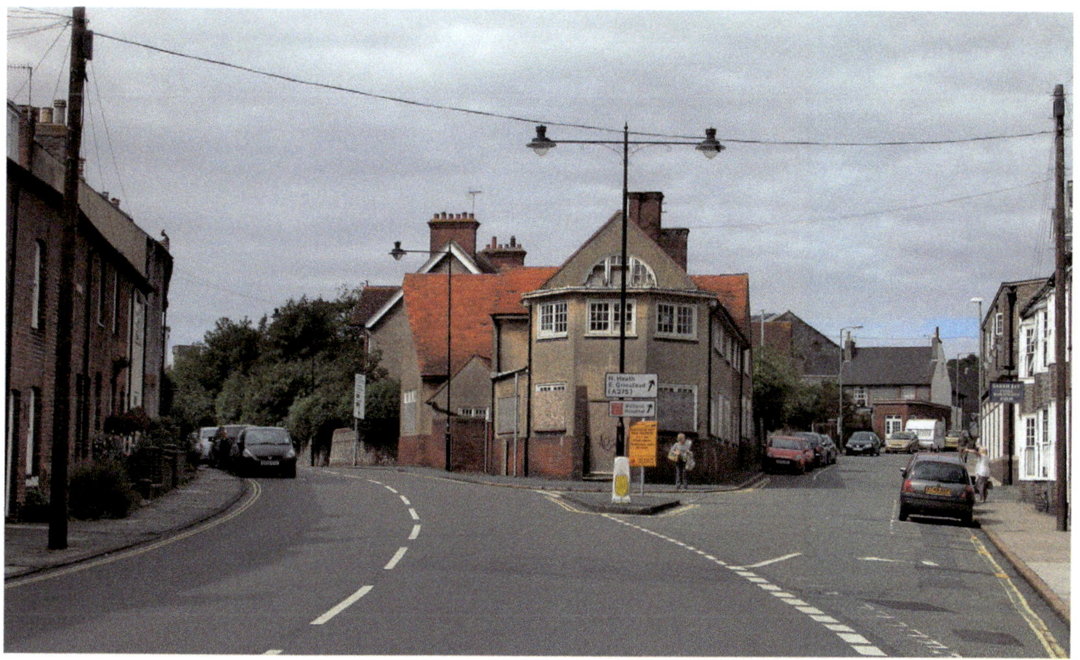

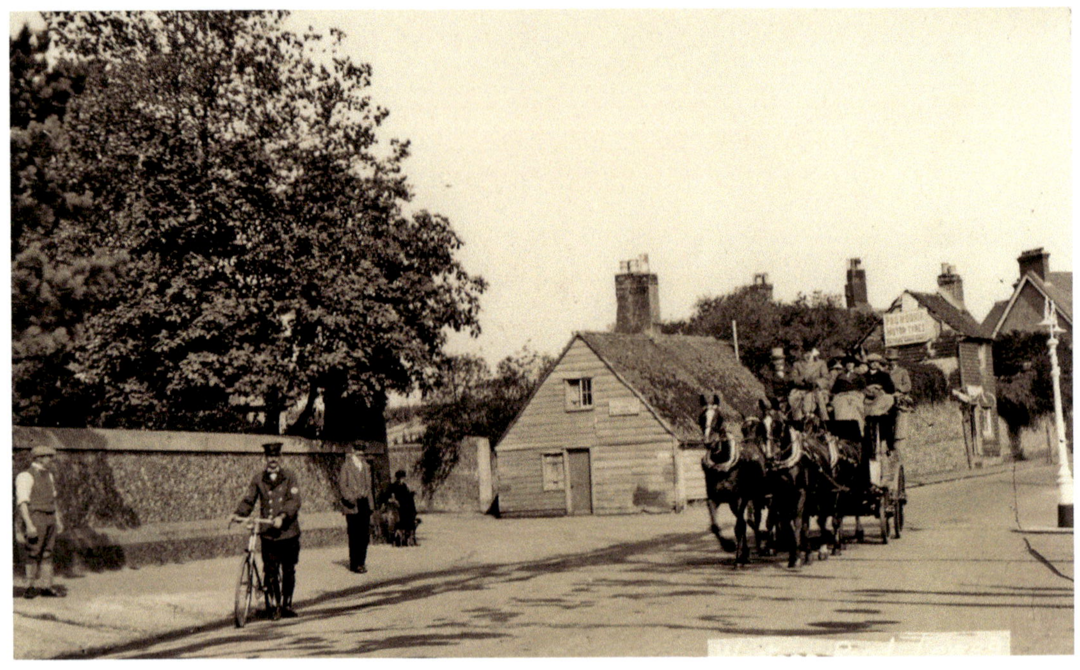

The Berkeley Stagecoach at the Prison

The stagecoach is at the top of Western Road and is crossing into Brighton Road on its return journey from The White Hart Hotel to The Old Ship, Brighton. To the left, beyond the prison's flint wall, is the main road to East Grinstead. Beyond is the triangle of land which once contained the leper hospital, The Windmill, cottages and latterly Western Road Primary School. The Victoria Institute and Parish Room of St Anne passed to the Roman Catholic diocese in 1977 and became the Canon O'Donnell Centre.

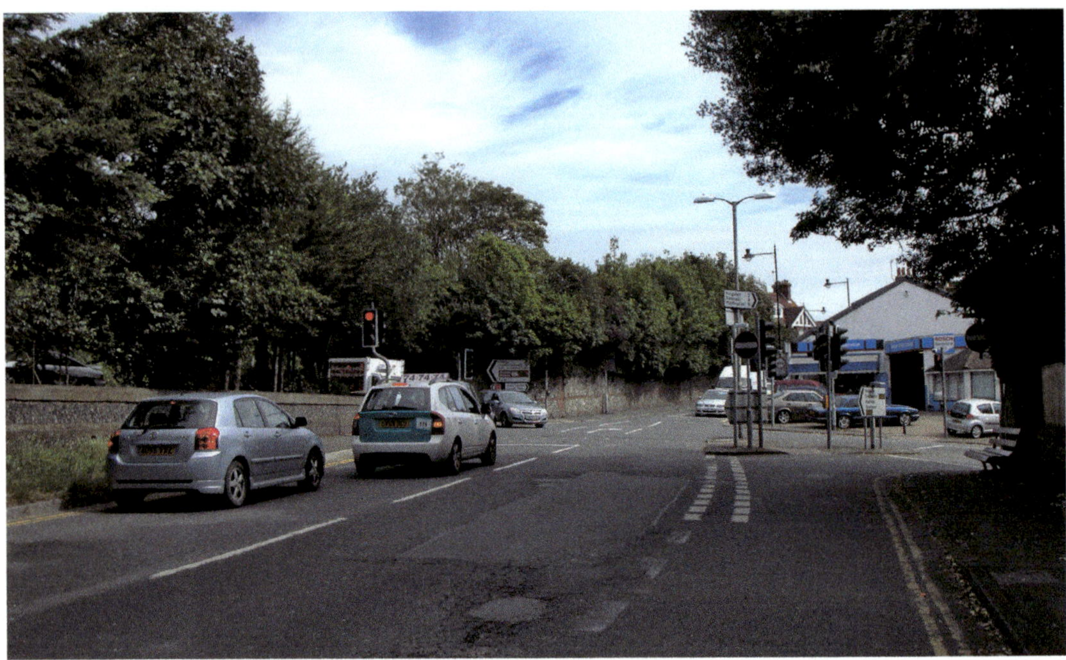

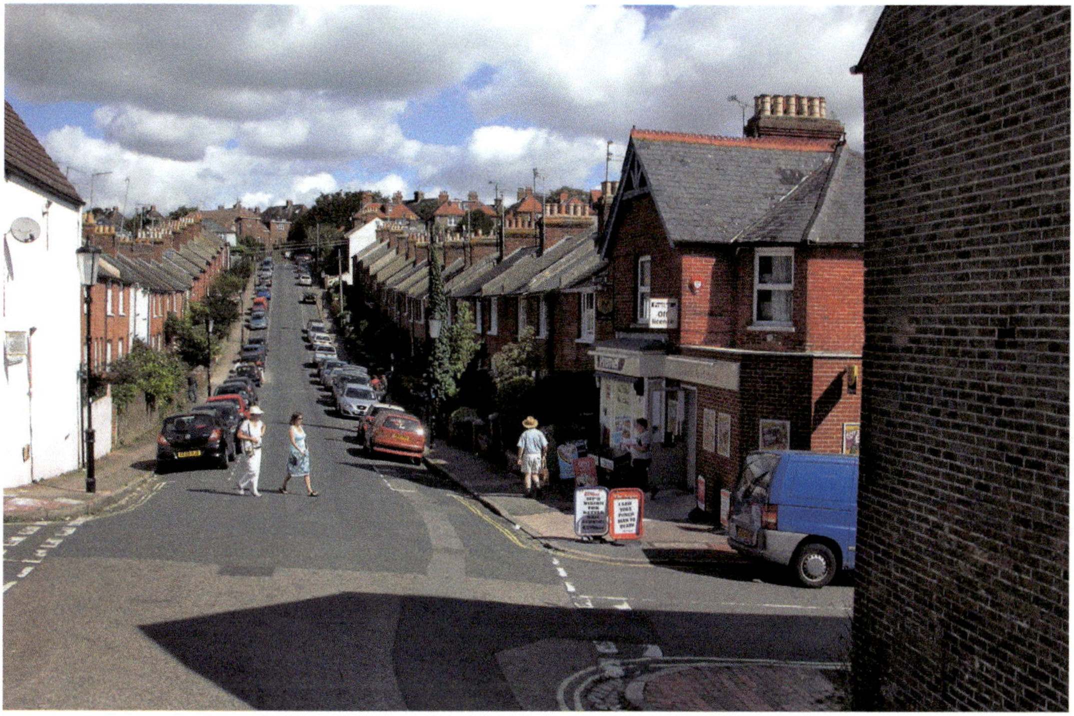

Leicester Road

We drop down to Leicester Road and a scene which has hardly changed except for the cars. It honours Simon de Montfort, Earl of Leicester, who is the only person to have two Lewes streets named after him. The year 2014 will see the 750th anniversary of his victory at the Battle of Lewes.

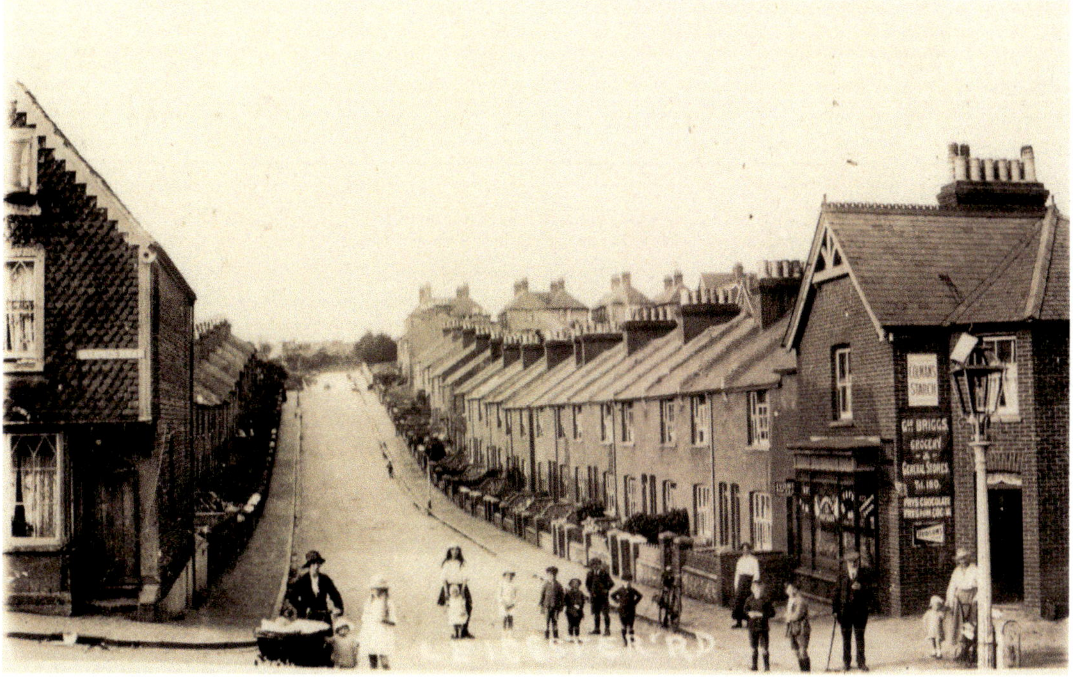

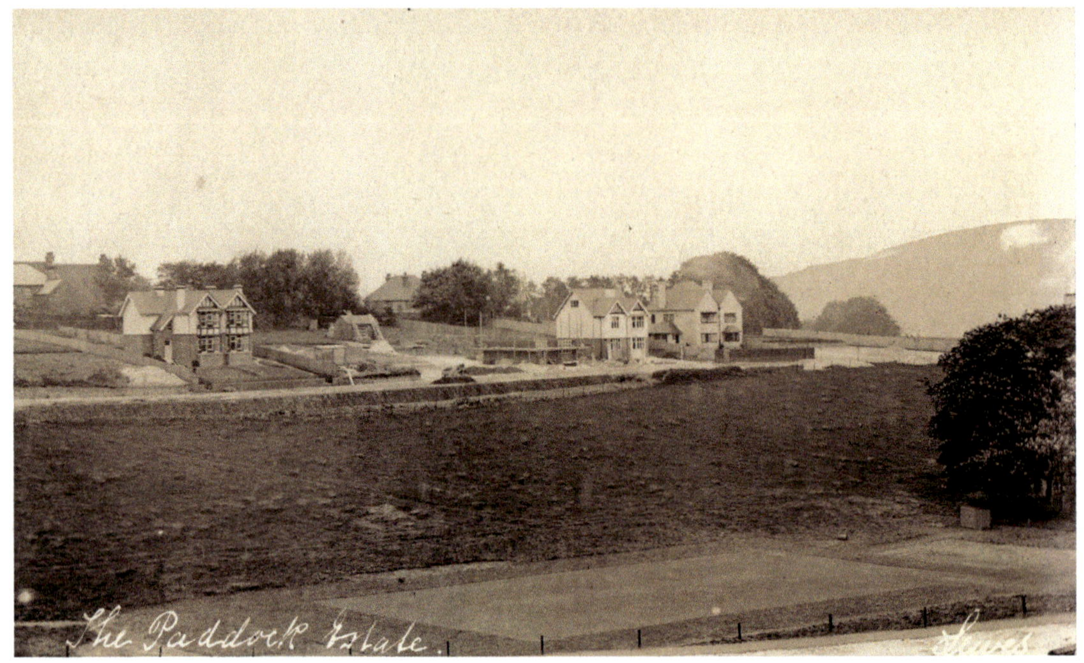

The Avenue

The development of the Paddock and Wallands Estates began in the 1880s and accelerated into the early twentieth century, expanding Lewes to the north-east. In 1907 The Avenue is progressing, and my photograph in 2012 suggests it might soon be finished! Its original name was D'Albiac Avenue, after the family who owned the Paddock Park land, but this was shortened a year later at the request of the new residents.

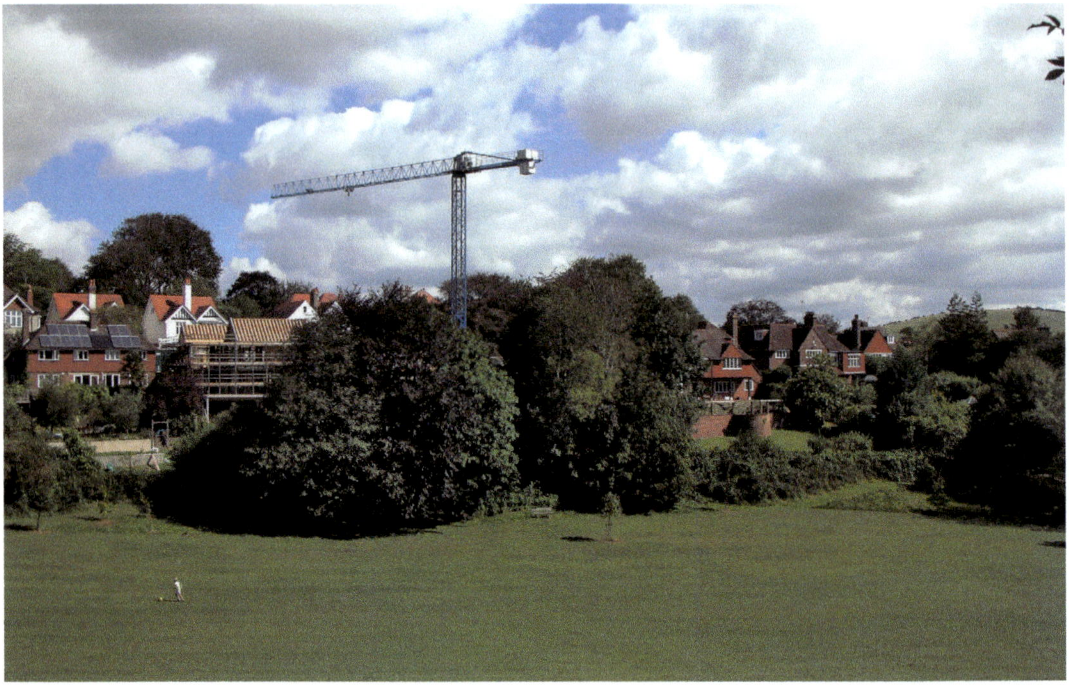

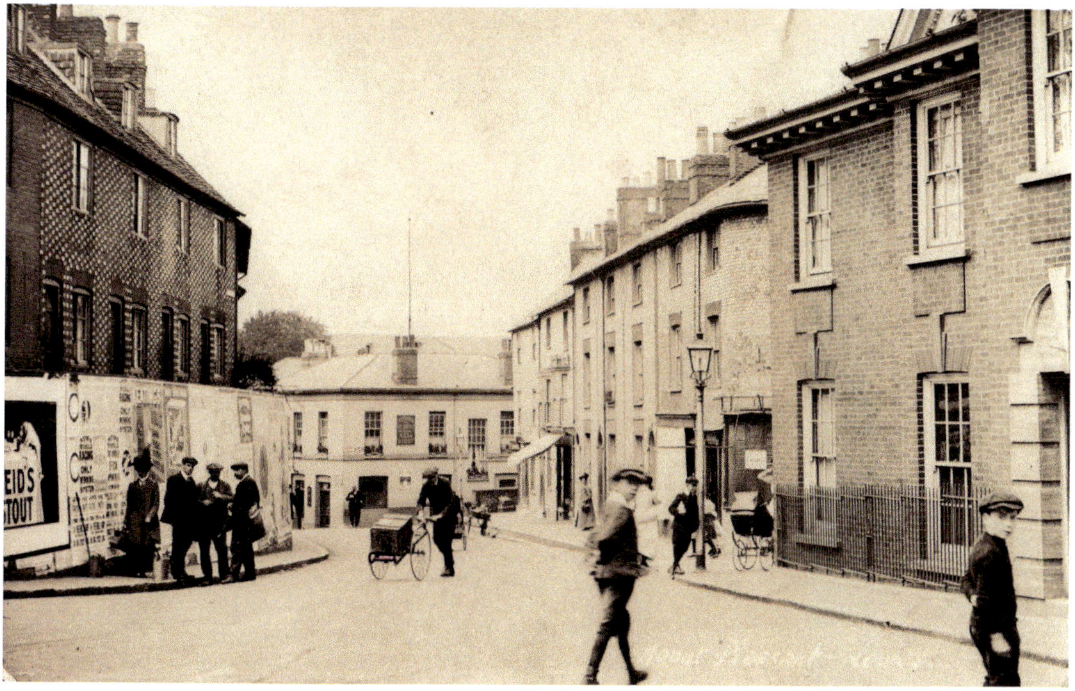

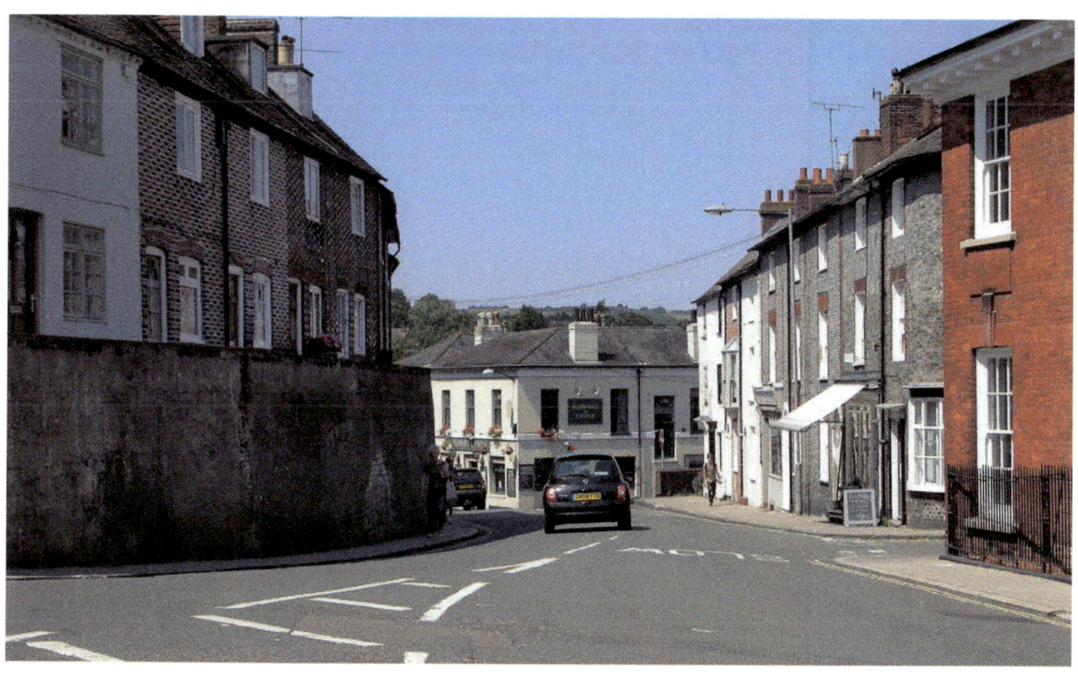

White Hill and Mount Pleasant

The Elephant & Castle, seen in the middle-background, dominates and the police station is on the right. White (Chalk) Hill was built across the Paddock Valley in 1821 for the Offham Turnpike Trustees by lowering the hills on either side and using the chalk to fill the valley, so creating the causeway. The public house followed in 1838. The 'Elephant' part of its name is probably taken from the crest of Tamplins, the brewers, and 'Castle' because it could be clearly seen at that time.

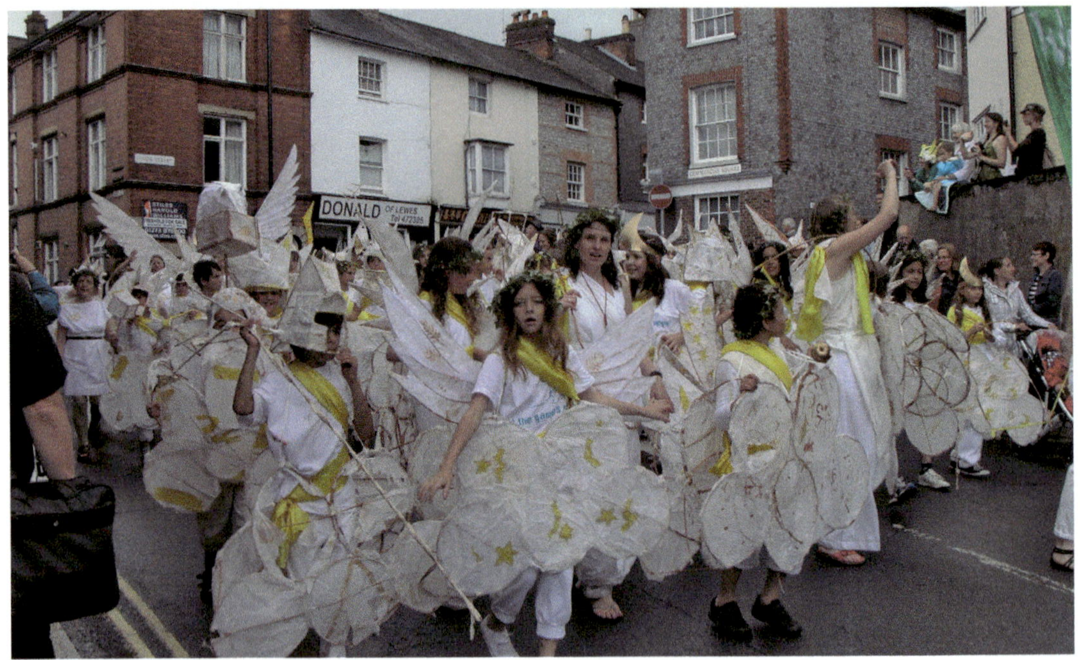

Commercial Square

Behind is Commercial Square and on Empire Day 1908, policemen, and most of the town, marched down (or is it up?) Fisher Street to a service in St John Sub Castro church. The name was given in the 1850s because of the wide range of businesses in the area, of which, except for those in Fisher Street, only a few now exist. The buildings of the Beard's Star Brewery, which gave its name to the lane in the nineteenth century, are in the background. The 2012 Patina, celebrating moving on to secondary school, passes by from West Street.

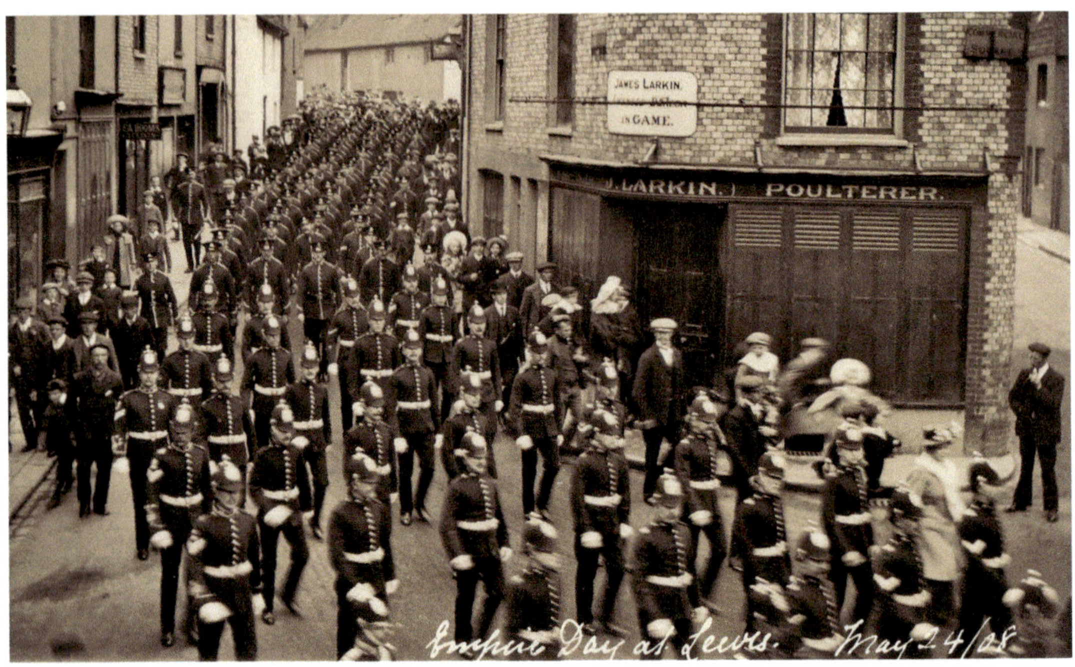

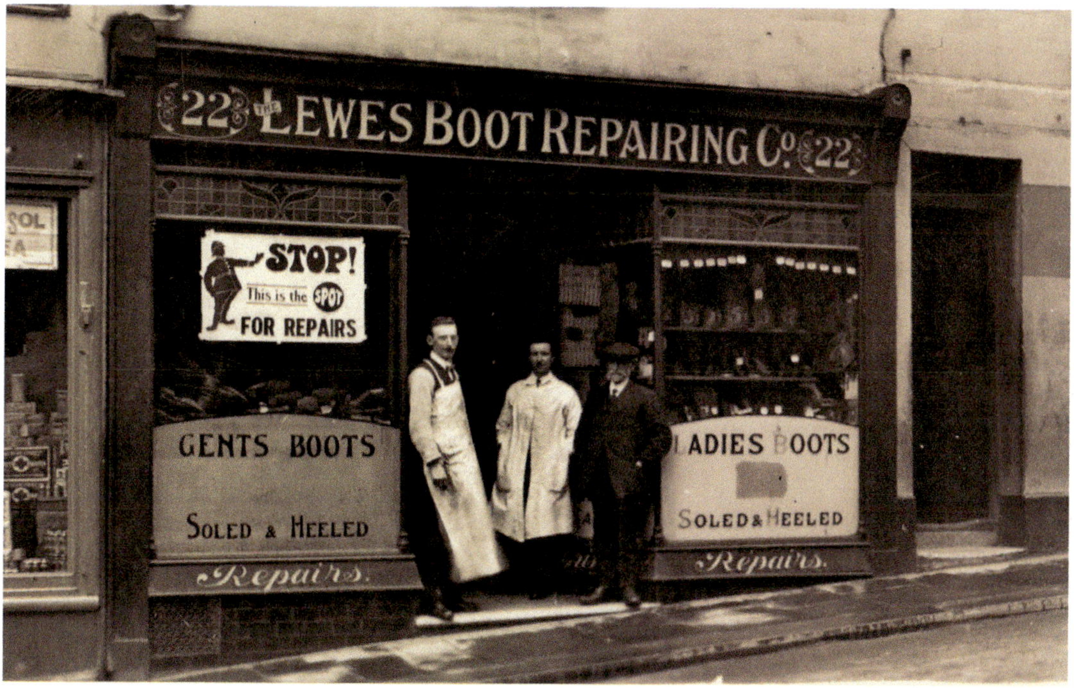

Fisher Street

At 22 Fisher Street was the Lewes Boot Repairing Co. owned by P. W. Griffin, who lived at 2 Paddock Terrace. The street is first noted in property deeds of 1383 and could be named after William Fyssher, who paid tax on a house here in 1340.

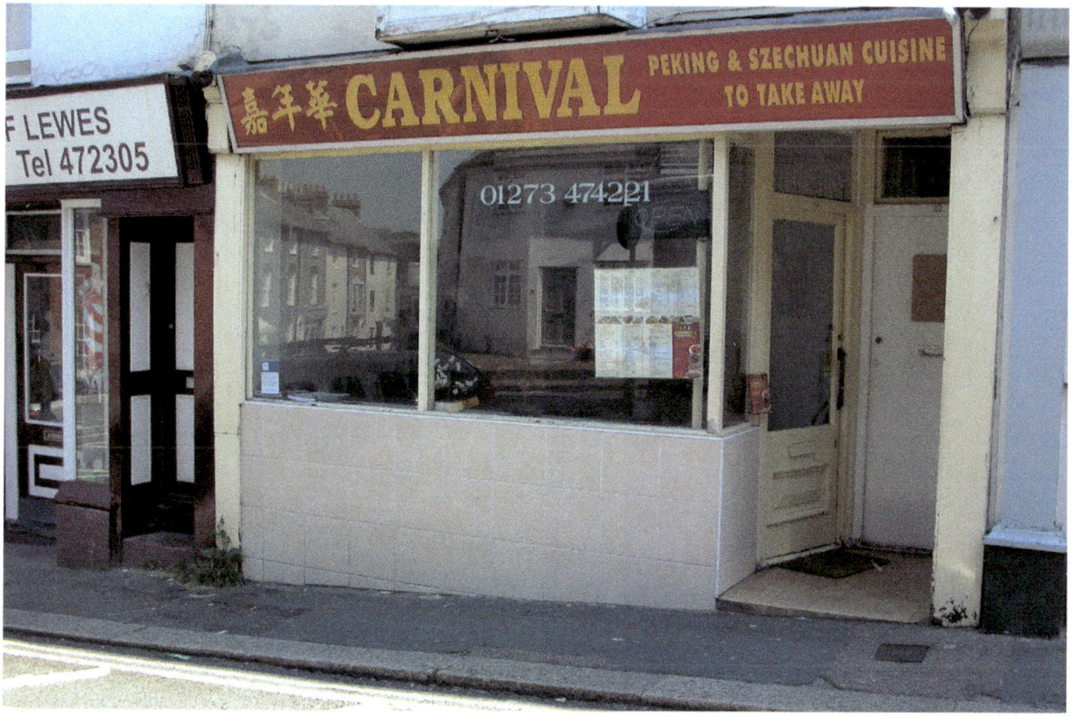

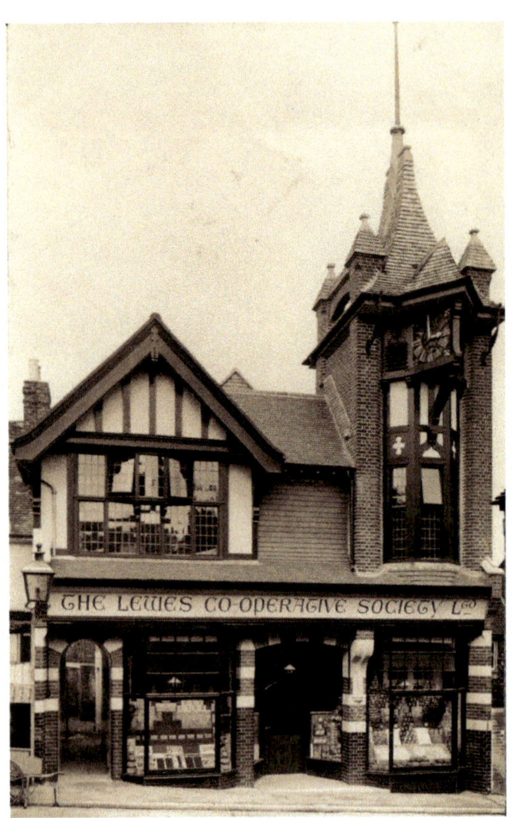

Lewes Co-operative Society

West Street once extended to the Paddock Valley but now runs from Commercial Square to North Street. At Nos 3/4 was the Lewes Co-operative Industrial & Provident Society Ltd. It was established in 1864 by a group of working men buying groceries in bulk and retailing to themselves at market prices. In 1908 there were 1,181 members, who enjoyed a dividend of 1s 10d in the pound. It closed in the 1980s when Wallis & Wallis turned it into their fine auction house, but without the clock steeple.

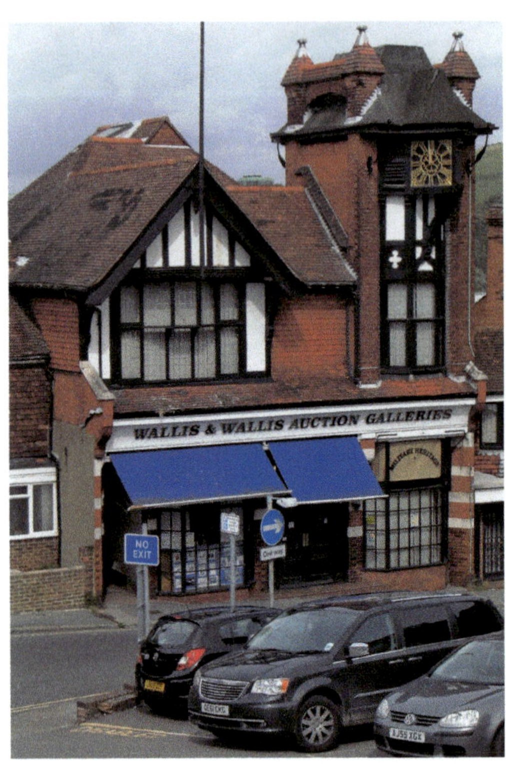

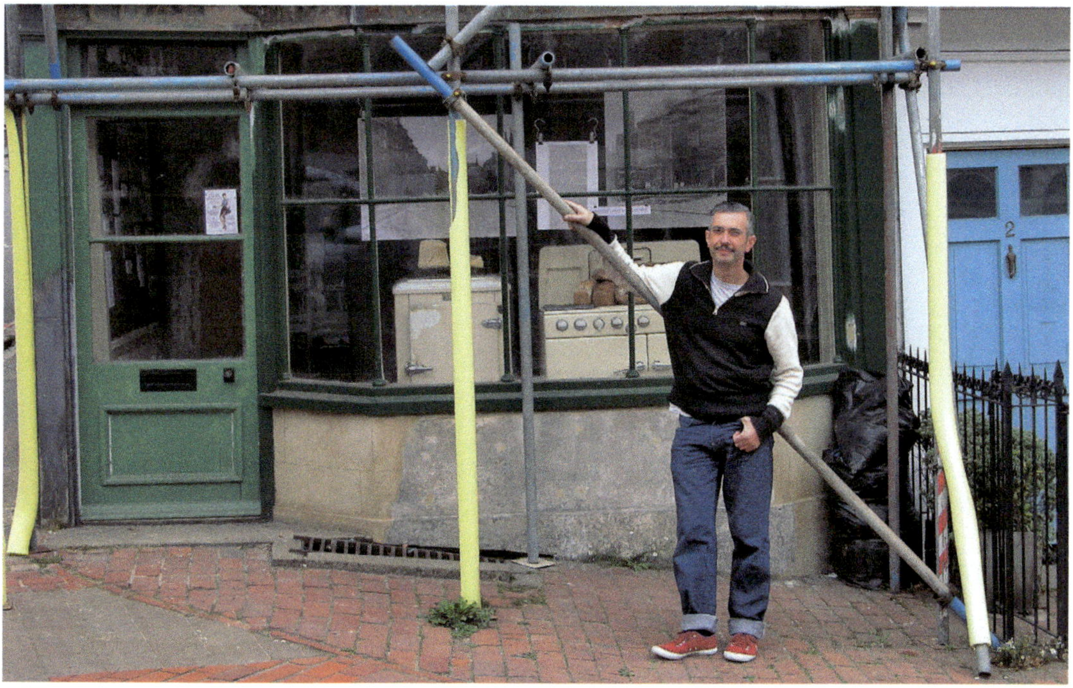

Urry & Sons

Lewes abounded with carriers and Richard Urry operated out of Sun Street before moving to 1 North Street in 1934, where he also sold coal and furniture. It later became a sweet shop and gunsmith's. The cottage was built in 1805 and narrowly avoided demolition in the 1960s along with most of upper North Street. Over the past eleven years it has been lovingly restored at great personal expense by Lewis Orchard. The Urry's name-board over the shop will be refurbished.

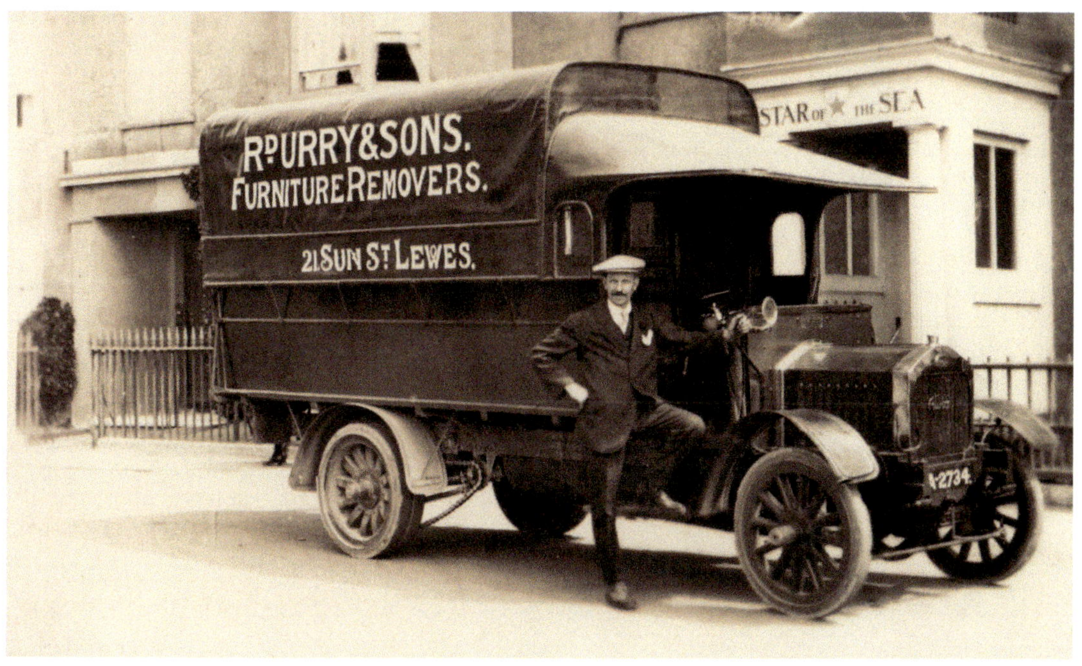

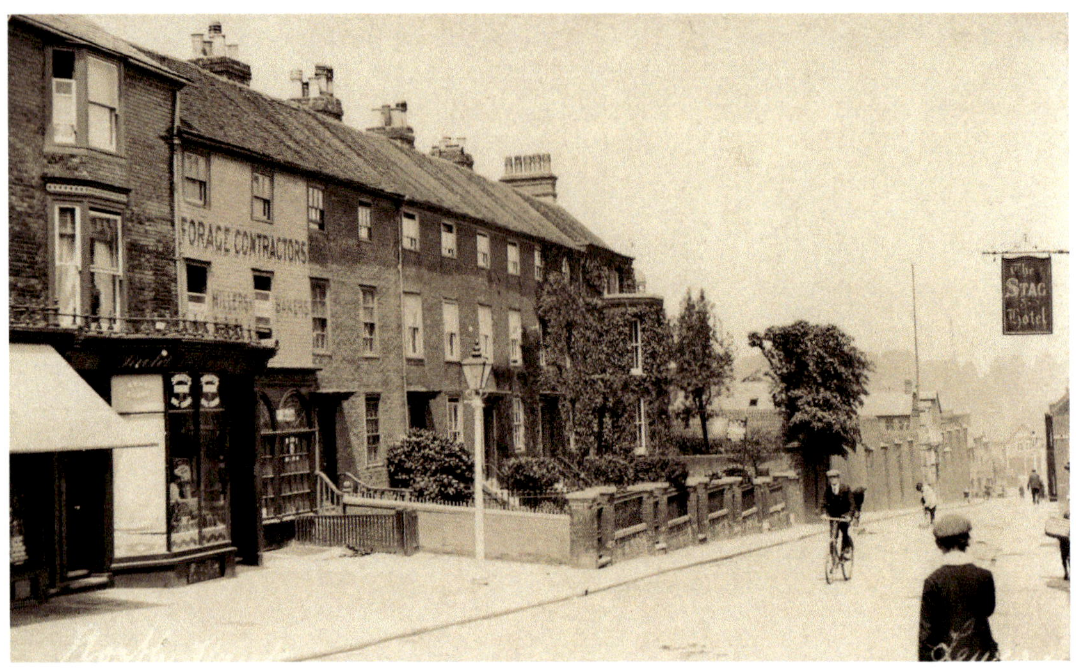

Upper North Street

North Street matches Malling Street for the degree of change it has endured. Developed in the 1790s, it survived largely unchanged until 1943. The fine terrace beyond the shops gave way to the building of the telephone exchange in the 1960s. The Naval Prison below, originally built as a house of correction and then used for Crimean prisoners, was also demolished at this time. It has been a car park since, and the Lewes police station, which opened in 2010, shares the site.

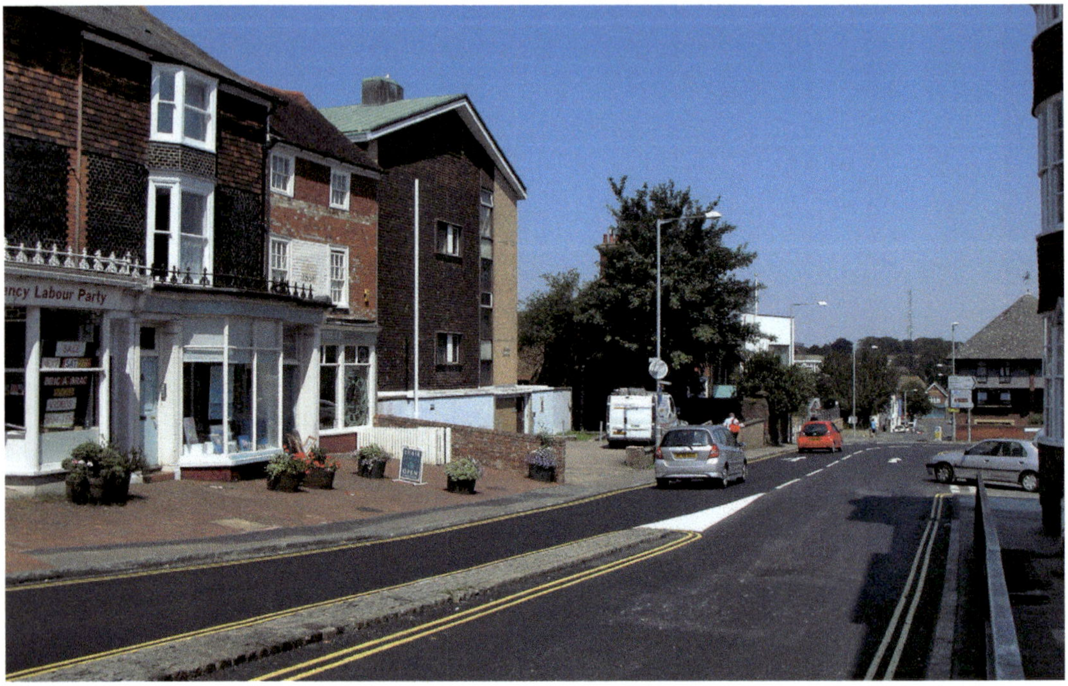

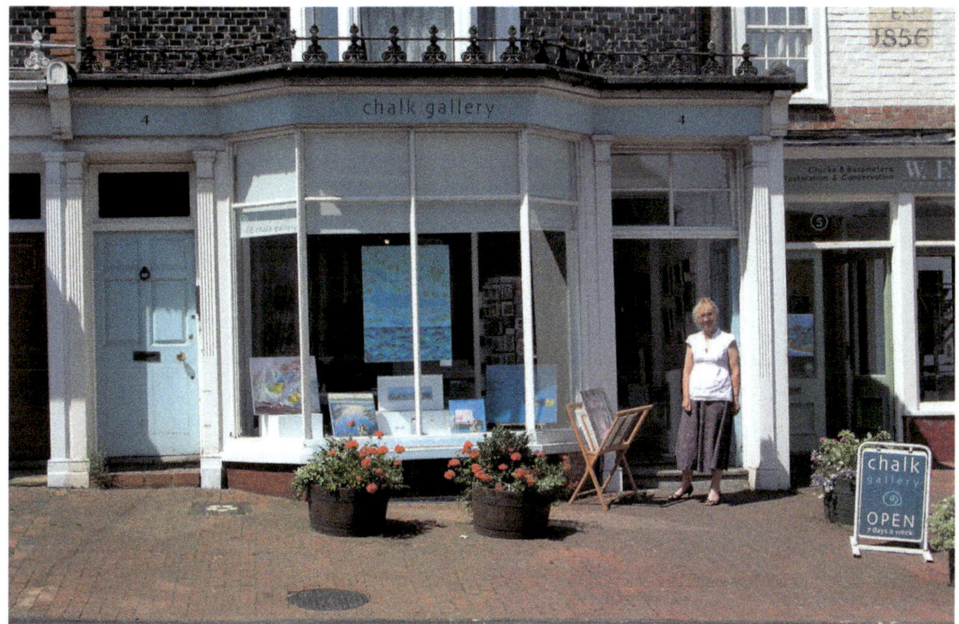

Stevenson's Shop in North Street

The shops have largely survived. Mr F. W. Curtis had the grocer's shop at No. 3 (now the Labour Party office and formerly Jenner's cheese shop) and R. Stevenson Ltd, forage contractor, miller and baker was at Nos 4/5. The company moved to Railway Lane in the 1990s and were replaced by an antiques emporium. Chalk Gallery, a co-operative of twenty-one local artists, is now in residence. Francis Knight, one of the artists, was on duty when I took the photograph.

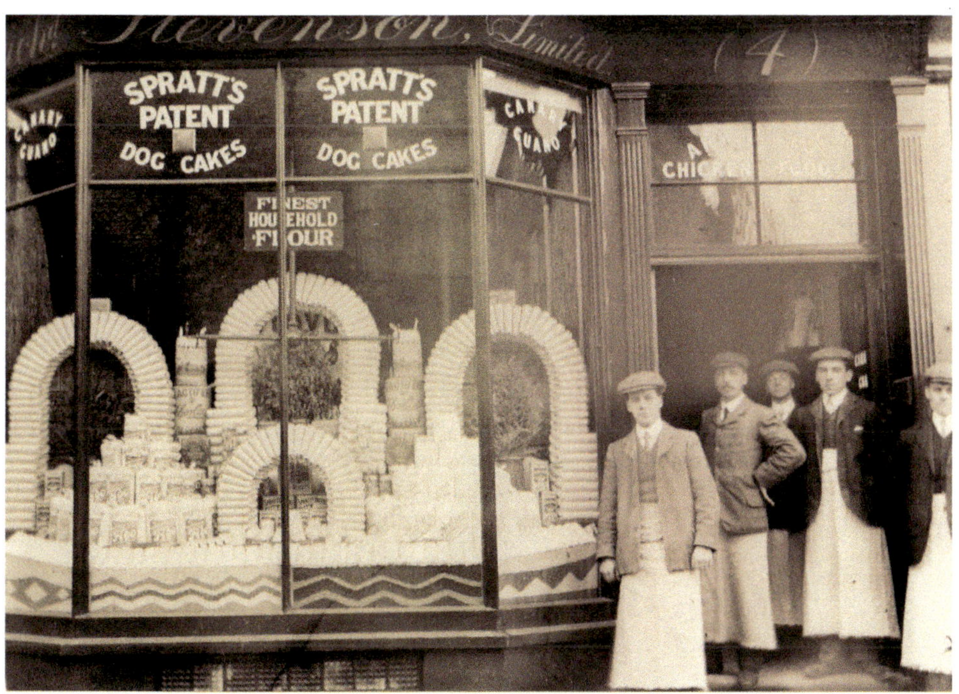

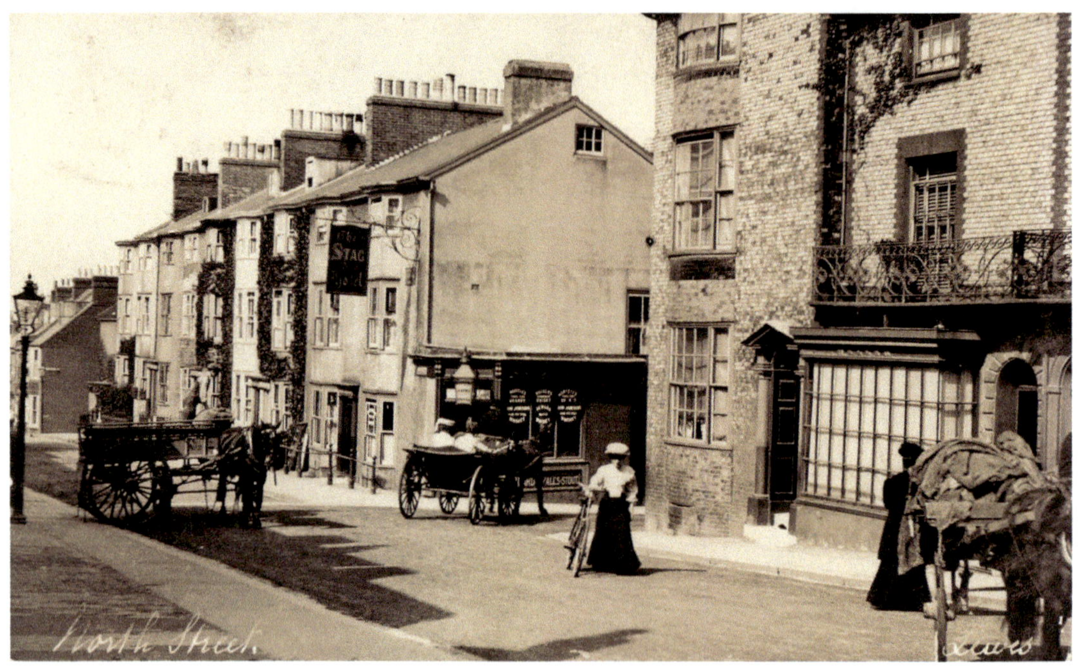

The Stag Hotel, North Street

Lewes largely avoided the many coastal raids during the Second World War. However, on 20 January 1943 the Luftwaffe dropped high explosives on the town and backed them up with cannon and machine gun fire. The Stag Hotel took a direct hit, which killed two people, and was finally destroyed by fire, as was the fine terrace beyond, when the gas main erupted that evening. The fine buildings in the foreground, with their black mathematical tiles, thankfully survived. The hotel site is a car park today.

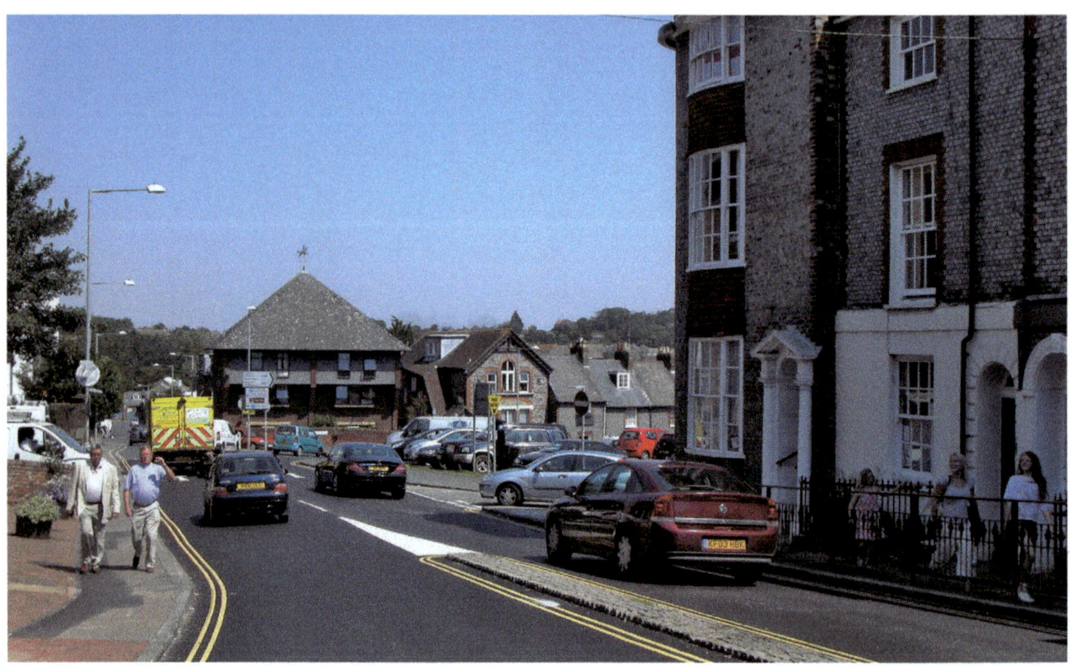

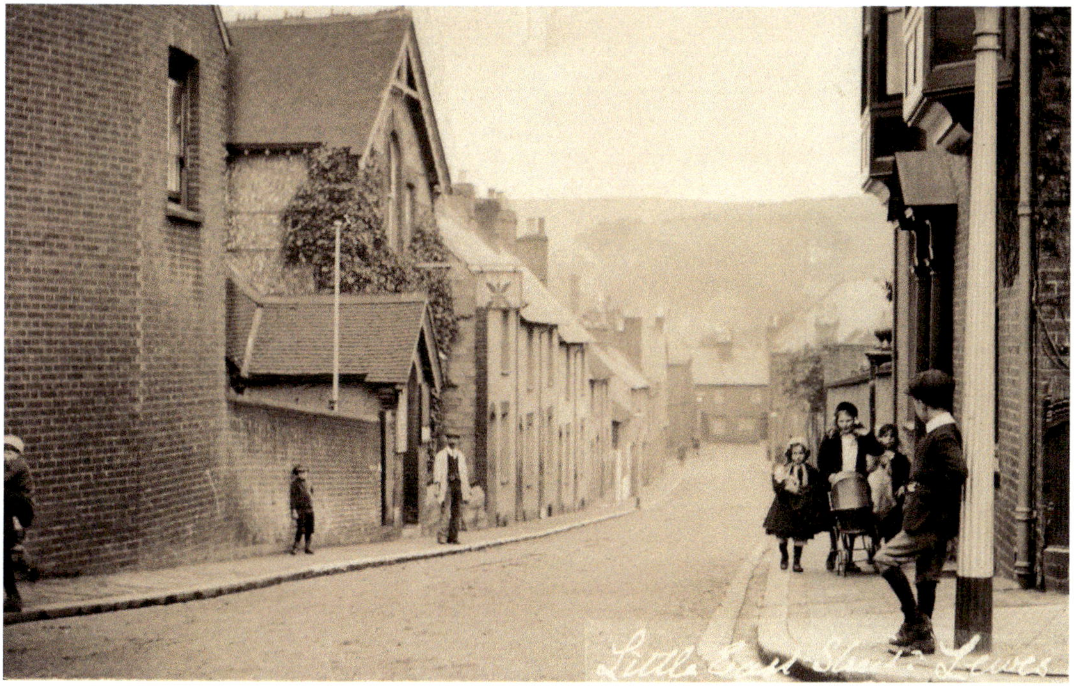

Little East Street

Sadly only half of the houses survive. The south side of the street was demolished in the 1960s to accommodate the dual carriageway, which links to the Phoenix Causeway below. The Providence chapel, with its sign on the left, has been converted into flats. All the peace and quiet suggested by the boy leaning on the lamppost has gone, as has the George Inn, which stood at the junction with Lancaster Street.

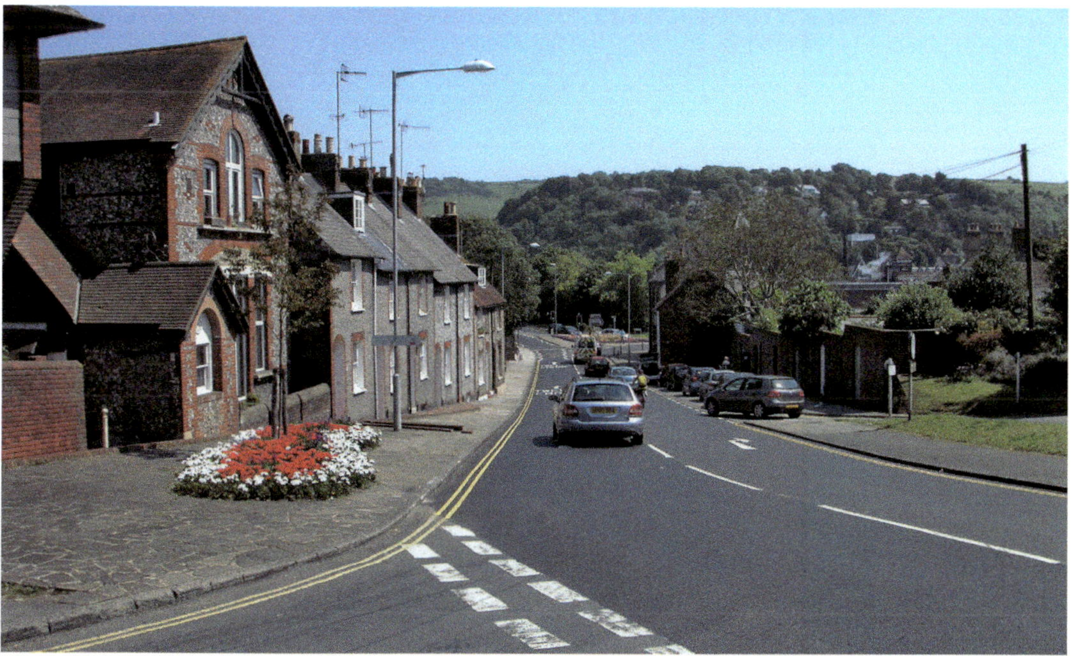

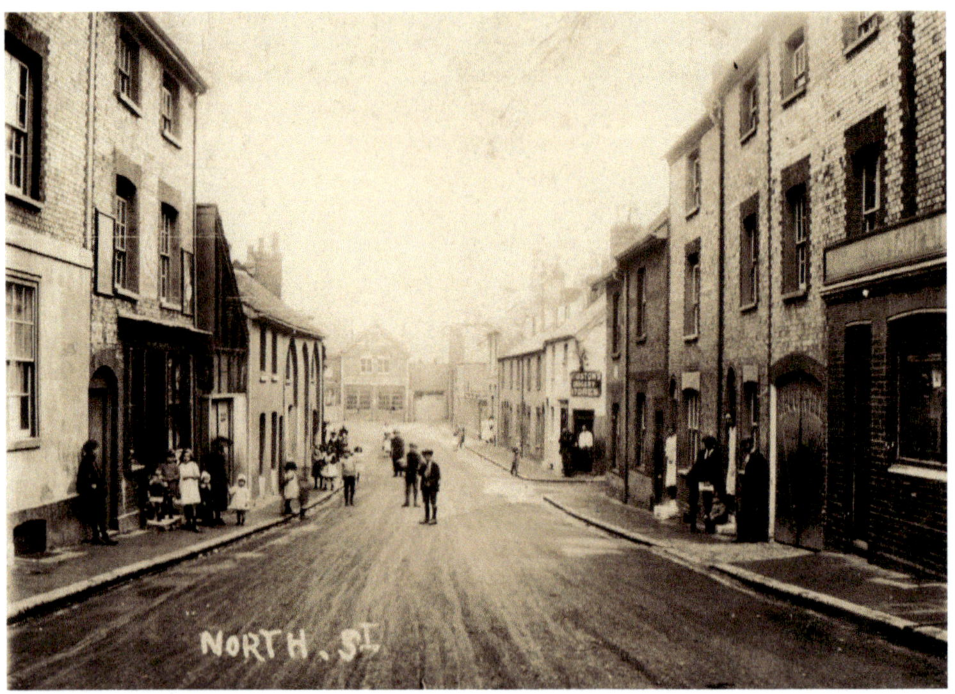

Lower North Street

This was an honest, working-class and highly populated area of Lewes. Backing on to the river with the Commercial and Every's Wharves, it was also the most industrialised. It was decimated by a succession of slum clearances following the building of the Landport Estate just before the Second World War and the demise of the Phoenix Ironworks. It was a largely self-contained community with shops, pubs, baths and employment at Every's.

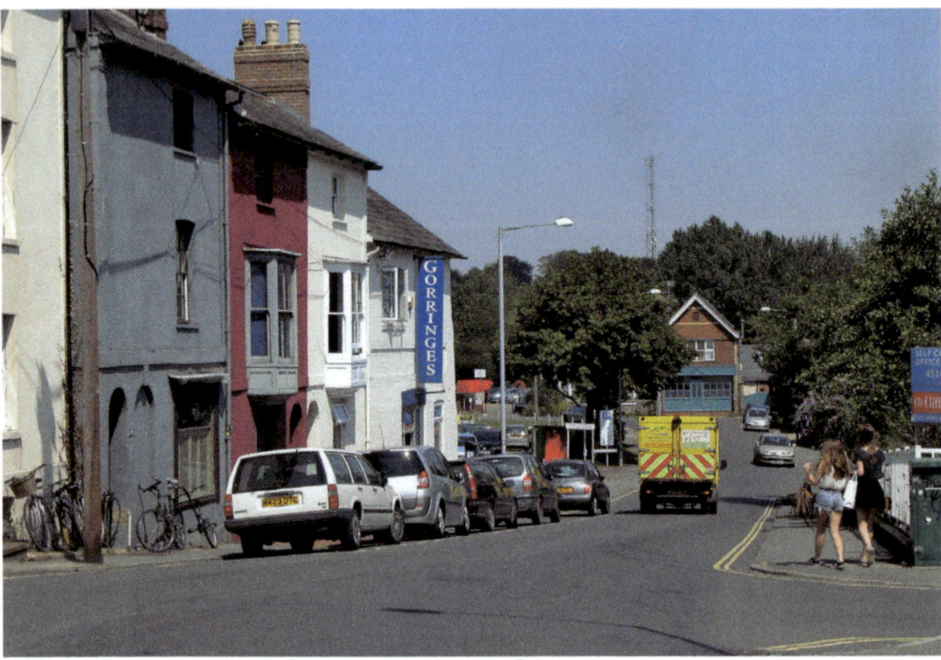

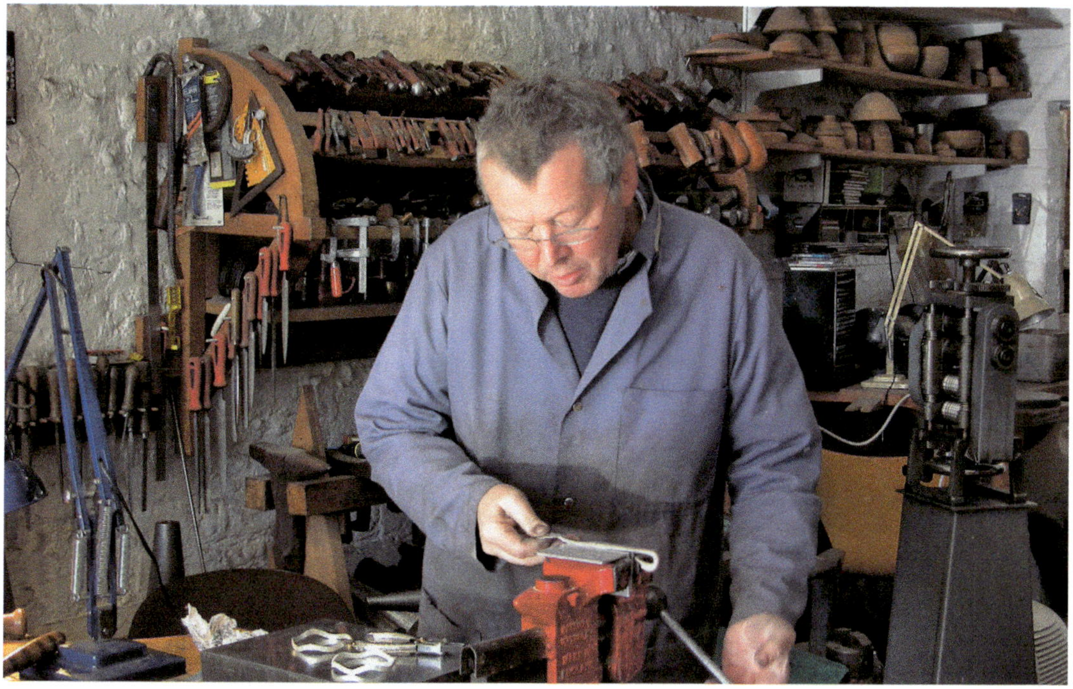

Lewes Fire Station

Following the Great Fire in 1904 (see page 45), Lewes Fire Brigade was modernised and a new station built in 1907 at the bottom of North Street. Cliffe had their own brigade in the nineteenth century and their station, to the side of Cliffe church, has been the premises of Simon Beer since 1999. He is another of Lewes' master craftsmen and trained under the renowned David Mellor. The water tank, fed from the roof, is still under the floor.

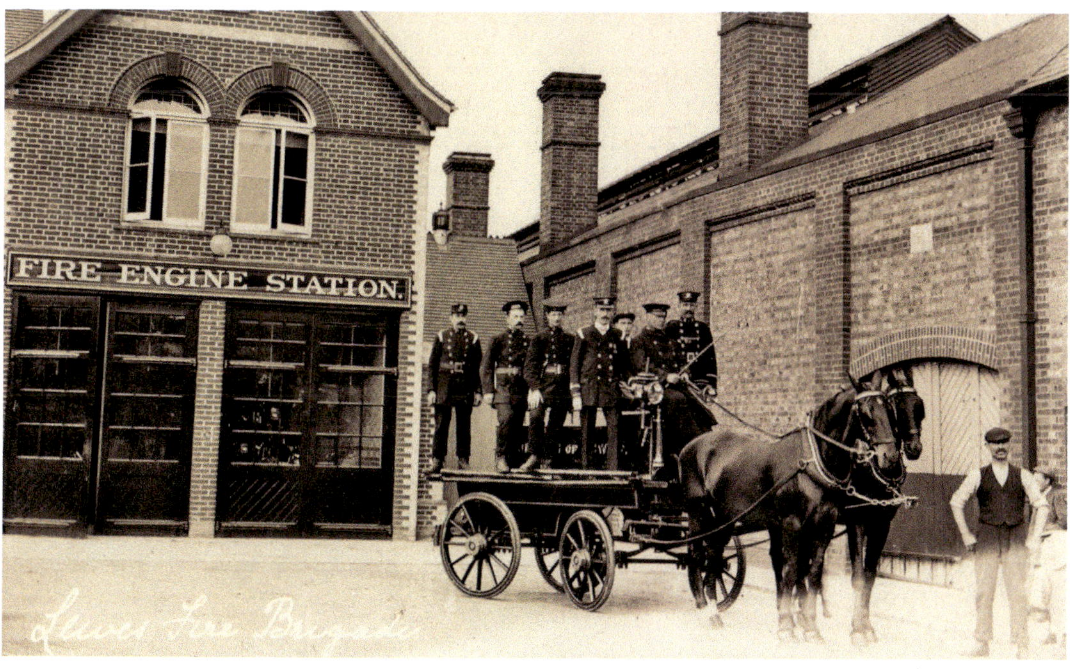

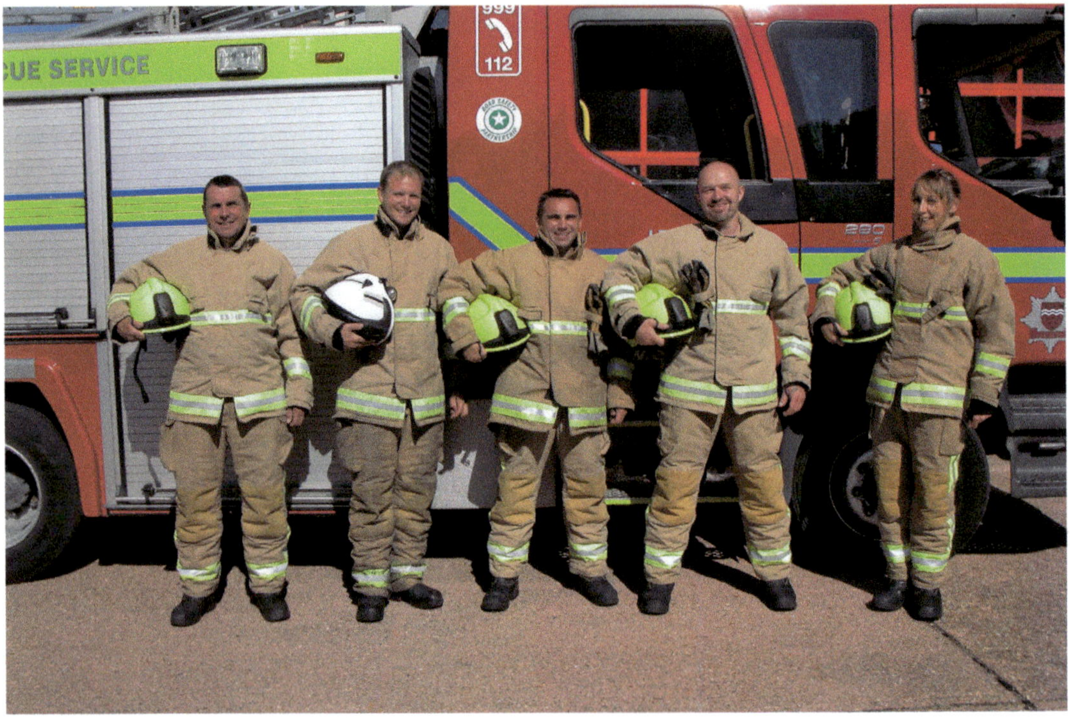

Lewes Fire Brigade

Lewes Fire Brigade proudly stand with their steam tender in 1907. Green Watch at Lewes Fire Station kindly donned fire kit to strike a similar pose for me. From the left they are Ricky Ross, David Washington (Watch Manager), Sean Oakman, Steve Dartnell and Julie Skeffington. Two of the watch were absent. They all refused to wear moustaches for my photograph.

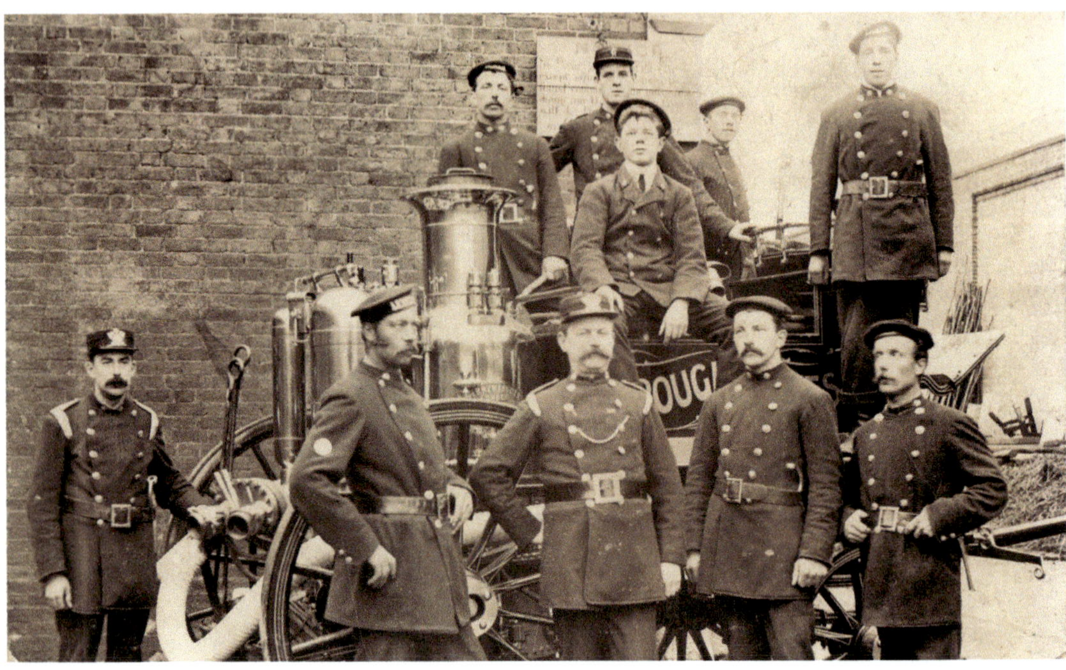

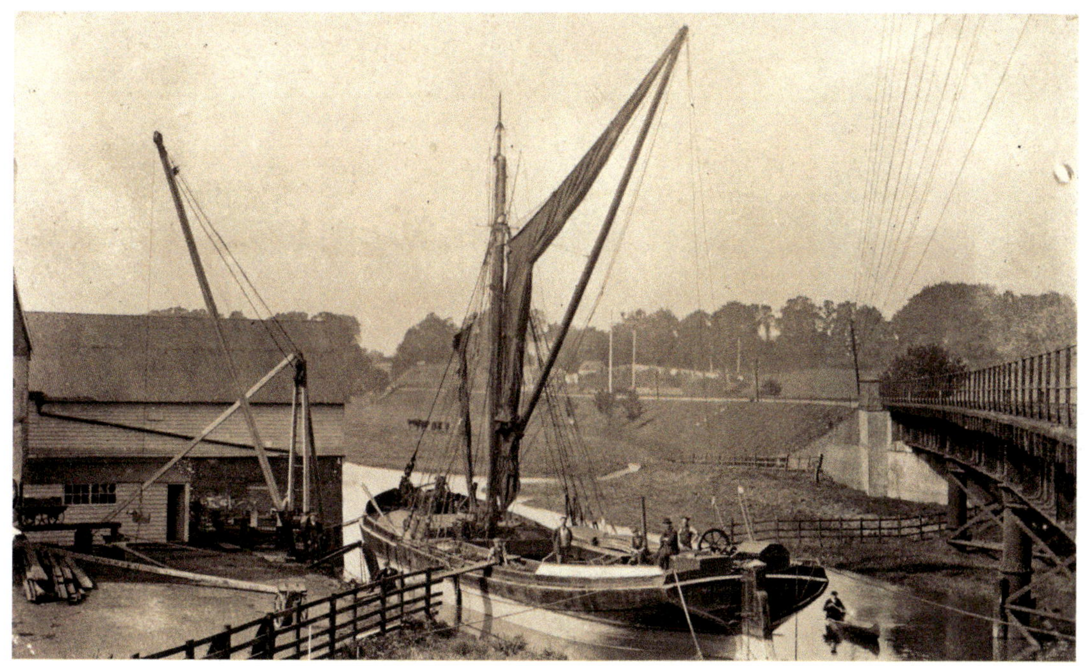

Phoenix Ironworks

The Ironworks was established by John Every in 1832 and finally settled in North Street a few years later. Many of the raw materials and finished products were transported by barges such as the one shown at the company's wharf. Every's was one of the town's largest employers and survived until it was asset-stripped and closed in the 1980s. The bridge, which carried the railway to Uckfield, sweeps round on the right, pretty much on the line of the Phoenix Bridge, from which I took the photograph.

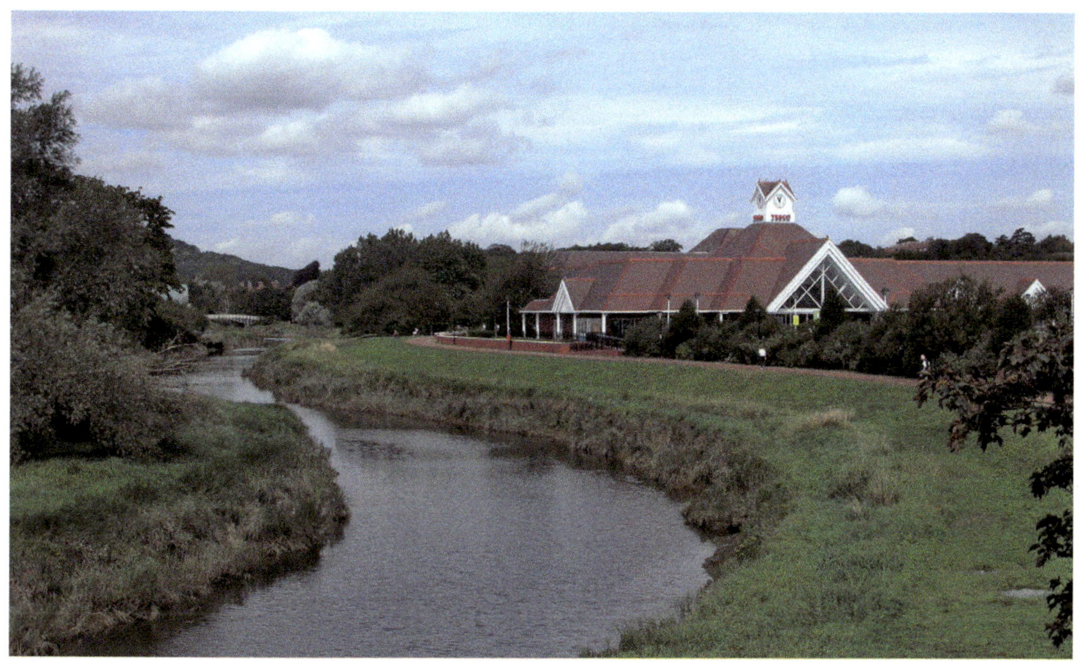

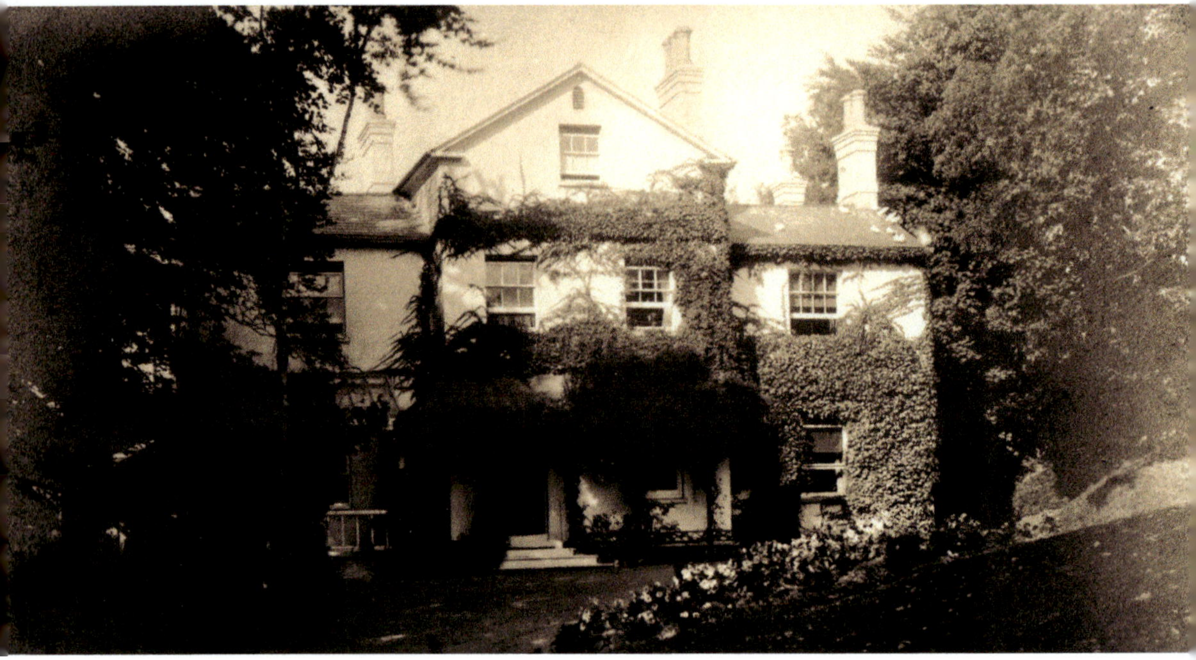

Southover Rectory

The Rectory in Rotten Row is still a superb building, although sadly it is boarded up, pending decisions on the future of the building and its site. For a long time it was St Anne's Special School but it has been empty since the closure. Local community action has brought pressure to bear on its owner, the County Council, to bring the building back into use but plans are still awaited.

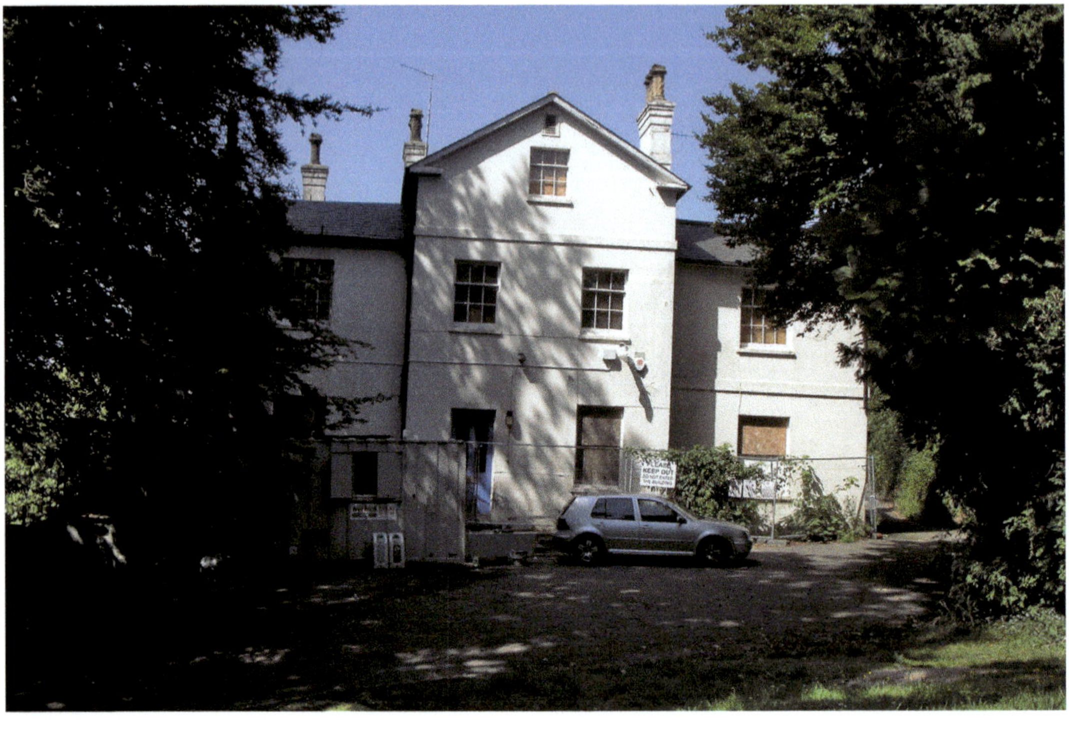

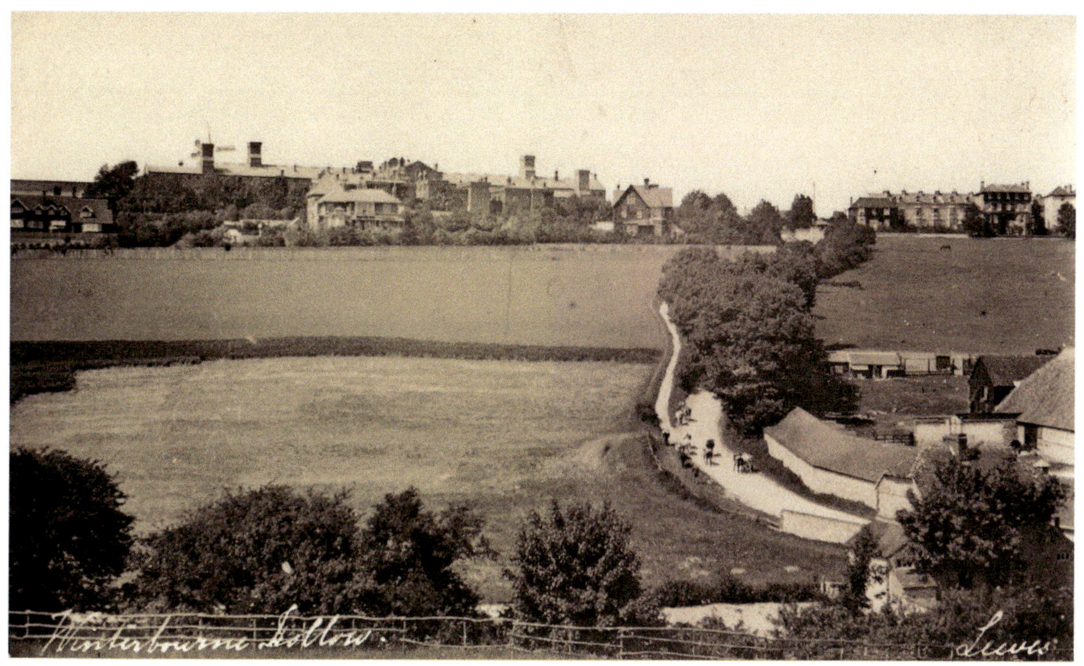

The Prison from Winterbourne

The Cheetham card captures the rural nature of the Winterbourne area and the limit of the town's development to the west, which finished at the prison. A century on and there is extensive housing in the valley, along the south of the Brighton Road to Hope in the Valley and the Houndean Estate on the north side down to Horndean. The town cemetery has little space left.

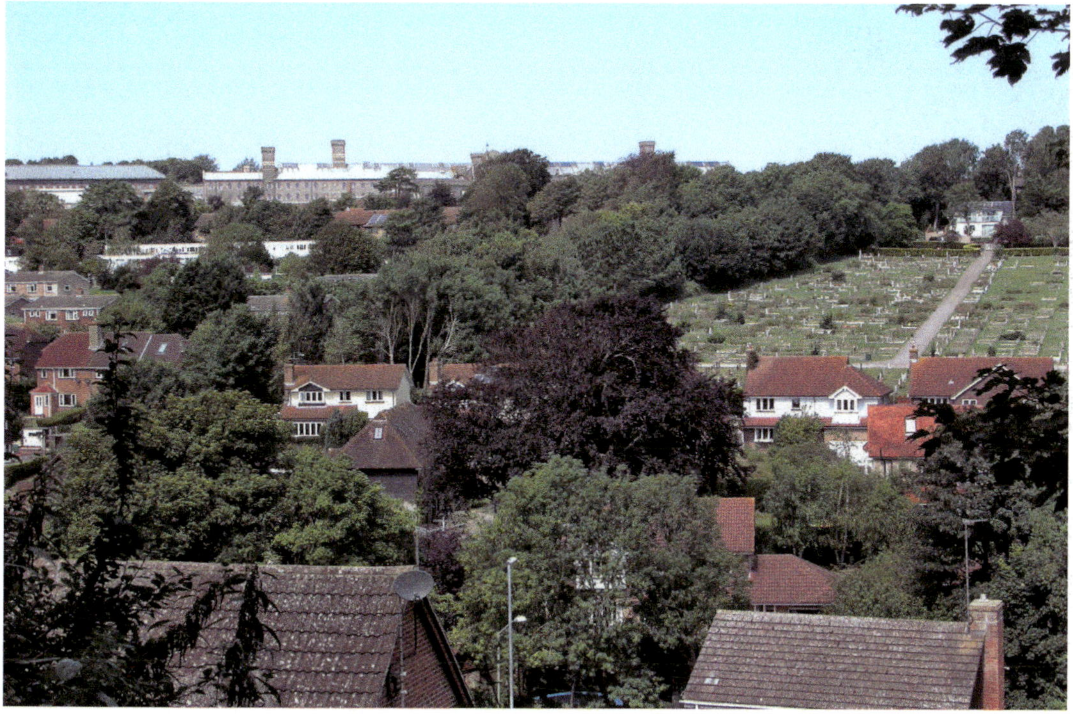

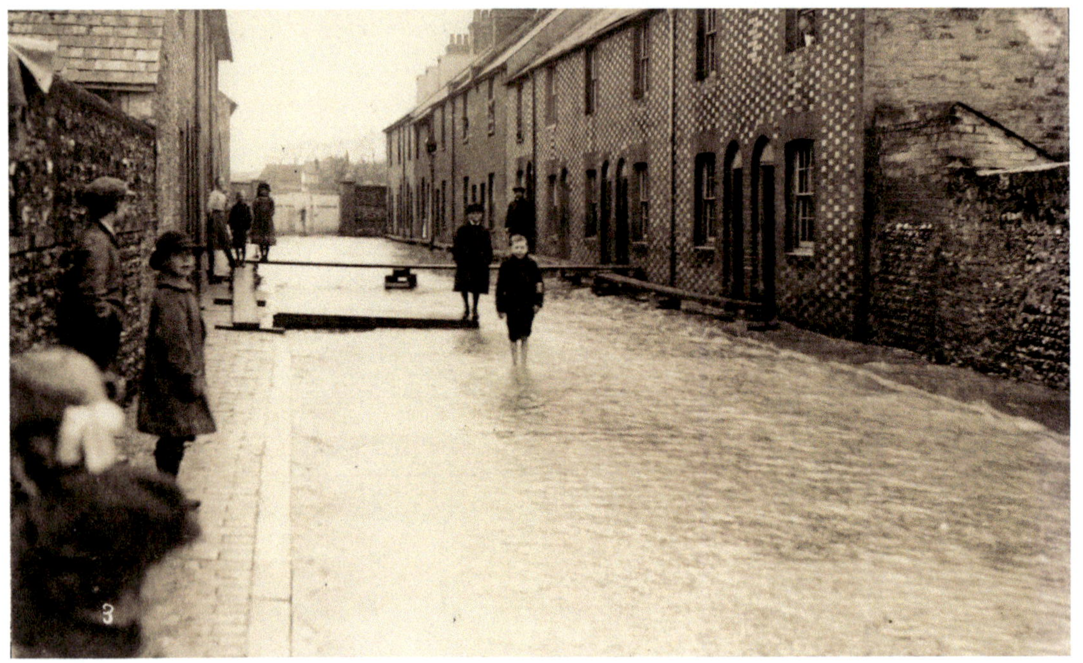

Spring Gardens Flooding

The major flooding of Lewes in 2000 is a horrible recent memory. Unfortunately, in earlier times it was a regular occurrence for those living adjacent to the course of the Winterbourne stream. In 1915, the residents of Spring Gardens don't seem unduly concerned by the stream running down the middle of the street. Demolished under slum clearance in the 1960s, the pavement by the side of St Pancras Stores shows the line of the Gardens, which ran west through the gate into the Winterbourne recreation area.

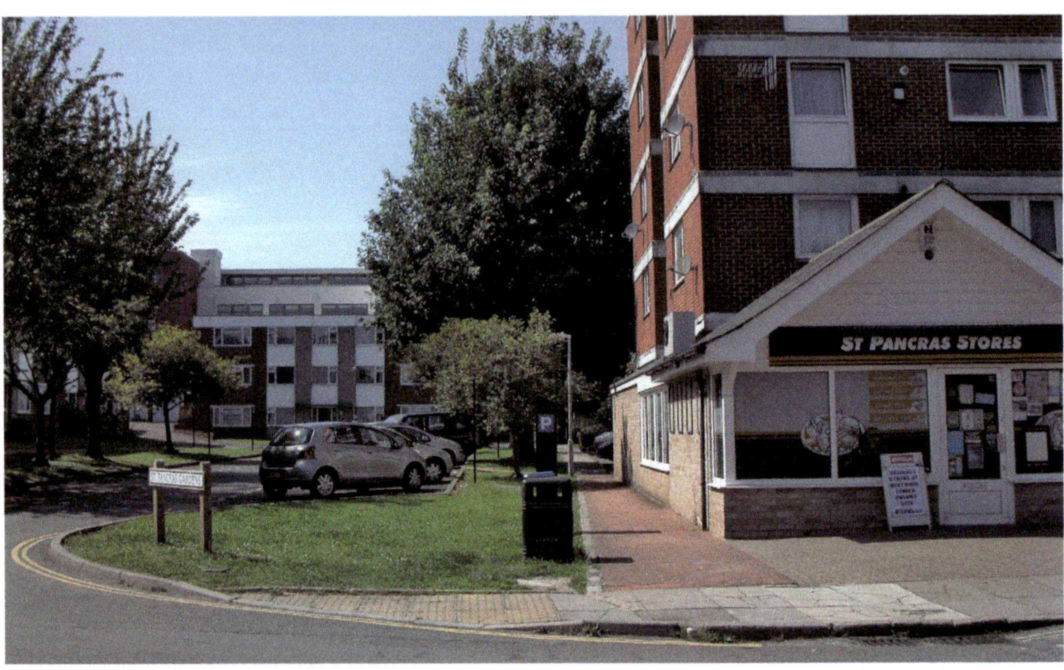

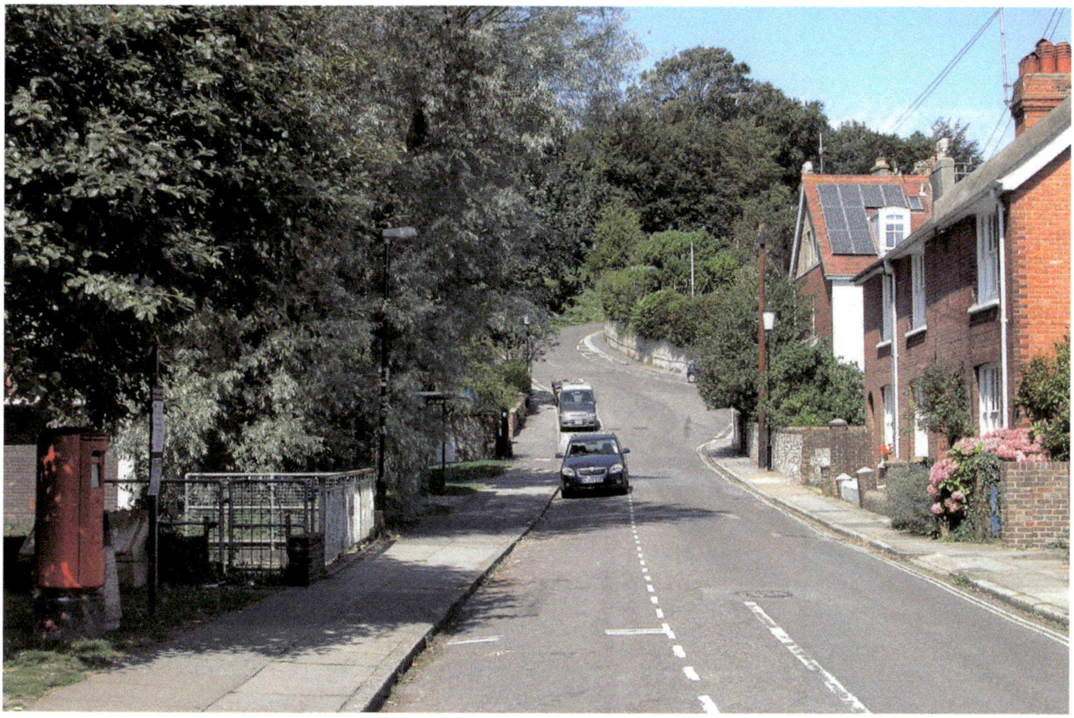

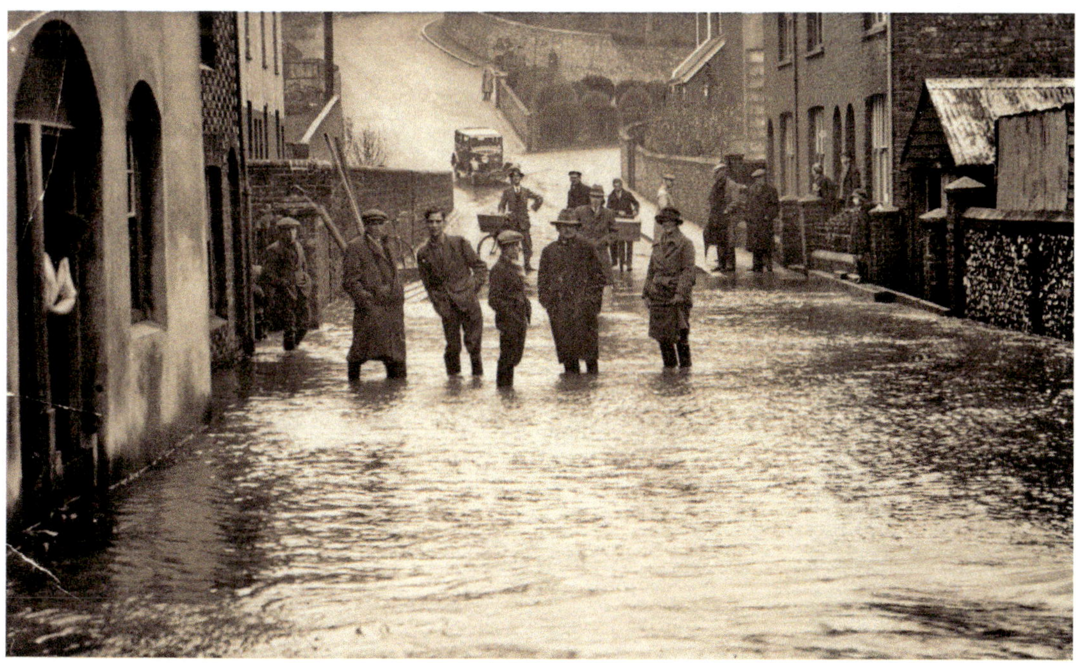

St Pancras Lane Flooding

Twenty-one years later, and probably on many occasions between, it's the turn of the St Pancras Lane community to be flooded. The view is north to the junction with Rotten Row and Grange Road. Again the residents seem nonplussed and, while the delivery boys have wisely decided to go no further, I'm not too sure about the intentions of the approaching car.

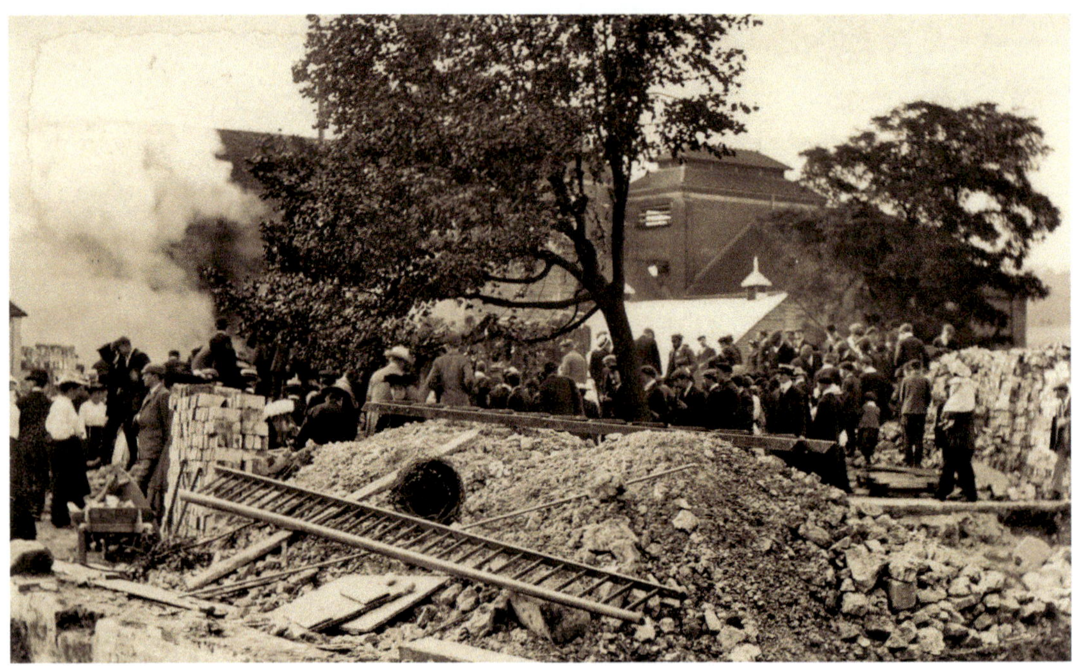

Southover Breweries

Two old Lewes breweries stood close to each other in Southover. The first was owned by the Verrall family from the seventeenth century and they lived in the Old Brewery house, part of which can be seen on the left of my photograph. It was later famously occupied by Charlie Watts of the Rolling Stones. Brewing stopped in 1897 and the works were demolished on 16 September 1905 into 300 tons of rubble and masonry. The second brewery can be seen in the background.

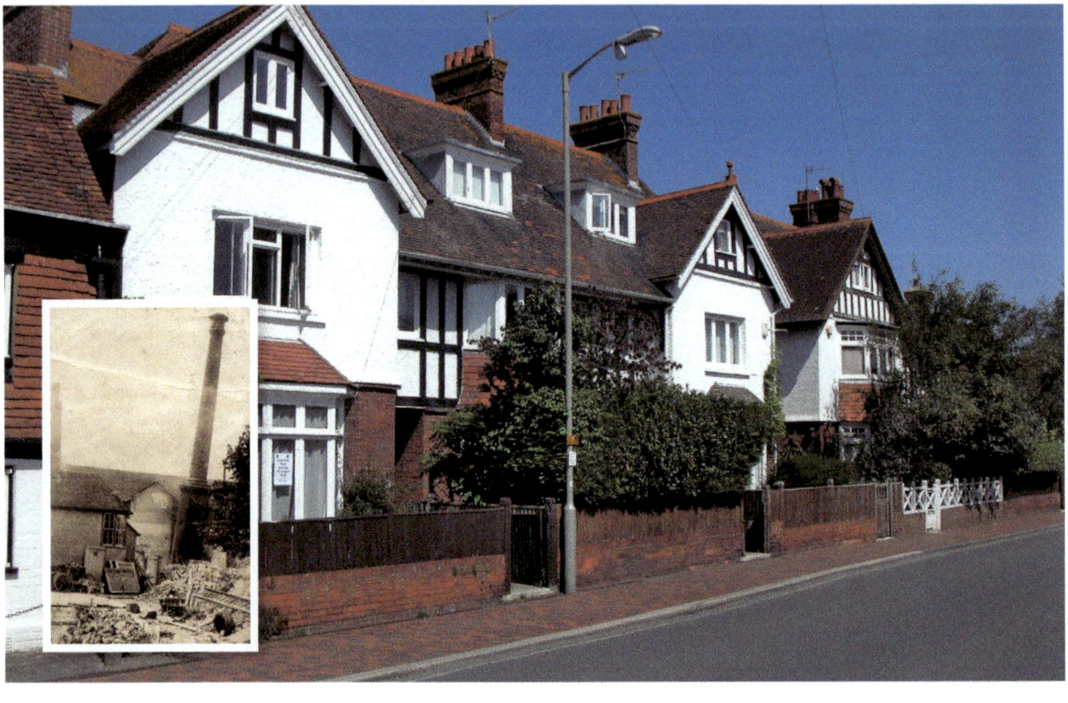

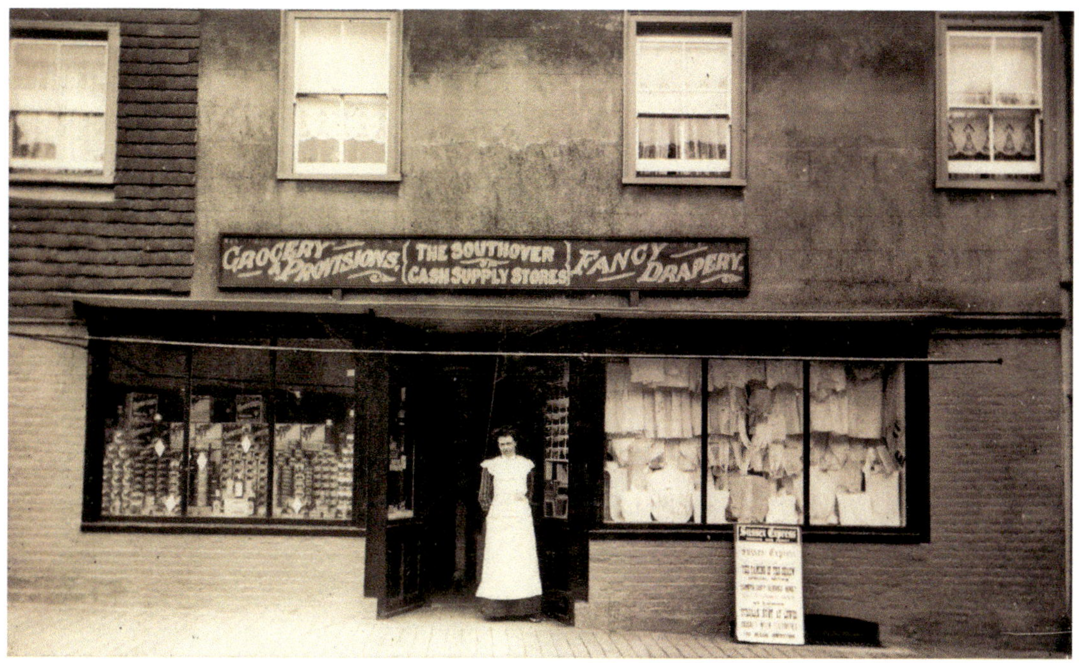

Southover Shopping Centre

Shops were everywhere in Lewes in the Victorian and Edwardian periods and Southover was no exception. The Southover Cash Supply Stores seems to be an early form of convenience store, providing just about everything except credit, given the stern look of its owner. I believe it was in the orange house shown in my photograph.

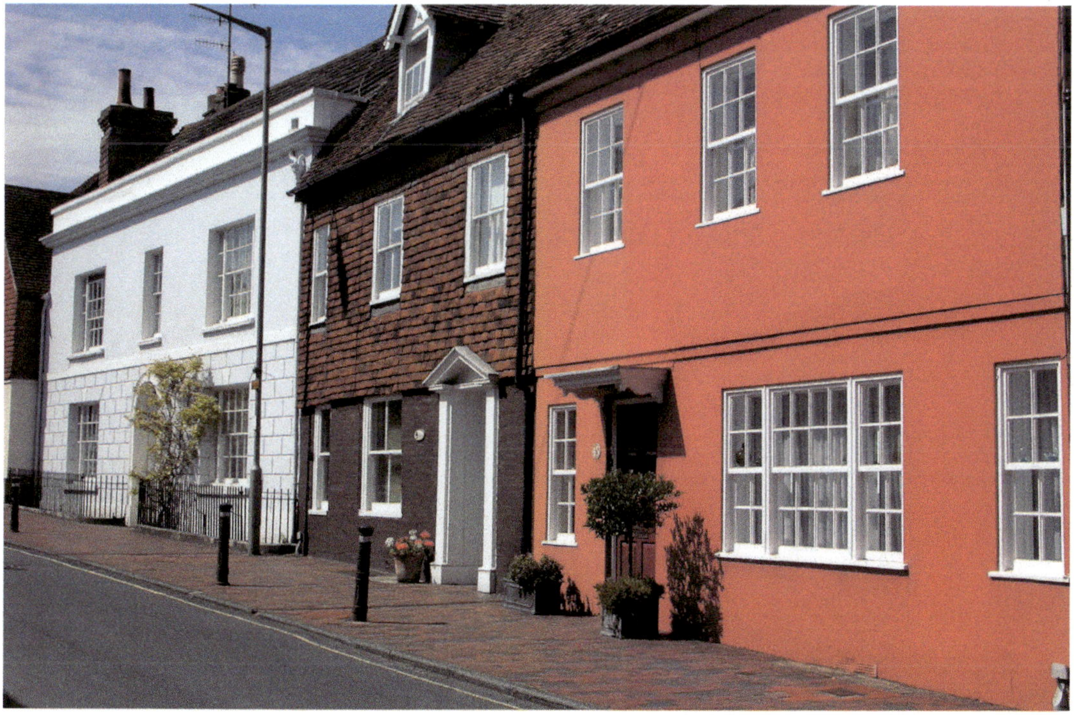

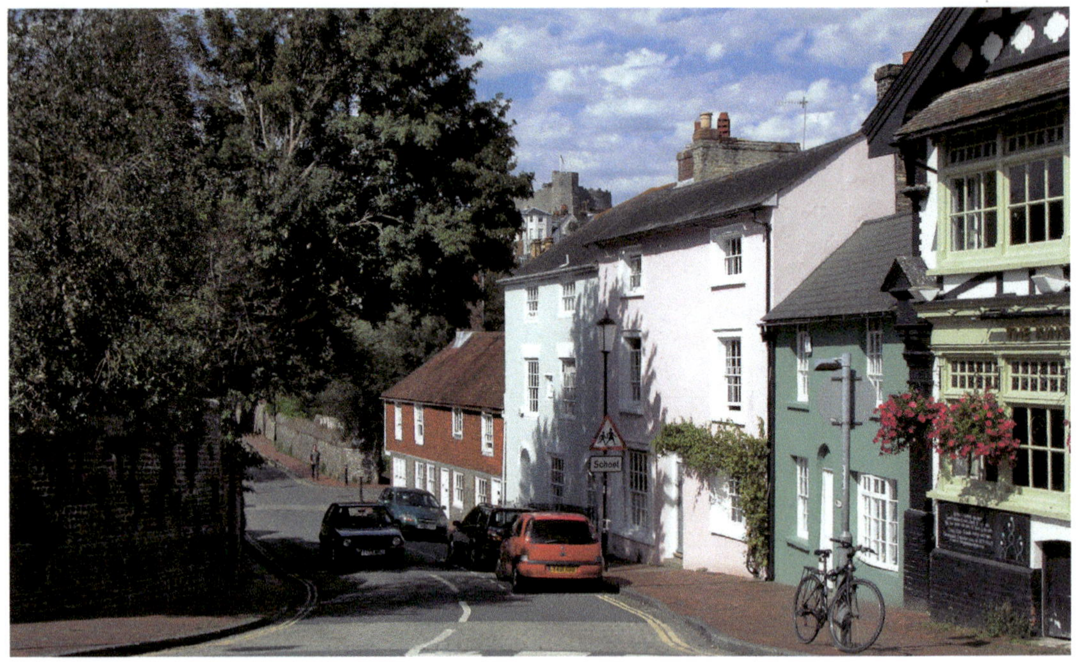

King's Head, Southover

The King's Head is on the corner of Priory Street and opposite Priory Crescent. It was probably established in Tudor times as a hostel linked to the priory. There is a Stuart reference to the Chequer tavern standing where the tile-hung cottages are. The large fig tree on the left still drops its fruit each year onto the pavement.

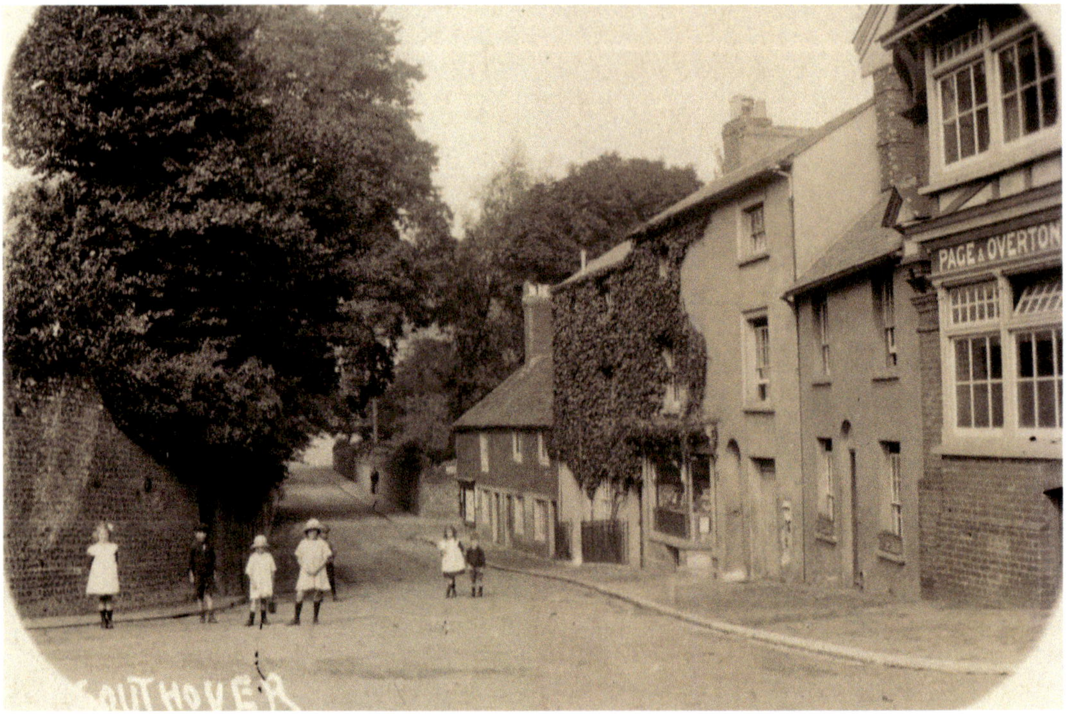

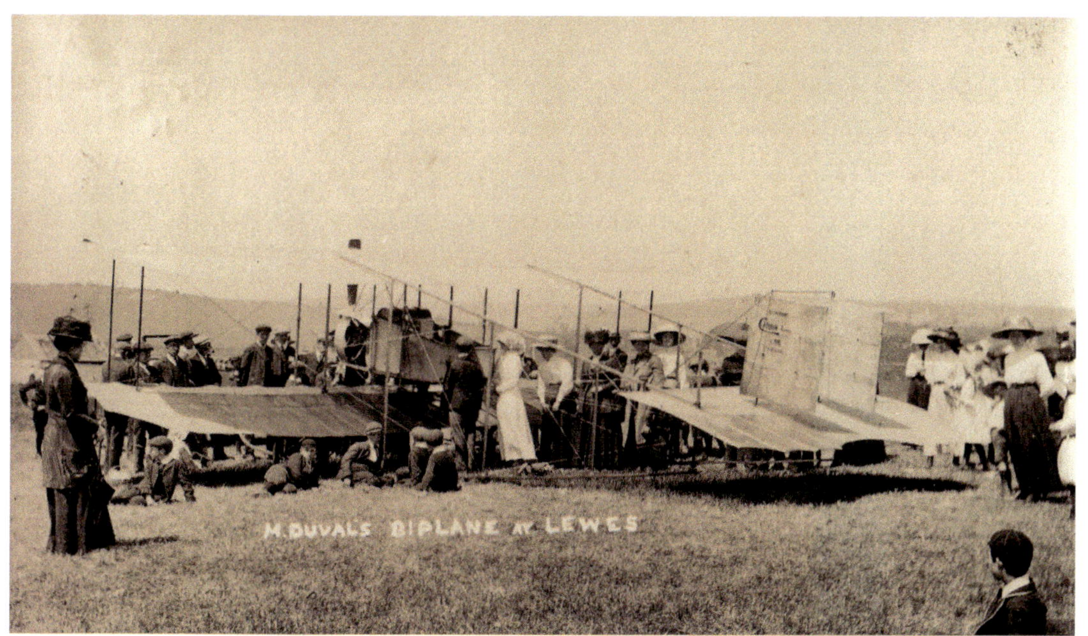

Flying Visit, Southover

In July 1911 at Rise Farm, Southover, Monsieur Duval made a forced landing while taking part in the Great European Air Race from Paris via Dover and Brighton (Shoreham Airport) to Hendon. Eleven aviators competed for £2,500, won by Beaumont. Unfortunately, mechanical problems led to Duval's withdrawal but not before, as the local paper reported, 'the planes of the machine were covered with the signatures of Lewes people'. Paragliders on Caburn continue with man's desire to fly.

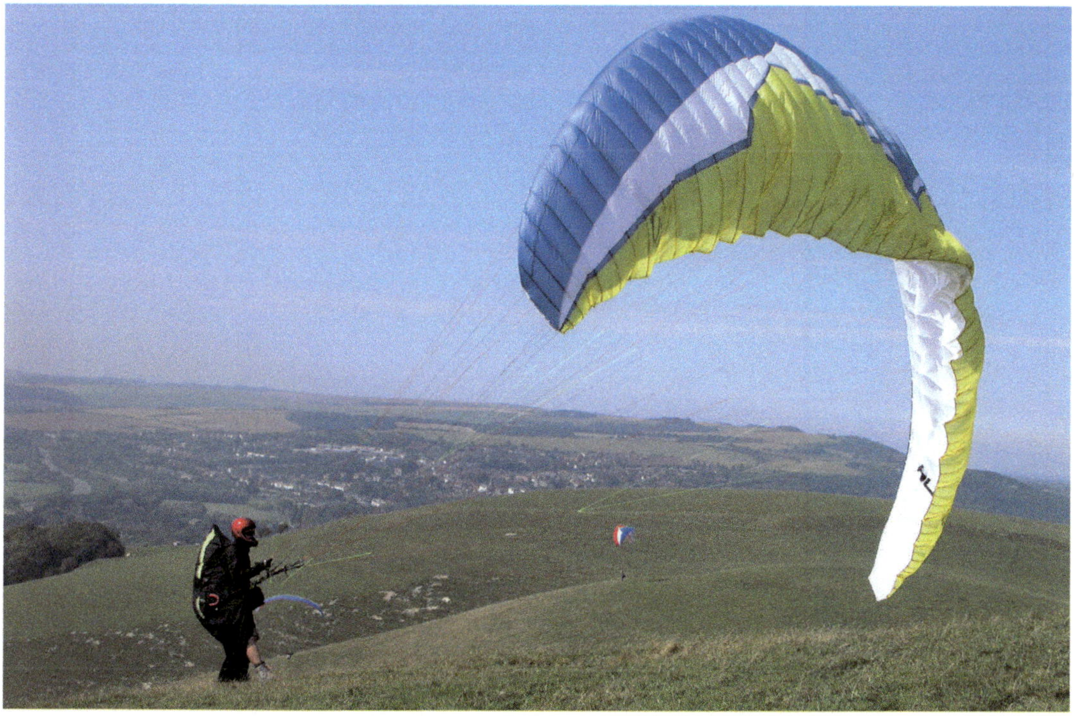

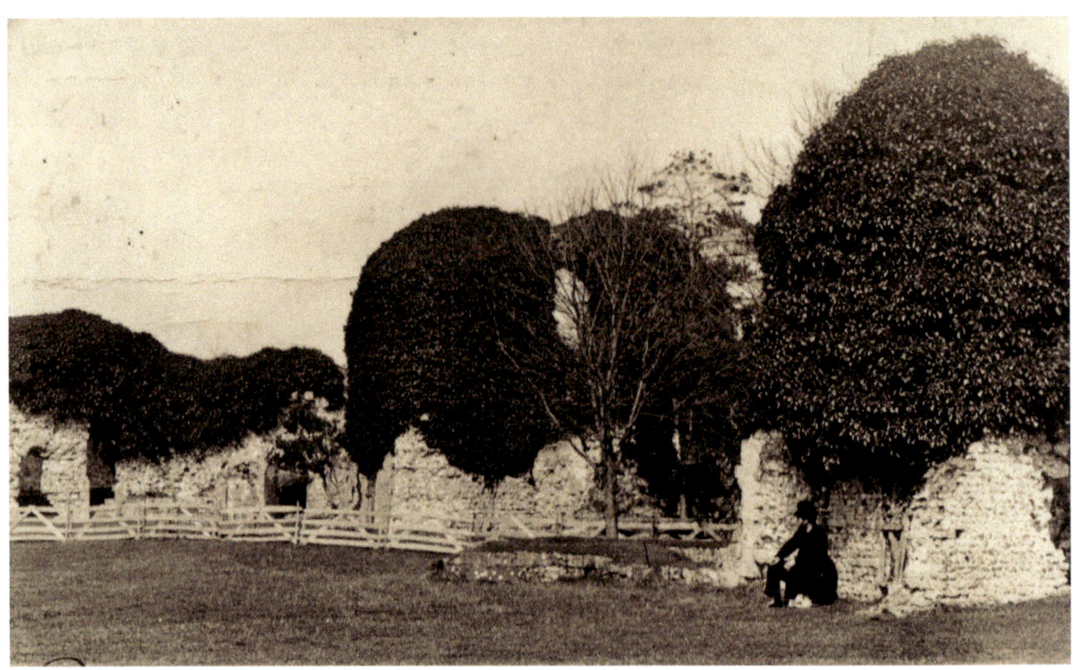

Cluniac Priory, Southover

The Southover Priory site reopened last year, after a major effort by the trustees, with English Heritage funding. The site now gives an excellent interpretation of the Cluniac Priory established by William de Warenne and his wife Gundrada in the 1080s. Its church was bigger than Chichester Cathedral. King Henry VIII claimed it in 1537 and had it destroyed soon after.

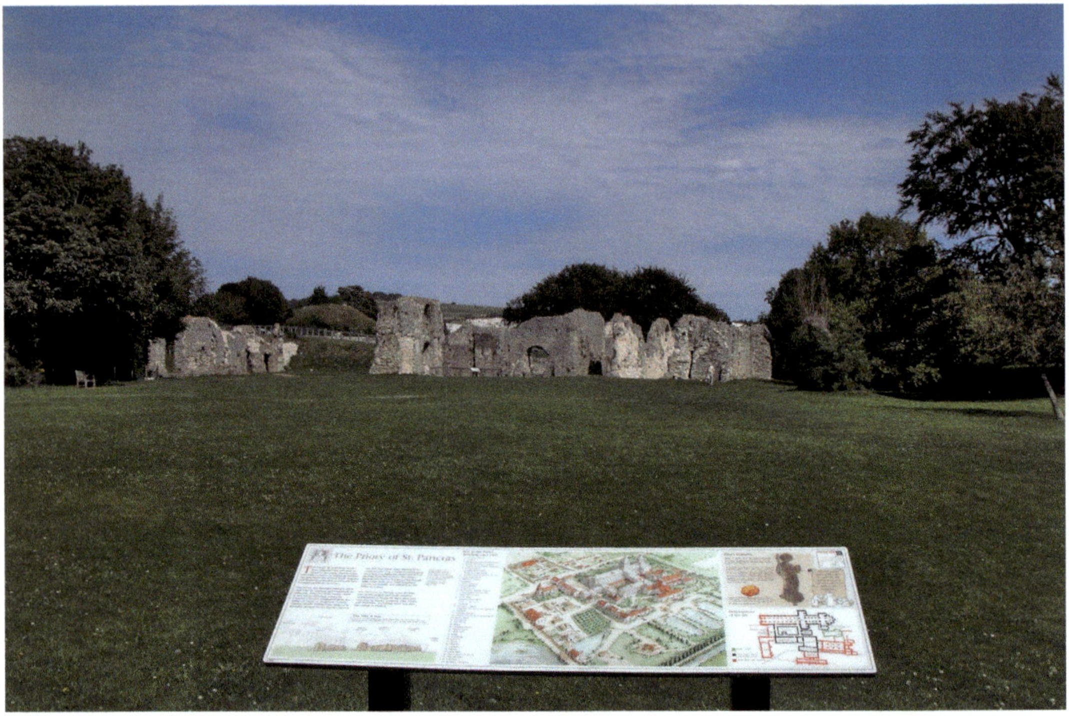

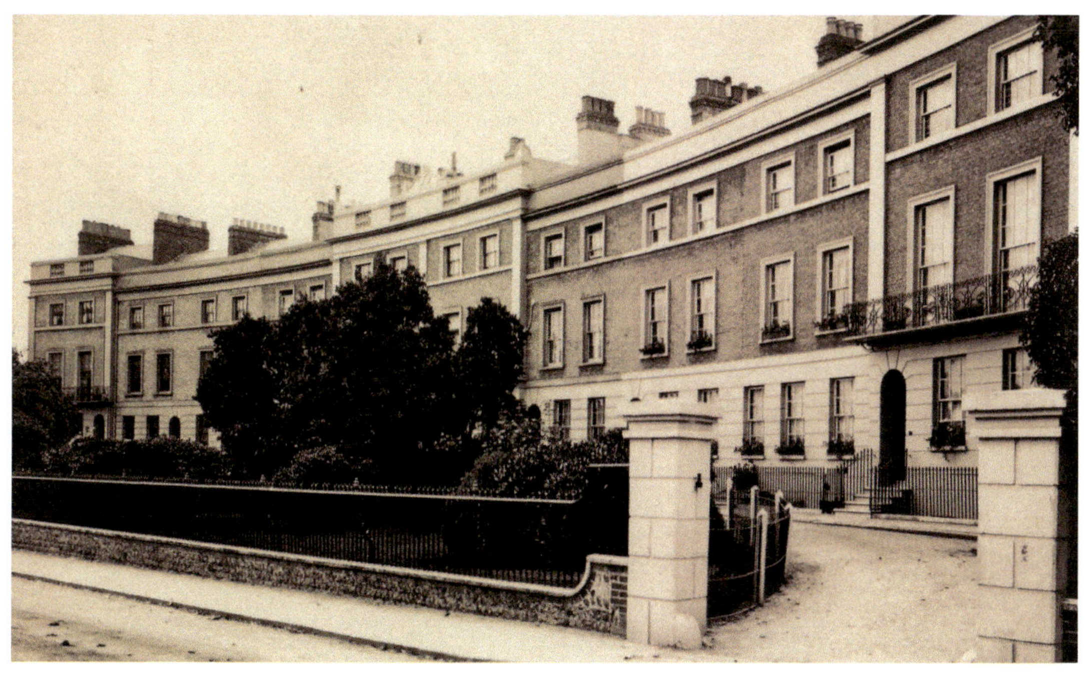

Priory Crescent

Built in two parts from opposite ends in 1832 and 1852, the keen eye can see the different brickwork of Nos 3 to 5. Pevsner was dismissive and judged it as, 'townish and out of place'. The first observation is probably true but the second is difficult to appreciate given it's magnificent sweep, although, as can be seen from the castle tower, it is on the edge of town.

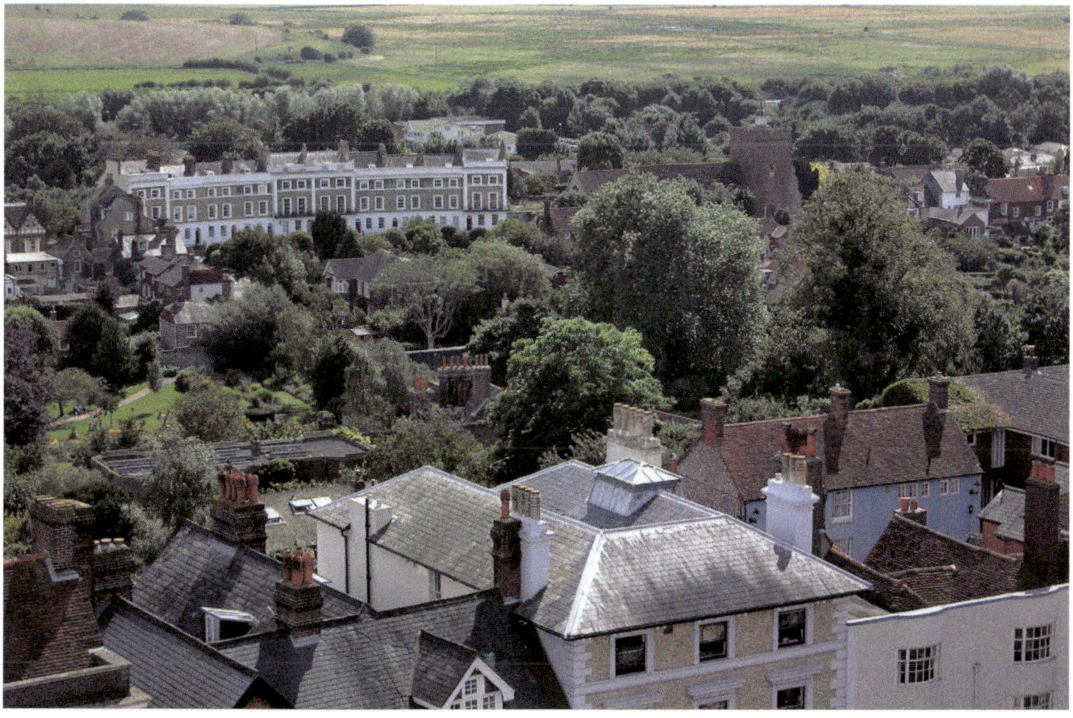

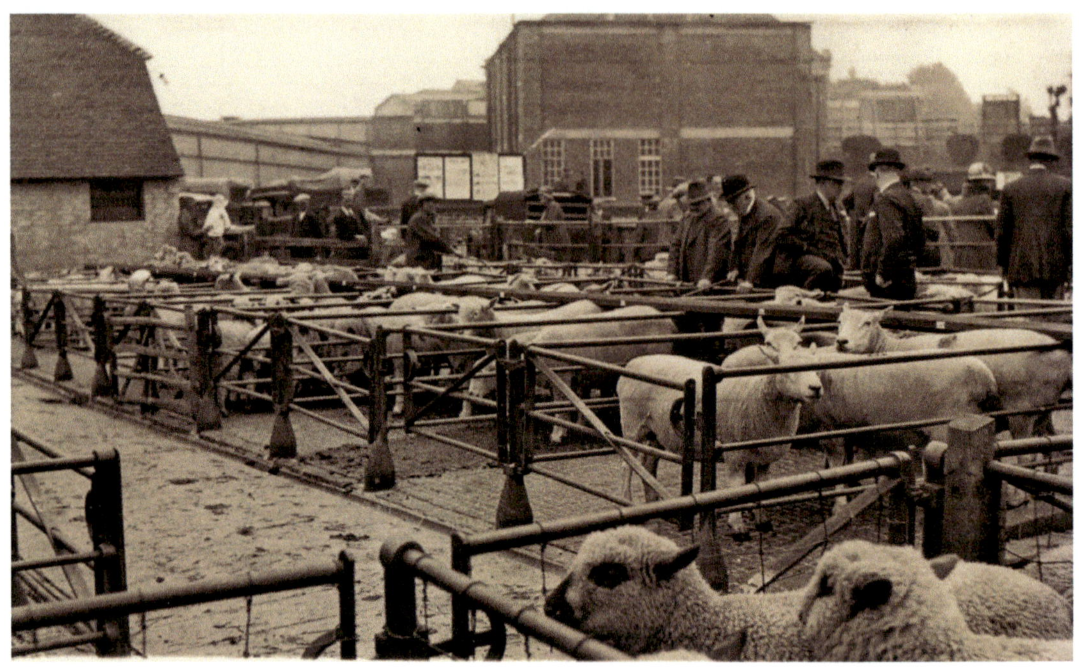

Lewes Market

Garden Street, formerly known as Gardeners Street, was named after the market gardens that once stretched across to the railway station. Lewes Market is shown in the 1920s postcard. It moved to this site in 1882 from the High Street via a brief sojourn in the Pells area. It closed in 1992 and most of the site was developed as Tanner's Brook. Julian Dawson continues to run his weekly antiques and furniture auction each Monday and has tried to convince me that he does not feature in the earlier photograph.

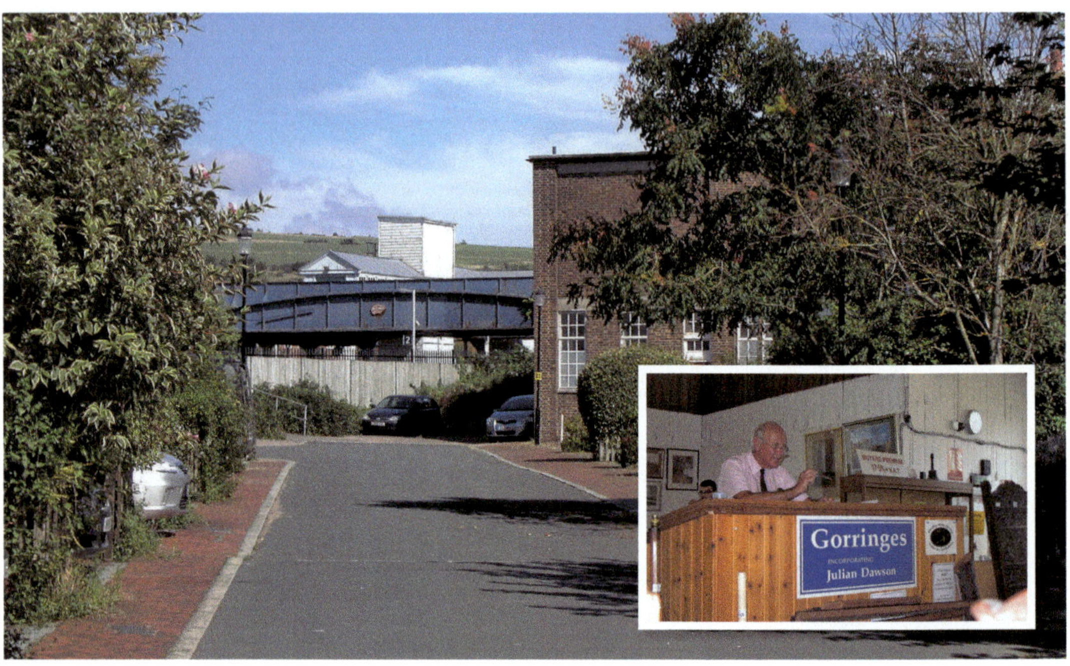

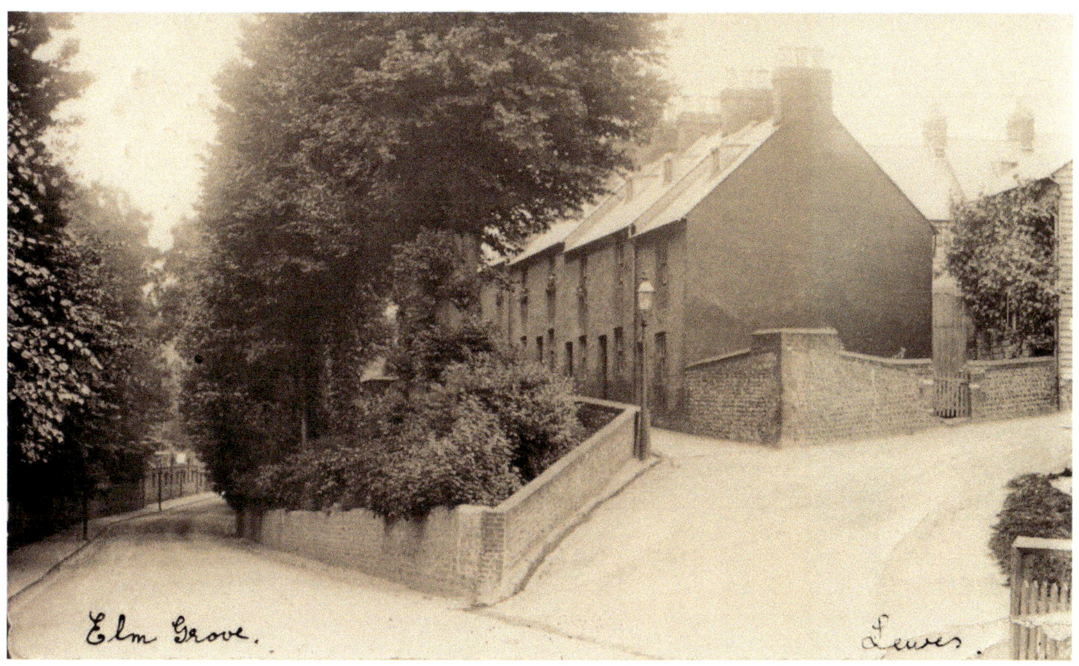

Elm Grove, Southover Road

This was another terrace of Victorian cottages lost in the name of slum clearance in the 1930s. As with many others, they would now be desired bijou properties had they survived for another thirty years. The modern black building overlooking the railway tunnel on the London line replaced The Grapevine tavern, which was also demolished in the 1930s.

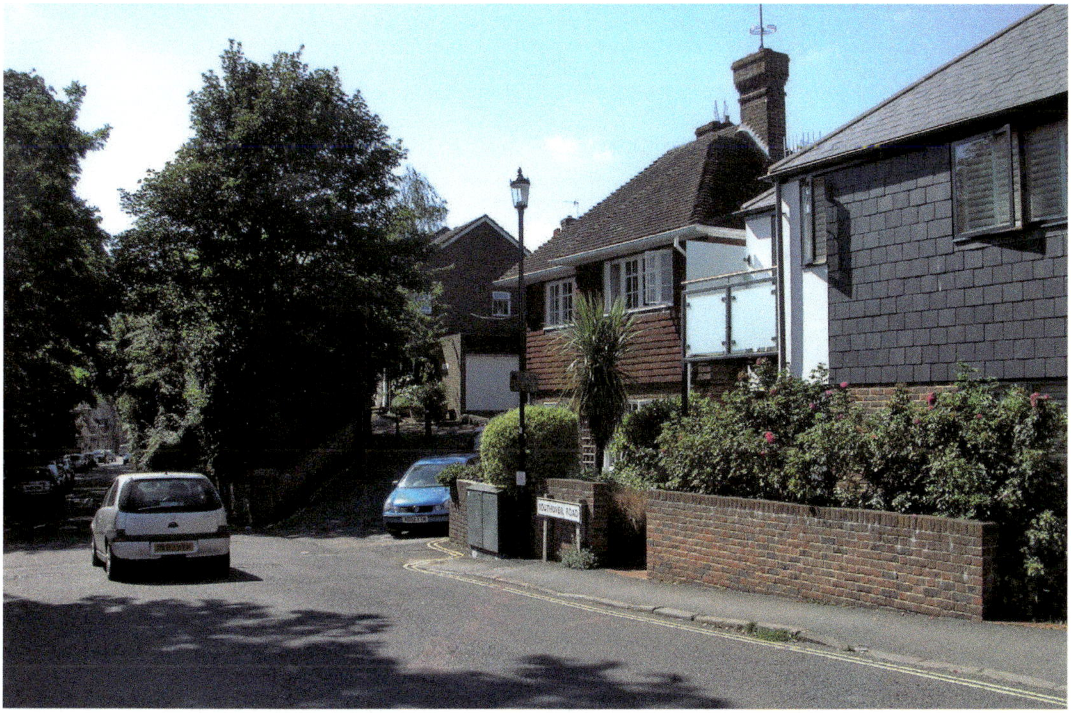

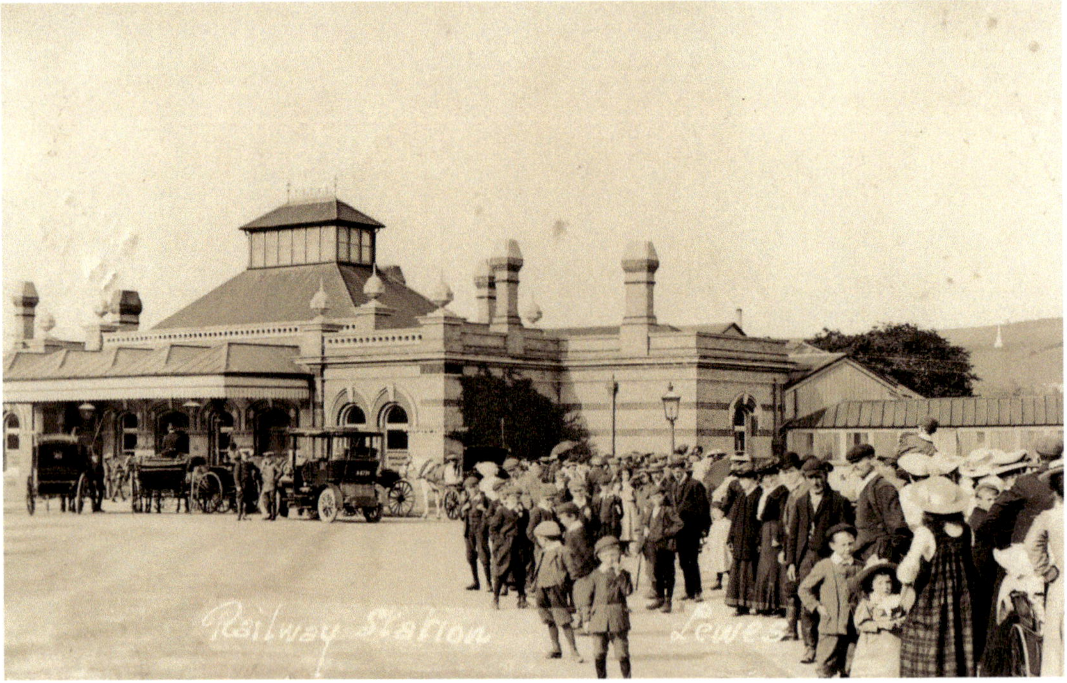

Second and Third Railway Stations

The railway station relocated to this site in 1857 and had a series of extensions and improvements before the original façade was restored in the mid-1980s. It was originally at the platform level in Pinwell Lane, but had its upper levels added about twenty years later.

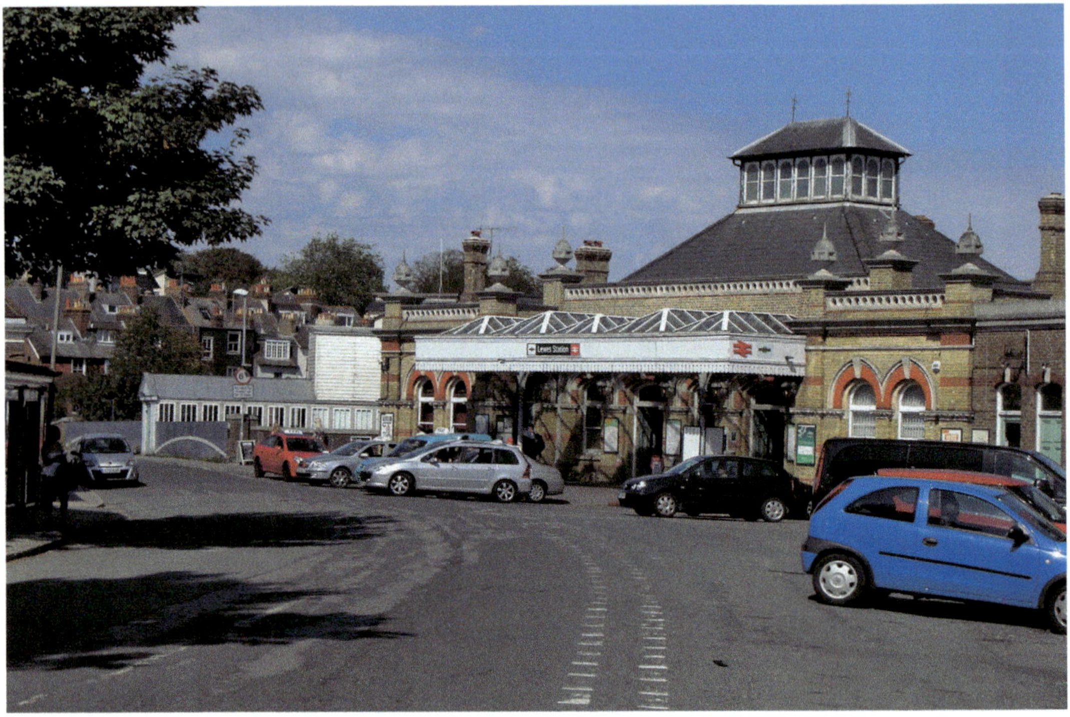

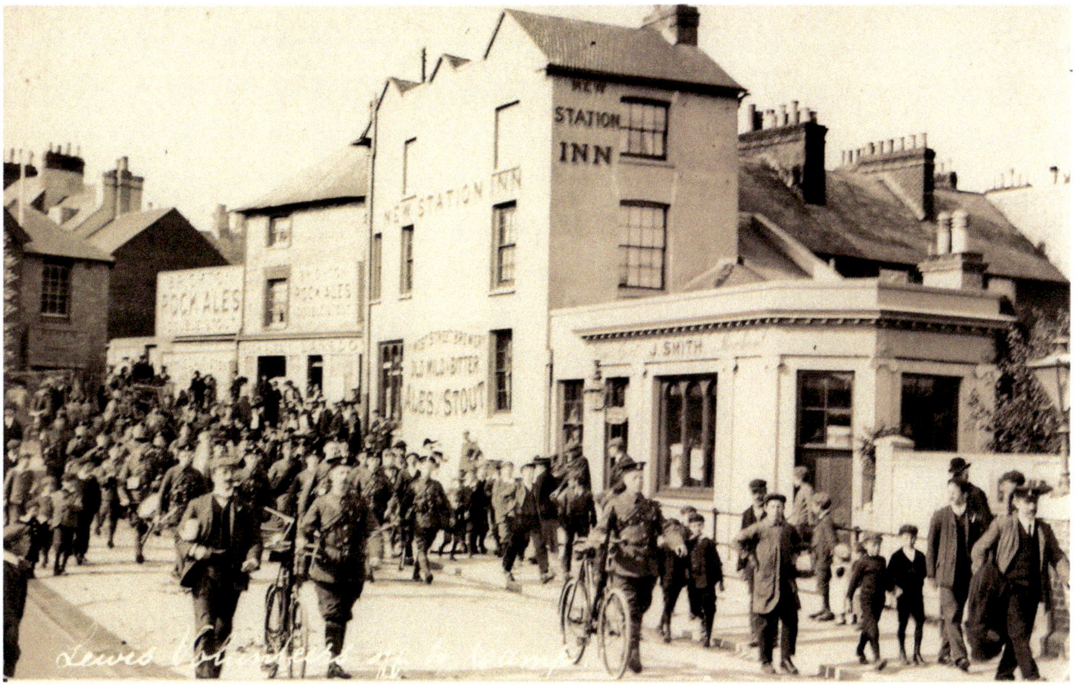

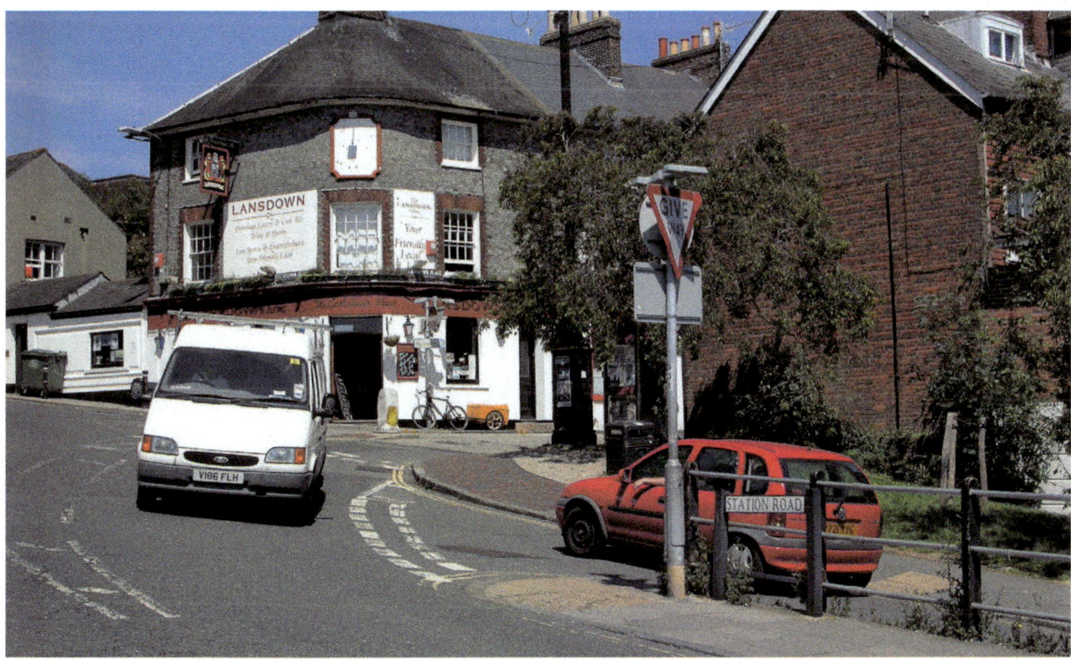

The New Station Inn

Standing on the corner with Station Road, this was a substantial building with accommodation. It was closed and demolished in 1963 to give traffic a better view around the corner to the railway station. The Lansdowne Arms and Central School are in the background. The postcard shows the Lewes volunteers, probably Territorials of the Sussex County Regiment, off to their annual training camp in Hampshire or Kent.

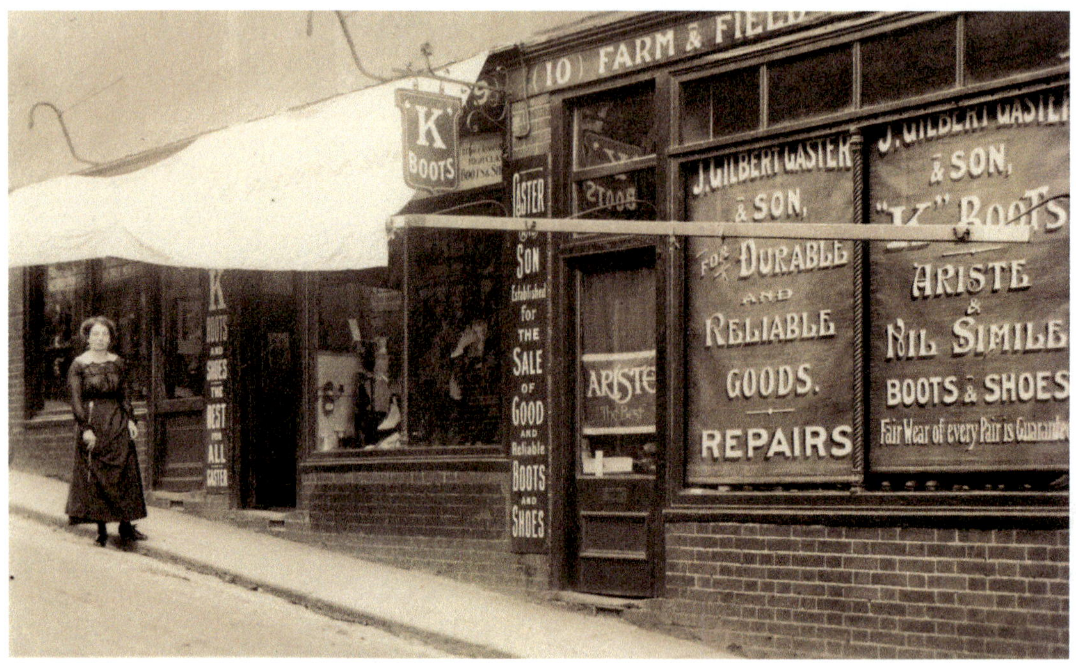

Up Station Street

This was known as St Mary Street until the building of the second railway station in 1857 and was named after St Mary-in-Foro church, which stood on the top corner with the High Street. The imposing premises of J. Gilbert Gaster & Son occupied Nos 8–10, the site of which fronted Ruggs Garage and is now under the McCarthy Stone sheltered housing development.

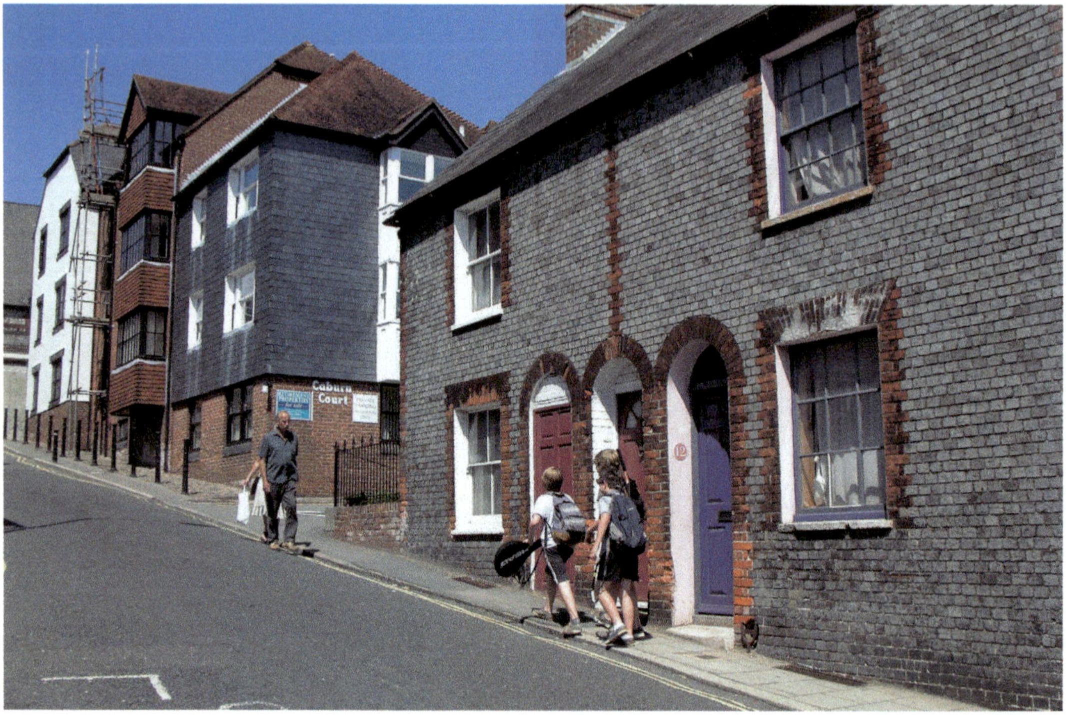

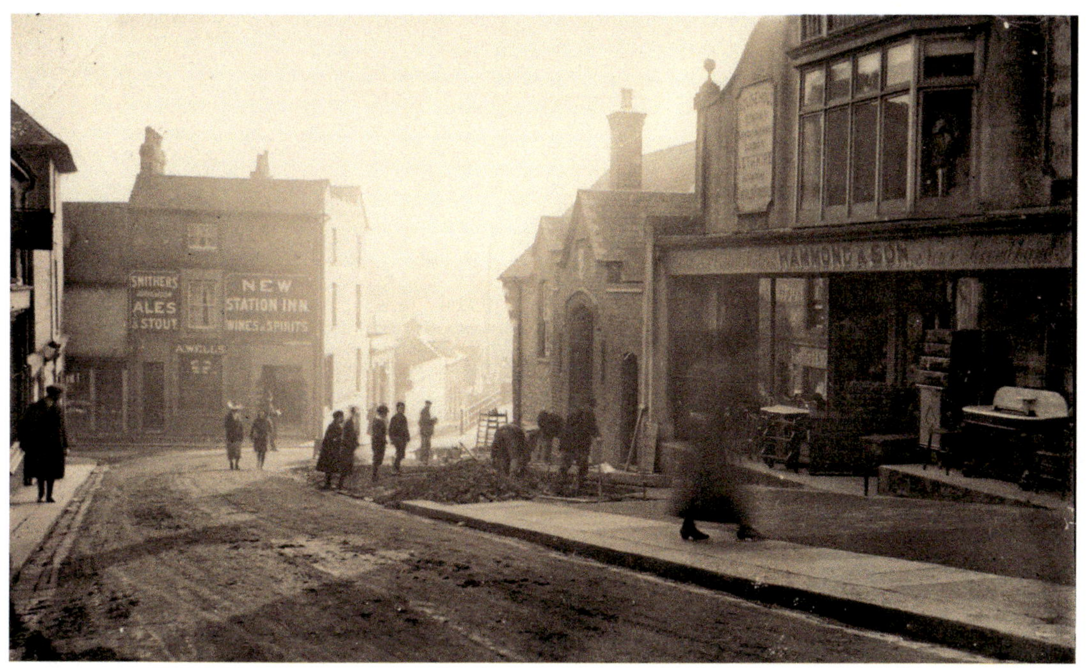

Down Station Street

Looking back to Lansdowne Place we get another view of the New Station Inn, built in 1857 when the railway station was relocated from Friars Walk. The imposing premises on the right were occupied by Hammond & Son, the furnishing and removal firm, for more than seventy years. It looks as though a gang is widening the pavement. This is still a lively commercial area, including good restaurants and cafés.

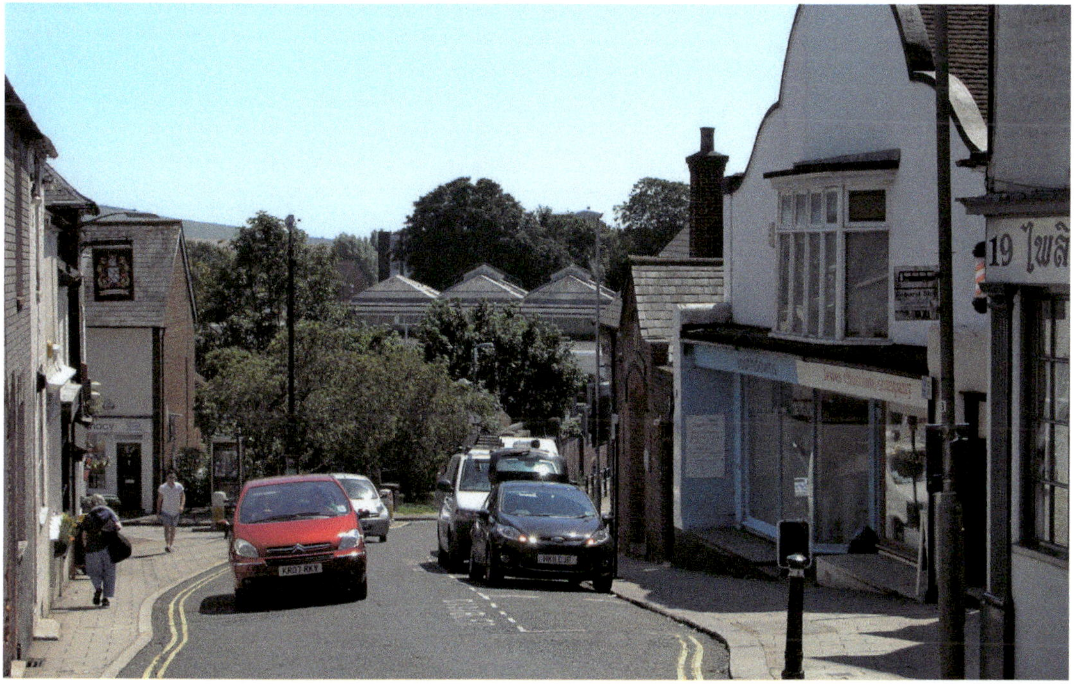

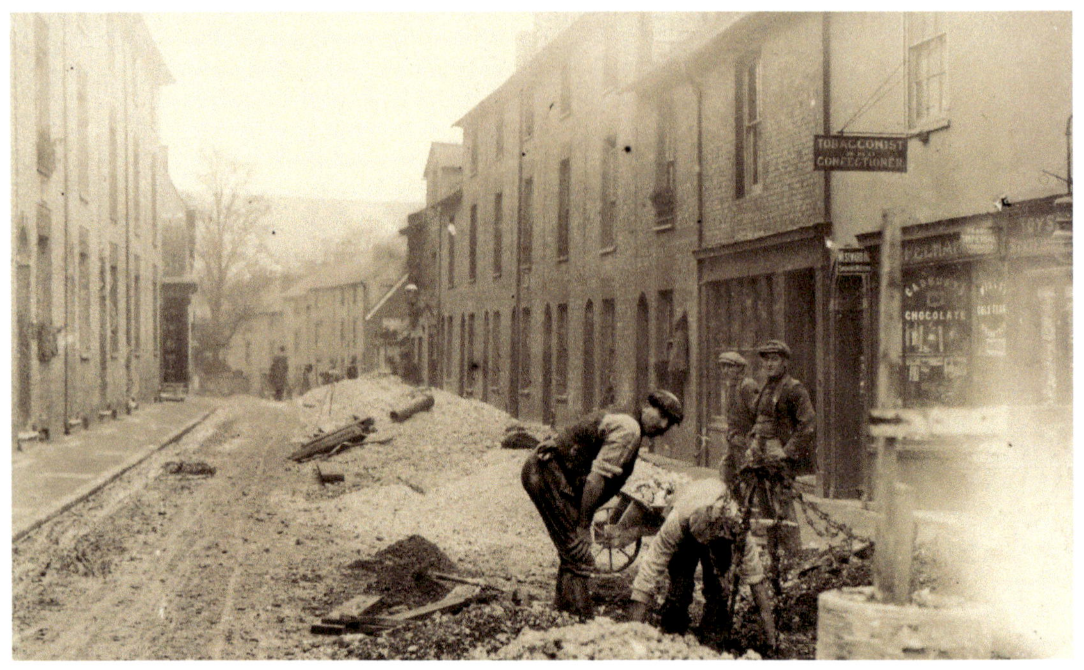

Lansdowne Place from the West

Digging up Lewes' roads is not a modern phenomenon. Here the electricity cables are being laid in 1907, following the building of the Electricity Works adjacent to Bear Yard. A sweet shop then called Cronin's survives, while the chemist's has replaced another called Milham's. The Edwardian street had the premises of four dressmakers and at least seven boarding houses.

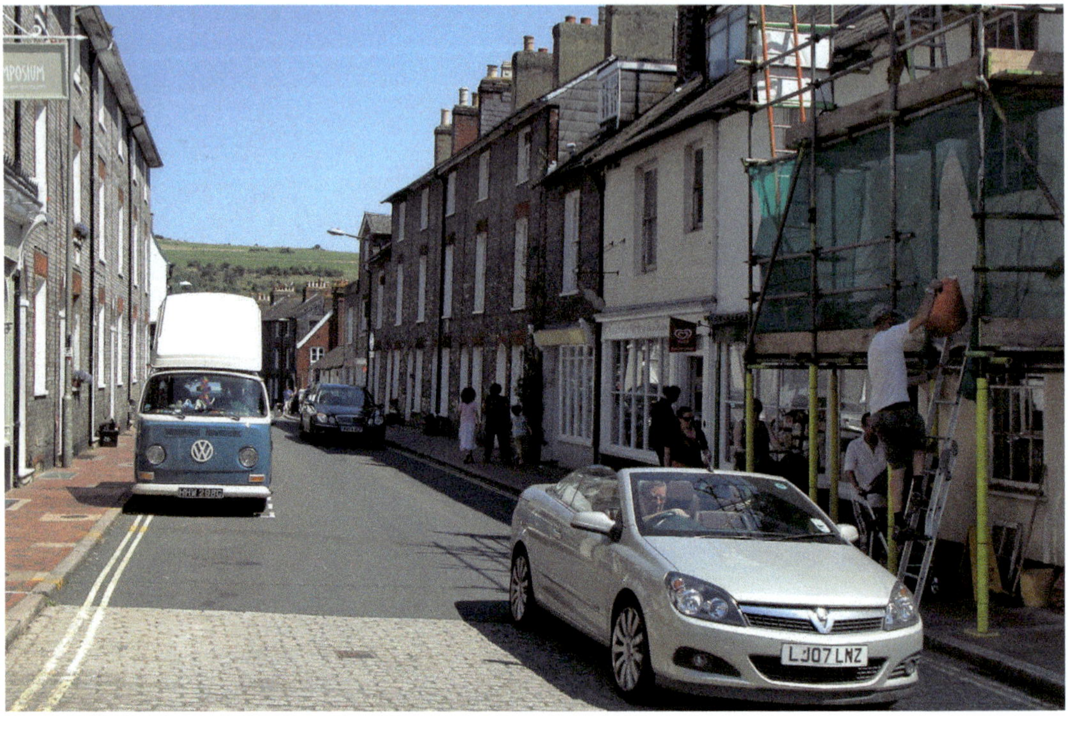

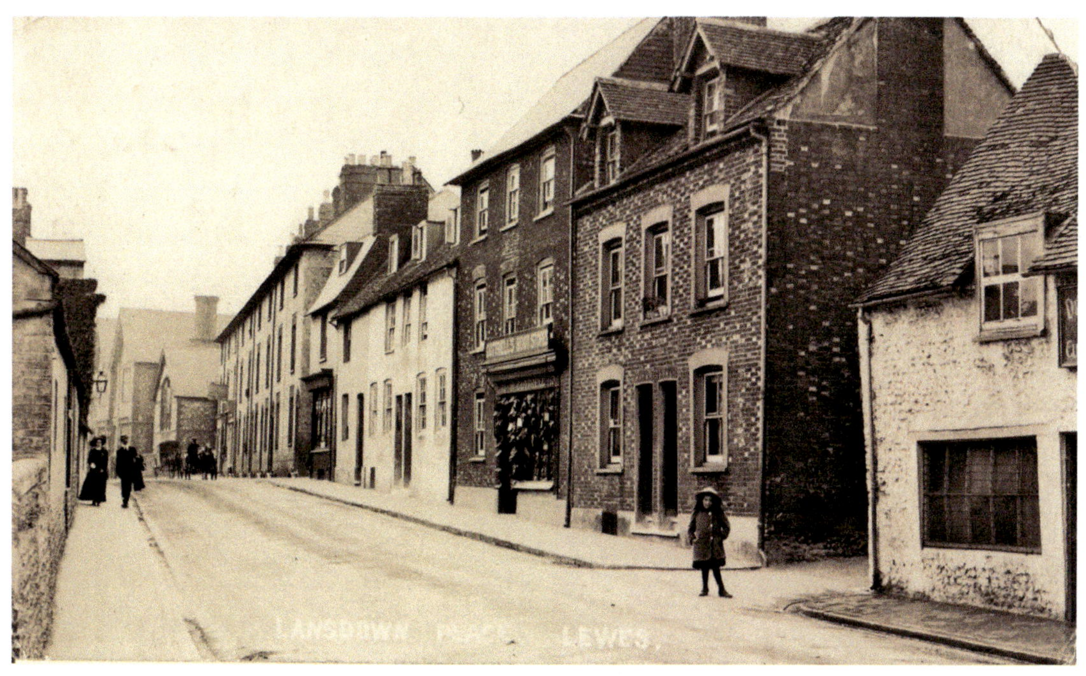

Lansdowne Place from the East

Developed from 1827, the individual nature of the houses has been lost under the white paint. The medieval house in the foreground was replaced in 1934 by the property now occupied by Laporte's café with its lovely garden.

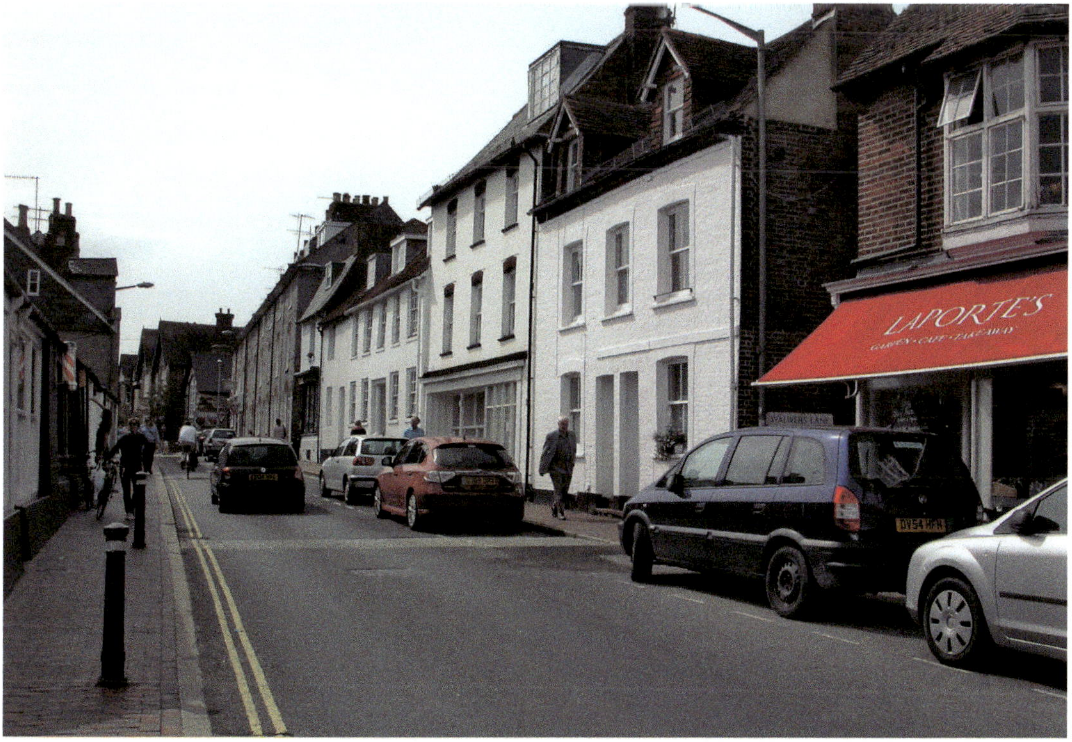

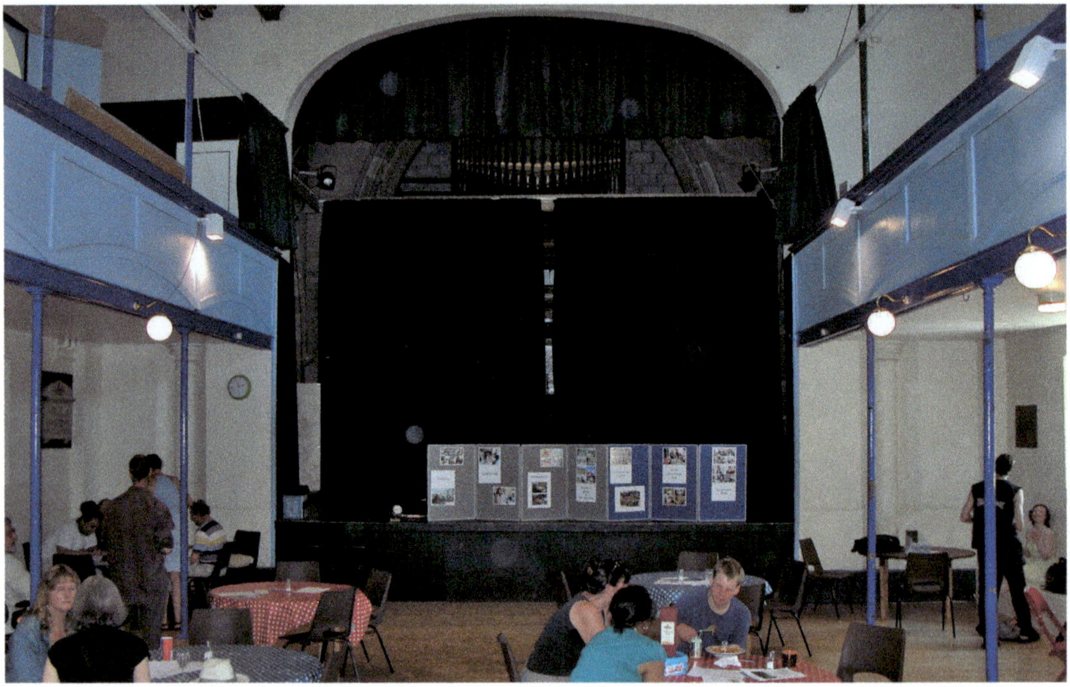

All Saints Church

The church, with its sixteenth-century tower, is a familiar sight in Friars Walk but its Victorian interior is more unusual. The pews have gone, but the fine window by Henry Holiday and the organ are hidden behind the curtain. It is a lively community asset to the town and my photograph shows the weekly Wednesday Café run by the Oyster Club.

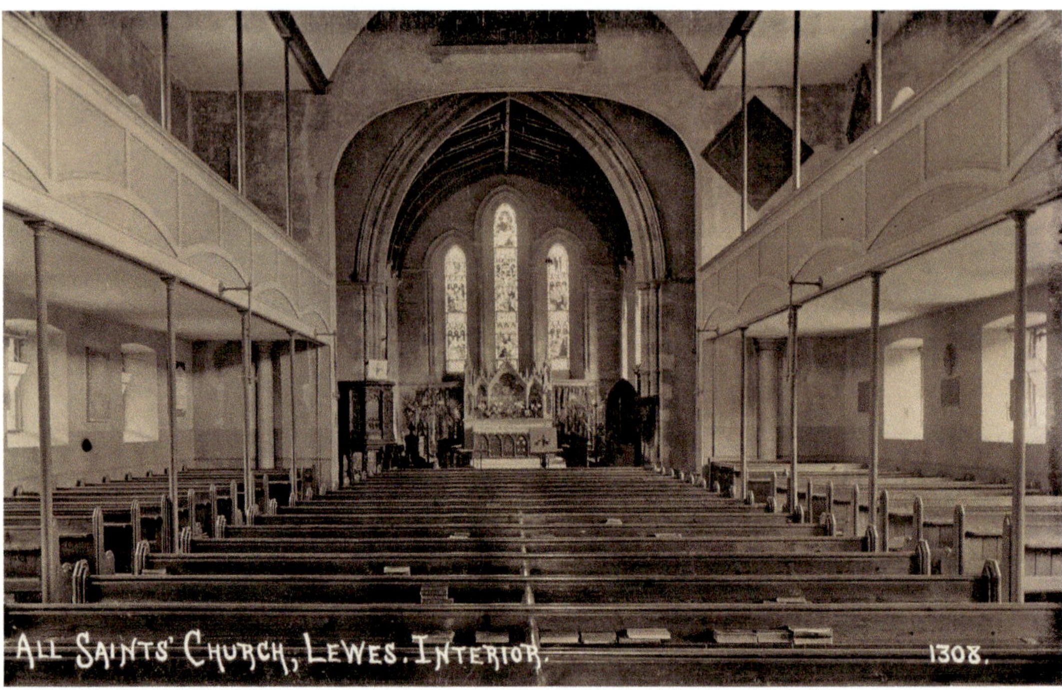

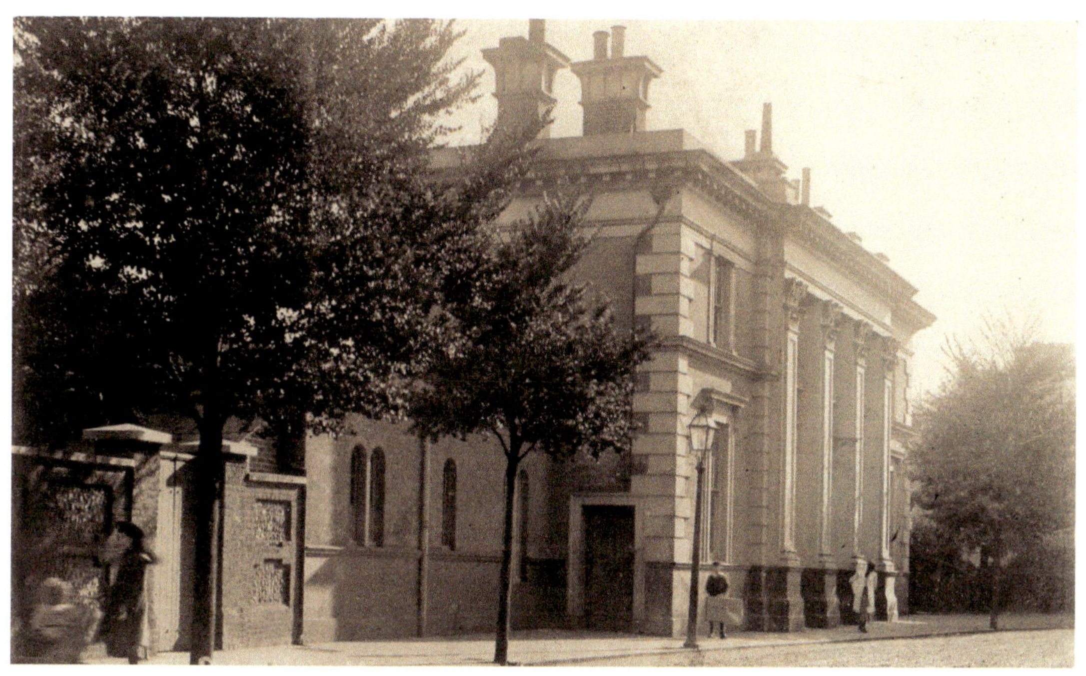

The First Railway Station

There have been three railway stations since 1846. This is the first terminus, which stood in Friars Walk until 1857 and was replaced in part by the Magistrates Courts. The second station was built on Pinwell Lane beside the London line and the third and current a few years later. The first line came in from Brighton and, two weeks later, went on to Hastings. In 1847, the route through to Keymer Junction provided a direct line to London.

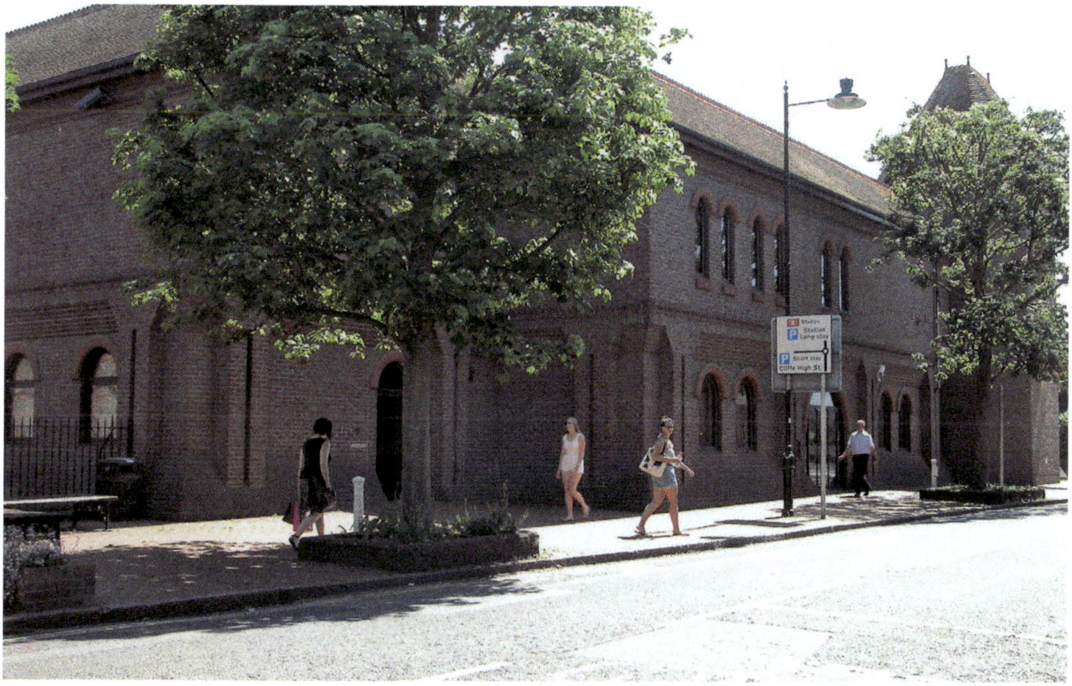

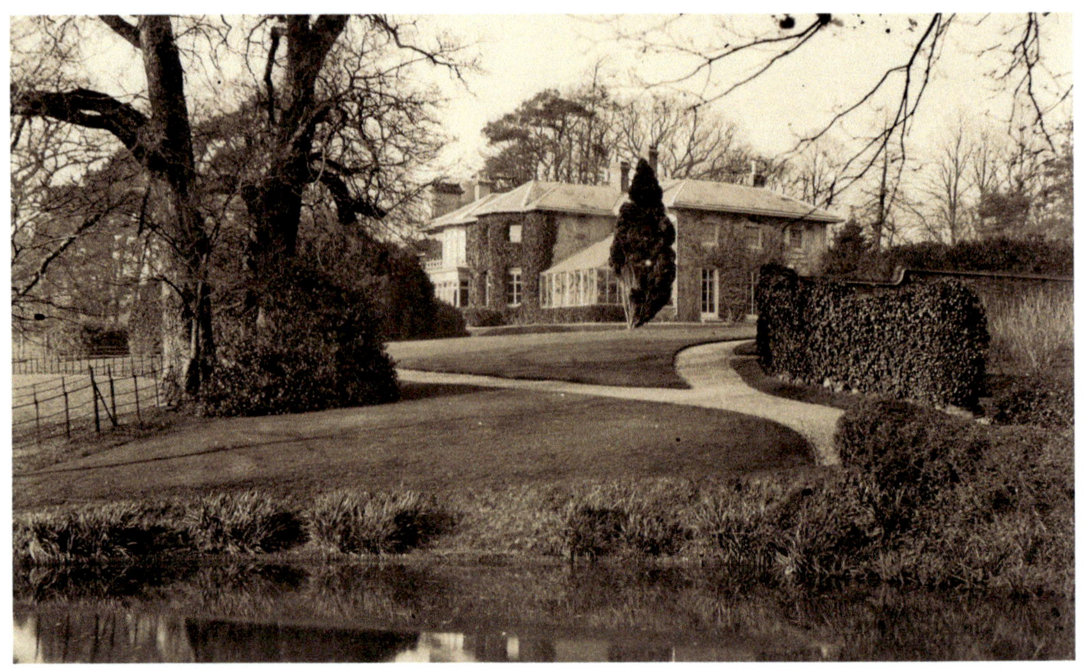

This was the grand home of Burwood Godlee. The wonderful grounds were dissected by the railway line to Uckfield in 1868. Other than a few foundations and odd walls nothing remains, and the grounds are in the good care of the Railway Land Trust. The impressive Linklater Pavilion on its boundary was opened last year.

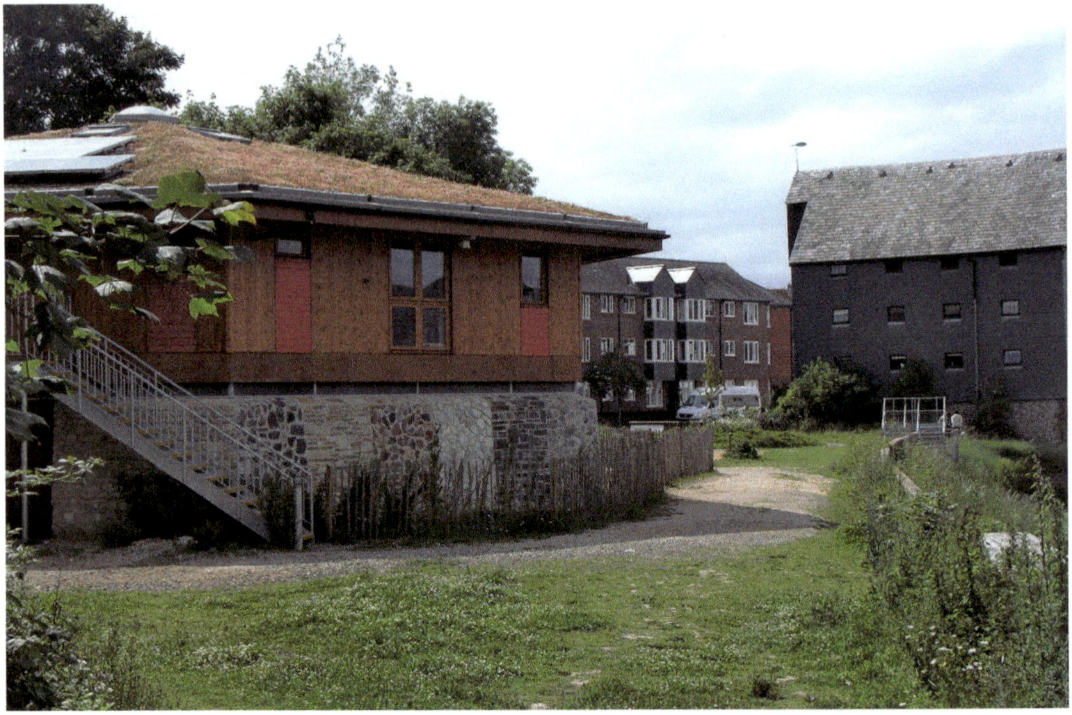

Ashcombe Mill

The Mill was destroyed in a storm on 28 March 1916. Its six sweeps were rare and it had been renovated by the Sussex Archaeological Society four years before its demise. It first appeared on maps in 1823, but was never used extensively for milling. James Tasker has recently built a replica on the site just off Juggs Lane. The remaining sweeps will be fitted next spring and it will soon become his family home. This is by far the best addition to the Lewes landscape for decades.

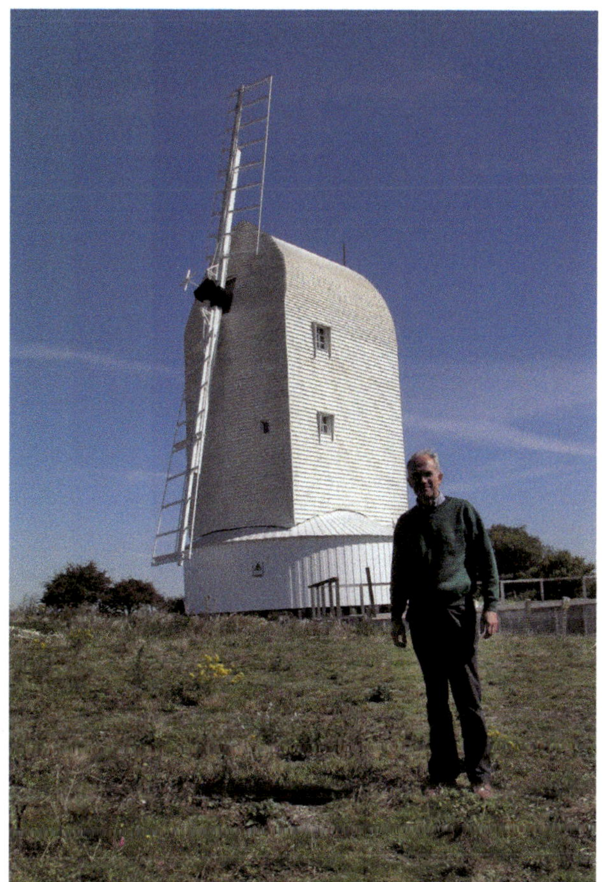

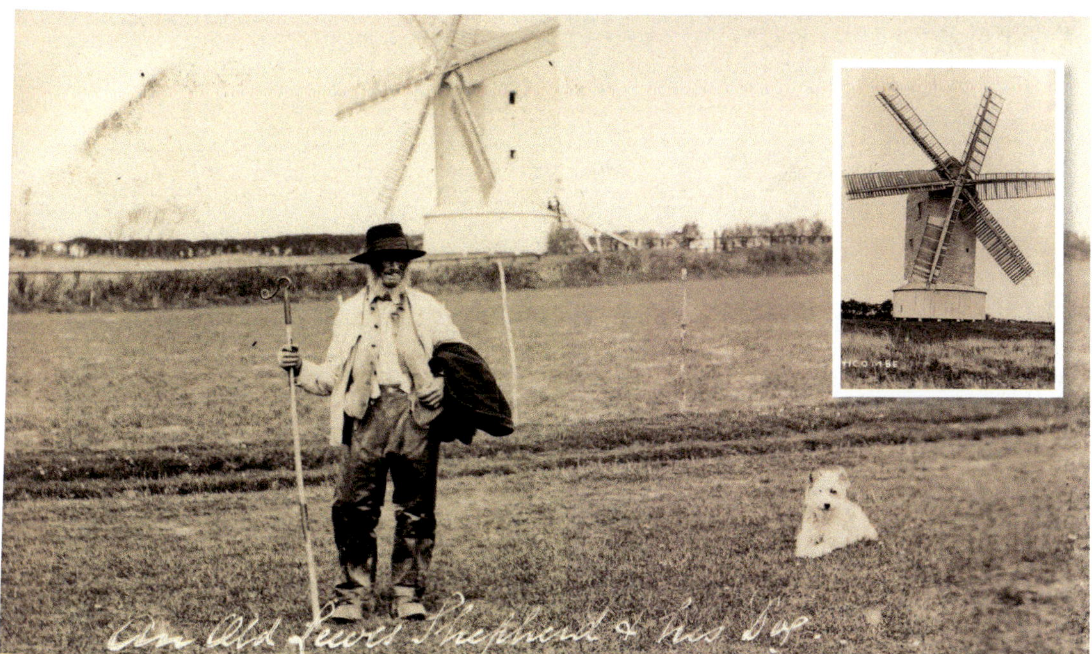

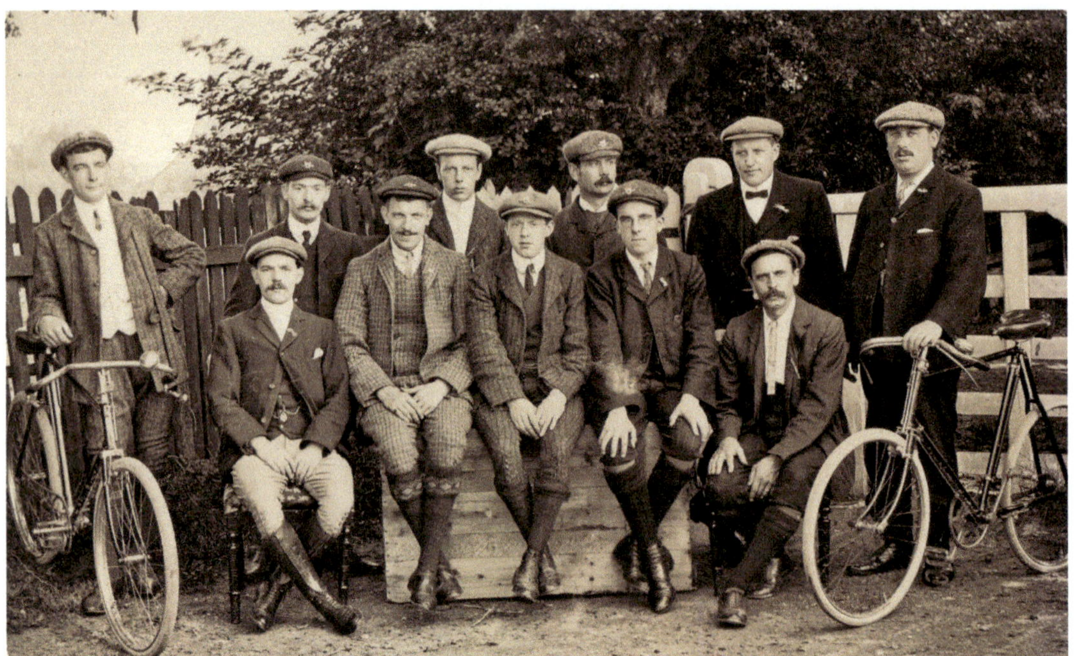

Lewes Victoria Cycling Club
The cyclists relax after their exertions and I will now do the same after producing this little book.

Acknowledgements

Thanks go to the people of Lewes who feature in this book and who willingly and with patience posed for my photographs, and the many others who showed an interest in my project.

Tom Reeves for allowing me to use postcards of which Edward Reeves & Son own the copyright.

The following authors, whose books on aspects of Lewes provide so much valuable information for local historians, researchers and writers: Colin Brent; Diana Crook; Kim Clark; L. S. Davey; Walter Godfrey; John Houghton; Helen Poole; Graham White.

www.sussexpostcard.info, a brilliant website developed by Rendel Williams.

Sophie Haynes, John Saunders and Linda Cairns for help with developing this book.